Learning Bootstrap

Second Edition

Unearth the potential of Bootstrap 4 to create highly responsive and beautiful websites using modern web techniques

Matt Lambert

BIRMINGHAM - MUMBAI

Learning Bootstrap 4

Second Edition

First published: December 2014

Second edition: August 2016

Production reference: 1220816

Published by Packt Publishing Ltd.

Livery Place

35 Livery Street

Birmingham B3 2PB, UK.

ISBN 978-1-78588-100-8

www.packtpub.com

Credits

Author

Matt Lambert

Reviewer

Sherwin Robles

Commissioning Editor

Wilson Dsouza

Acquisition Editor

Dharmesh Parmar

Content Development Editor

Prashanth G Rao

Technical Editor

Murtaza Tinwala

Copy Editor

Safis Editing

Project Coordinator

Ulhas Kambali

Proofreader

Safis Editing

Indexer

Tejal Daruwale Soni

Production Coordinator

Melwyn Dsa

Graphics

Abhinash Sahu

About the Author

Matt Lambert is a designer and developer with more than 16 years of experience. He currently works full-time as a senior product designer for CA Technologies in Vancouver, BC, Canada.

In his free time, he is an author, artist, and musician. In 2005, Matt founded Cardeo Creative, which is a small web design studio based in Vancouver. He works with a select list of clients on a part-time basis while producing his own products on the side.

To date, Matt has self-published three additional development books titled: *Mastering Bootstrap, CSS3 Handbook,* and the *Freelance Startup Guide*. He is also the author of *Bootstrap Site Blueprints Volume II, Packt Publishing.*

About the Reviewer

Sherwin Robles is a web application developer from the Philippines with a solid 5 years of experience of designing, developing, and implementing automated solutions. Most of his projects are built with the CakePHP framework with the help of Bootstrap, which makes development even faster. In April 2015 he joined INIGOTECH, a company that aims to make your ideas into reality.

His expertise is rooted in research and development endeavors on the subject of achieving improved levels of dependability from Internet and computing systems.

www.PacktPub.com

eBooks, discount offers, and more

Did you know that Packt offers eBook versions of every book published, with PDF and ePub files available? You can upgrade to the eBook version at `www.PacktPub.com` and as a print book customer, you are entitled to a discount on the eBook copy. Get in touch with us at `customercare@packtpub.com` for more details.

At `www.PacktPub.com`, you can also read a collection of free technical articles, sign up for a range of free newsletters and receive exclusive discounts and offers on Packt books and eBooks.

`https://www2.packtpub.com/books/subscription/packtlib`

Do you need instant solutions to your IT questions? PacktLib is Packt's online digital book library. Here, you can search, access, and read Packt's entire library of books.

Why subscribe?

- Fully searchable across every book published by Packt
- Copy and paste, print, and bookmark content
- On demand and accessible via a web browser

Table of Contents

Preface 1

Chapter 1: Introducing Bootstrap 4 7

Introducing Bootstrap 7

Bootstrap 4 advantages 8

Improved grid system and flexbox 8

Card component 8

Rebooting normalize.css 9

Internet Explorer 8 support dropped 9

Other updates 9

Implementing framework files 9

Inserting the JavaScript files 10

The starter template 10

HTML5 DOCTYPE 11

Structuring the responsive meta tag 12

Normalizing and Rebooting 12

Taking the starter template further 12

Using a static site generator 12

Converting the base template to a generator 13

Installing Harp.js 13

Adding Sass in Harp 14

Setting up the project 14

Inserting the CSS 14

Inserting the JavaScript 14

Other directories 14

Setting up the layout 15

Compiling your project 16

Previewing your project 16

Deploying your project 16

Installing Surge 17

Using Surge to deploy your project 17

Summary 17

Chapter 2: Using Bootstrap Build Tools 19

Different types of tools 19

Installing Node.js 20

Updating npm 20

Installing Grunt 22

Download the Bootstrap source files 23
Installing Ruby 23
Installing the Bundler gem 25
Running the documentation 26
Setting up the static site generator 26
Why use Harp.js 27
Installing Harp.js 27
Setting up the blog project 28
css 28
fonts 28
img 28
js 29
partial 29
EJS files 29
Setting up the JSON files 29
Creating the data JSON file 30
Setting up the layout 31
Setting up the header 32
Setting up the footer 34
Creating our first page template 35
Compiling your project 35
Running your project 36
Viewing your project 36
A note about Sass 38
Summary 38
Chapter 3: Jumping into Flexbox 39
Flexbox basics and terminology 39
Ordering your Flexbox 40
Stretching your child sections to fit the parent container 42
Changing the direction of the boxes 42
Wrapping your Flexbox 44
Creating equal-height columns 46
Setting up the Bootstrap Flexbox layout grid 52
Updating the Sass variable 52
Setting up a Flexbox project 53
Adding a custom theme 54
Creating a basic three-column grid 55
Creating full-width layouts 57
Designing a single blog post 58

Summary 61

Chapter 4: Working with Layouts 63

Working with containers 63
Creating a layout without a container 65
Using multiple containers on a single page 65
Inserting rows into your layout 66
Adding columns to your layout 67
Extra small 67
Small 67
Medium 67
Large 68
Extra large 68
Choosing a column class 68
Creating a simple three-column layout 68
Mixing column classes for different devices 70
What if I want to offset a column? 71
Coding the blog home page 72
Writing the index.ejs template 72
Using spacing CSS classes 73
Testing out the blog home page layout 74
Adding some content 75
What about mobile devices? 77
Using responsive utility classes 79
Coding the additional blog project page grids 79
Updating _data.json for our new pages 79
Creating the new page templates 80
Coding the contact page template 80
Adding the contact page body 81
Coding the blog post template 84
Adding the blog post feature 84
Adding the blog post body 85
Converting the mailing list section to a partial 86
Summary 89

Chapter 5: Working with Content 91

Reboot defaults and basics 91
Headings and paragraphs 92
Lists 92
Preformatted text 92
Tables 92
Forms 92

Learning to use typography 93
Using display headings 93
Customizing headings 94
Using the lead class 94
Working with lists 95
Coding an unstyled list 95
Creating inline lists 97
Using description lists 97
How to style images 98
Making images responsive 98
Using image shapes 99
Aligning images with CSS 99
Coding tables 101
Setting up the basic table 101
Inversing a table 102
Inversing the table header 103
Adding striped rows 104
Adding borders to a table 104
Adding a hover state to rows 105
Color-coating table rows 106
Making tables responsive 107
Summary 107
Chapter 6: Playing with Components 109
Using the button component 109
Basic button examples 109
Creating outlined buttons 110
Checkbox and radio buttons 111
Creating a radio button group 112
Using button groups 114
Creating vertical button groups 114
Coding a button dropdown 115
Creating a pop-up menu 116
Creating different size drop-down buttons 117
Coding forms in Bootstrap 4 118
Setting up a form 118
Adding a select dropdown 119
Inserting a textarea tag into your form 121
Adding a file input form field 121
Inserting radio buttons and checkboxes to a form 122
Adding a form to the blog contact page 124
Updating your project 124

Additional form fields 126
Creating an inline form 126
Hiding the labels in an inline form 127
Adding inline checkboxes and radio buttons 127
Changing the size of inputs 128
Controlling the width of form fields 129
Adding validation to inputs 130
Using the Jumbotron component 132
Adding the Label component 134
Using the Alerts component 135
Adding a dismiss button to alerts 136
Using Cards for layout 137
Moving the Card title 139
Changing text alignment in cards 140
Adding a header to a Card 141
Inverting the color scheme of a Card 143
Adding a location card to the Contact page 146
Updating the Blog index page 148
Adding the sidebar 151
Setting up the Blog post page 154
How to use the Navs component 157
Creating tabs with the Nav component 158
Creating a pill navigation 159
Using the Bootstrap Navbar component 160
Changing the color of the Navbar 161
Making the Navbar responsive 162
Adding Breadcrumbs to a page 164
Adding Breadcrumbs to the Blog post page 164
Using the Pagination component 165
Adding the Pager to the Blog post template 166
How to use the List Group component 166
Summary 168
Chapter 7: Extending Bootstrap with JavaScript Plugins 169
Coding a Modal dialog 169
Coding the Modal dialog 170
Coding Tooltips 172
Updating the project layout 172
How to use Tooltips 172
How to position Tooltips 174

Adding Tooltips to buttons 175
Updating the layout for buttons 175
Avoiding collisions with our components 176
Using Popover components 177
Updating the JavaScript 177
Positioning Popover components 178
Adding a Popover to a button 179
Adding our Popover button in JavaScript 179
Using the Collapse component 180
Coding the collapsable content container 180
Coding an Accordion with the Collapse component 181
Coding a Bootstrap Carousel 184
Adding the Carousel bullet navigation 185
Including Carousel slides 186
Adding Carousel arrow navigation 187
Summary 188
Chapter 8: Throwing in Some Sass 189
Learning the basics of Sass 189
Using Sass in the blog project 190
Updating the blog project 190
Using variables 191
Using the variables in CSS 192
Using other variables as variable values 193
Importing partials in Sass 194
Using mixins 196
How to use operators 197
Creating a collection of variables 198
Importing the variables to your custom style sheet 198
Adding a color palette 199
Adding some background colors 199
Setting up variables for typography 200
Coding the text color variables 201
Coding variables for links 202
Setting up border variables 202
Adding variables for margin and padding 203
Adding mixins to the variables file 203
Coding a border-radius mixin 204
Customizing components 206
Customizing the button component 206

Extending the button component to use our color palette 207
Writing a theme 210
Common components that need to be customized 210
Theming the drop-down component 211
Customizing the alerts component 213
Customizing the typography component 215
Summary 216
Chapter 9: Migrating from Version 3 217
Browser support 217
Big changes in version 4 217
Switching to Sass 217
Updating your variables 218
Updating @import statements 218
Updating mixins 219
Additional global changes 220
Using REM units 220
Other font updates 221
New grid size 221
Migrating components 221
Migrating to the Cards component 222
Using icon fonts 222
Migrating JavaScript 222
Miscellaneous migration changes 223
Migrating typography 223
Migrating images 223
Migrating tables 223
Migrating forms 224
Migrating buttons 224
Summary 224
Index 225

Preface

Bootstrap, the most popular frontend framework built to design elegant, powerful, and responsive interfaces for professional-level web pages, has undergone a major overhaul. Bootstrap 4 introduces a wide range of new features that make frontend web design even more simple and exciting. In this comprehensive tutorial, we'll teach you everything you need to know to start building websites with Bootstrap 4 in a practical way. You'll get a feel of build tools such as Node, Grunt, and more to start building your project. You'll discover the principles of mobile-first design to ensure your pages can adapt to fit any screen size and meet the responsive requirements of the modern age. You'll get to play with Bootstrap's grid system and base CSS to ensure your designs are robust and beautiful, and that your development process is speedy and efficient. Then, you'll find out how you can extend your current build with some cool JavaScript plugins, and throw in some Sass to spice things up and customize your themes. If you've tinkered with Bootstrap before and are planning on migrating to the latest version, we'll give you just the right tricks to get you there. This book will make sure you're geared up and ready to build amazingly beautiful and responsive websites in a jiffy.

What this book covers

`Chapter 1`, *Introducing Bootstrap 4*, will be a quick overview of what Bootstrap is, what's new in Bootstrap 4, and why a developer should take the time to learn about the new framework. We'll also discuss the basic files and templates needed for any web page. I'll also cover the different ways you can download or build a Bootstrap project.

`Chapter 2`, *Using Bootstrap Build Tools*, will teach the user how to use build tools such as Node, Grunt, and Autoprefixer to build their own projects.

`Chapter 3`, *Jumping into Flexbox*, will give a quick explanation of what a flexbox layout is compared to traditional layouts. Also, you will learn about the benefits of flexbox and when to use it. Then it will briefly explain how to create a flexbox layout using the new Bootstrap layout component and review it with the reader.

`Chapter 4`, *Working with Layouts*, will teach you the basic Bootstrap layout components and what is new in Bootstrap 4 in regard to them. For the components that are significantly different, the chapter will provide coded examples for the users.

`Chapter 5`, *Working with Content*, covers the new Bootstrap CSS reset named REBOOT. It will also cover typography, code, images, tables, and figure components.

`Chapter 6`, *Playing with Components,* will be one of the longer chapters in the book as it will cover a large amount of Bootstrap components. It will cover all remaining Bootstrap components, including Buttons, button groups, button drop-down, forms, input groups, drop-downs, jumbotron, labels, alerts, cards, navs, navbars, breadcrumbs, pagination, progress, and list groups.

`Chapter 7`, *Extending Bootstrap with JavaScript Plugin,* will cover any and all components in Bootstrap that rely on JavaScript. This will include Modal, Tooltips, Popovers, Collapse, and Carousel.

`Chapter 8`, *Throwing in Some Sass,* will explain how, in Bootstrap 4, the framework has moved from Less to Sass as its CSS preprocessor. It will cover the basics of using Sass in a Bootstrap theme and explain how you can customize or use existing variables or write your own.

`Chapter 9`, *Migrating from Version 3,* will cover the basic steps required to migrate a website from version 3 to 4 and point out some of the known trouble areas for doing this.

What you need for this book

To get started using Bootstrap 4 there are a few tools I would recommend installing on your computer. First of all you'll need a text editor like Sublime Text or Notepad. Secondly you'll need a command line tool. If you're on a MAC you can use Terminal which is included with OSX. If you're on Windows I would recommend downloading Cygwin. That's all you need to get started with the book. In `Chapter 2`, *Using Bootstrap Build Tools,* I'll cover the installation of a few other tools that we'll be using in our project like: Node.js, NPM, Grunt.js, Jekyll, Harp.js and Sass. If you already have those tools installed great! If not, don't worry we'll go through it step by step later in the book.

Who this book is for

If you want to learn to build enterprise-level websites efficiently with Bootstrap, this book is for you. You must have a basic and fundamental understanding of HTML, CSS, and JavaScript; however, there is no need to have prior Bootstrap experience.

Conventions

In this book, you will find a number of text styles that distinguish between different kinds of information. Here are some examples of these styles and an explanation of their meaning.

Code words in text, database table names, folder names, filenames, file extensions, pathnames, dummy URLs, user input, and Twitter handles are shown as follows: "Bootstrap has taken `normalize.css` and extended it with a new module. "

A block of code is set as follows:

```
<!DOCTYPE html>
<html lang="en">
  <head>
    <!-- Required meta tags always come first -->
    <meta charset="utf-8">
    <meta name="viewport" content="width=device-width, initial-scale=1,
shrink-to-fit=no">
```

Any command-line input or output is written as follows:

```
$ sudo npm install -g harp
```

New terms and **important words** are shown in bold. Words that you see on the screen, for example, in menus or dialog boxes, appear in the text like this: "The first is the white button labeled **Close**, which, when clicked, will close the Modal."

Warnings or important notes appear in a box like this.

Tips and tricks appear like this.

Reader feedback

Feedback from our readers is always welcome. Let us know what you think about this book—what you liked or disliked. Reader feedback is important for us as it helps us develop titles that you will really get the most out of.

To send us general feedback, simply e-mail `feedback@packtpub.com`, and mention the book's title in the subject of your message.

If there is a topic that you have expertise in and you are interested in either writing or contributing to a book, see our author guide at `www.packtpub.com/authors`.

Customer support

Now that you are the proud owner of a Packt book, we have a number of things to help you to get the most from your purchase.

Downloading the example code

You can download the example code files for this book from your account at `http://www.packtpub.com`. If you purchased this book elsewhere, you can visit `http://www.packtpub.com/support` and register to have the files e-mailed directly to you.

You can download the code files by following these steps:

1. Log in or register to our website using your e-mail address and password.
2. Hover the mouse pointer on the **SUPPORT** tab at the top.
3. Click on **Code Downloads & Errata**.
4. Enter the name of the book in the **Search** box.
5. Select the book for which you're looking to download the code files.
6. Choose from the drop-down menu where you purchased this book from.
7. Click on **Code Download**.

You can also download the code files by clicking on the **Code Files** button on the book's webpage at the Packt Publishing website. This page can be accessed by entering the book's name in the **Search** box. Please note that you need to be logged in to your Packt account.

Once the file is downloaded, please make sure that you unzip or extract the folder using the latest version of:

- WinRAR / 7-Zip for Windows
- Zipeg / iZip / UnRarX for Mac
- 7-Zip / PeaZip for Linux

The code bundle for the book is also hosted on GitHub at `https://github.com/PacktPublishing/Learning-Bootstrap-4`. We also have other code bundles from our rich catalog of books and videos available at `https://github.com/PacktPublishing/`. Check them out!

Downloading the color images of this book

We also provide you with a PDF file that has color images of the screenshots/diagrams used in this book. The color images will help you better understand the changes in the output. You can download this file from `https://www.packtpub.com/sites/default/files/downloads/LearningBootstrap4_ColorImages.pdf`.

Errata

Although we have taken every care to ensure the accuracy of our content, mistakes do happen. If you find a mistake in one of our books—maybe a mistake in the text or the code—we would be grateful if you could report this to us. By doing so, you can save other readers from frustration and help us improve subsequent versions of this book. If you find any errata, please report them by visiting `http://www.packtpub.com/submit-errata`, selecting your book, clicking on the **Errata Submission Form** link, and entering the details of your errata. Once your errata are verified, your submission will be accepted and the errata will be uploaded to our website or added to any list of existing errata under the Errata section of that title.

To view the previously submitted errata, go to `https://www.packtpub.com/books/content/support` and enter the name of the book in the search field. The required information will appear under the **Errata** section.

Piracy

Piracy of copyrighted material on the Internet is an ongoing problem across all media. At Packt, we take the protection of our copyright and licenses very seriously. If you come across any illegal copies of our works in any form on the Internet, please provide us with the location address or website name immediately so that we can pursue a remedy.

Please contact us at `copyright@packtpub.com` with a link to the suspected pirated material.

We appreciate your help in protecting our authors and our ability to bring you valuable content.

Questions

If you have a problem with any aspect of this book, you can contact us at `questions@packtpub.com`, and we will do our best to address the problem.

1
Introducing Bootstrap 4

Bootstrap is the most popular **HTML**, **CSS**, and JavaScript framework on the planet. Whether you are new to web development or an experienced master, Bootstrap is a powerful tool for whatever type of web application you are building. With the release of version 4, Bootstrap is more relevant than ever and brings a complete set of components that are easy to learn to use. In this book, I'll jump right into using Bootstrap, what's new in version 4, and strategies you can use to get the most out of the framework. In my opinion, the best way to learn to code is through real-world examples. As we progress through the book, we'll build a blog and portfolio website so that you will have a fully functional template once you're done. In this chapter, I'll cover the following topics:

- Why should you use Bootstrap?
- What's new in Bootstrap 4?
- The basic files and template required to start a project

Introducing Bootstrap

There are several reasons to use Bootstrap but let me boil it down to a few of the key reasons I recommend it. If you're like me, you're constantly starting new web projects. One of the most frustrating parts of getting a project off the ground is to reinvent the base HTML, CSS, and JavaScript for each project. It makes much more sense to reuse the same base code and then build on top of it. Some developers may prefer to write their own framework, and in some cases this may make sense. However, with most projects, I've found that it is easier to just use an existing framework. On top of the components that Bootstrap provides out-of-the-box, there are hundreds of other third-party components you can integrate it with, with a large community of other developers to help you.

Bootstrap is also a powerful prototyping tool in the start-up world. Often, you will want to vet an idea without investing tons of time into it. Bootstrap allows you to quickly build a prototype to prove out your idea without a large time commitment to build out a frontend that you might not end up using. Even better, if you're working in a team of developers, it is very likely everyone will be familiar with the framework. This will allow for code consistency from day one. No arguing over how to name the selectors or the best way to structure a CSS file. Most of the configuration is already set up for you and you can get on with creating your project faster.

Bootstrap 4 advantages

With the release of Bootstrap 4, there are a number of key updates to the framework. One of the biggest changes is the move from **Less,** which is a CSS preprocessor, to **Sass**. When Bootstrap first started out, there was no clear favorite when it came to preprocessors. Over the last couple of years, Sass has gained a bit of an edge, so this switch should come as no surprise. If you haven't used Sass before, don't worry; it is similar to Less and really easy to learn. In later chapters, I will cover Sass in greater depth.

Improved grid system and flexbox

Another big new feature in version 4 is the improved grid system and the inclusion of flexbox. For the regular grid, another grid level has been added to better target mobile devices, and media queries have been reworked too. Flexbox is the grid of the future and it's really exciting that it's been included. By default, the regular grid will work out-of-the-box but you can switch to the flexbox grid by switching a simple Sass variable to take advantage of this new layout component.

Card component

Bootstrap 4 sees the deprecation of components such as wells, thumbnails, and panels, and the introduction of the new card component. This is a good thing for a couple of reasons. First of all, it removes a few components that were similar and replaces them with a single card component. This makes the framework a little lighter and easier to learn for the new user. The card component has also seen an increase in popularity lately, so it makes sense to include it here. All one has to do is to look at the popularity of Google's **Material Design** to see how cards are a great component to use in a web application.

Rebooting normalize.css

One change that you might not notice immediately but is great nonetheless is the improvements to the built-in CSS reset. Bootstrap has taken `normalize.css` and extended it with a new module called **Reboot**. Reboot improves on Normalize and tightens up the default browser styling that needs to be reset for all web-based projects.

Internet Explorer 8 support dropped

I couldn't be happier to see that Bootstrap has dropped support for Internet Explorer 8 (IE8). The time has come to leave this browser in the past! If you need IE8 support, the recommendation is to continue using Bootstrap 3.

Other updates

All of the JavaScript plugins that come with Bootstrap have been rewritten in ES6, which allows for the use of the latest JavaScript functionality. The tooltip and popover components have been extended to use the Tether library. This is just scratching the surface, as there are a ton of other minor updates that have been built into the framework.

Implementing framework files

Before we get into building the basic template for a Bootstrap project, we should review the files that we need to include to make the framework run properly. At the very minimum, we require one CSS file and two JavaScript files. These files can either be served from the Bootstrap **Content Delivery Network** (**CDN**) or downloaded and included directly in our project. If you are using the CDN, simply include this line of code in the head of your file:

```
<link rel="stylesheet"
href="https://maxcdn.bootstrapcdn.com/bootstrap/4.0.0-alpha.2/css/bootstrap
.min.css" integrity="sha384-
y3tfxAZXuh4HwSYylfB+J125MxIs6mR5FOHamPBG064zB+AFeWH94NdvaCBm8qnd"
crossorigin="anonymous">
```

If you would like to include the CSS file yourself, go to `http://getbootstrap.com/` and download the framework. Extract the resultant ZIP file and locate the `/css` directory. Within this directory will be a number of CSS files. The only one you need to worry about is `bootstrap.min.css`. Locate that file and copy it to the `/css` directory of your own project. Once there, link it into the head of your document, which will look something like this:

```
<link rel="stylesheet" href="/path/to/your/file/bootstrap.min.css">
```

Inserting the JavaScript files

As I mentioned earlier, we need to include two JavaScript files to implement the framework properly. The files are the **jQuery** and **Bootstrap JavaScript** framework files. As with the CSS file, you can either do this through the use of a CDN or download and insert the files manually. The JavaScript files should be inserted at the bottom of your page right before the closing `</body>` tag. If you choose to use the CDN, insert the following lines of code:

```
<script
src="https://ajax.googleapis.com/ajax/libs/jquery/2.1.4/jquery.min.js"></sc
ript>
<script
src="https://maxcdn.bootstrapcdn.com/bootstrap/4.0.0-alpha.2/js/bootstrap.m
in.js" integrity="sha384-
vZ2WRJMwsjRMW/8U7i6PWi6AlO1L79snBrmgiDpgIWJ82z8eA5lenwvxbMV1PAh7"
crossorigin="anonymous"></script>
```

If you prefer to insert the files yourself, go back to the Bootstrap package you downloaded earlier and locate the `/js` directory. There will be a few files here but the one you want is `bootstrap.min.js`. You'll need to also head to `http://jquery.com` to download the jQuery framework file. Once you've done that, drop both files into the `/js` directory for your own project. Next, enter the following lines of code at the bottom of your page template. Make sure jQuery is loaded before `bootstrap.min.js`. This is critical; if you load them in the opposite order, the framework won't work properly:

```
<script src="/path/to/your/files/jquery.min.js"></script>
<script src="/path/to/your/files/bootstrap.min.js"></script>
```

That concludes the explanation of the key Bootstrap framework files you need to include to get your project started. The next step will be to set up the basic starter template so you can begin coding your project.

The starter template

The basic starter template is the bare bones of what you'll need to get a page going using Bootstrap. Let's start by reviewing the code for the entire template and then I'll break down each critical part:

```
<!DOCTYPE html>
<html lang="en">
  <head>
    <!-- Required meta tags always come first -->
    <meta charset="utf-8">
    <meta name="viewport" content="width=device-width, initial-scale=1,
shrink-to-fit=no">
    <meta http-equiv="x-ua-compatible" content="ie=edge">

    <!-- Bootstrap CSS -->
    <link rel="stylesheet"
href="https://maxcdn.bootstrapcdn.com/bootstrap/4.0.0-alpha.2/css/bootstrap
.min.css" integrity="sha384-
y3tfxAZXuh4HwSYylfB+J125MxIs6mR5FOHamPBG064zB+AFeWH94NdvaCBm8qnd"
crossorigin="anonymous">
  </head>
  <body>
    <h1>Hello, world!</h1>

    <!-- jQuery first, then Bootstrap JS. -->
    <script
src="https://ajax.googleapis.com/ajax/libs/jquery/2.1.4/jquery.min.js"></sc
ript>
    <script
src="https://maxcdn.bootstrapcdn.com/bootstrap/4.0.0-alpha.2/js/bootstrap.m
in.js" integrity="sha384-
vZ2WRJMwsjRMW/8U7i6PWi6AlO1L79snBrmgiDpgIWJ82z8eA5lenwvxbMV1PAh7"
crossorigin="anonymous"></script>
  </body>
</html>
```

HTML5 DOCTYPE

Like most projects nowadays, Bootstrap uses the HTML5 DOCTYPE for its template. That is represented by the following line of code:

```
<!DOCTYPE html>
```

Avoid using other DOCTYPES such as **XHTML** strict or transitional or unexpected issues will arise with your components and layouts.

Structuring the responsive meta tag

Bootstrap is a mobile-first framework so the following meta tag needs to be included to allow for responsive web design. To make sure your project renders properly on all types of devices, you must include this meta tag in the `<head>` of your project:

```
<meta name="viewport" content="width=device-width, initial-scale=1, shrink-
to-fit=no">
```

If you're interested in learning more about how responsive web design works in Bootstrap, you should check out the documentation at: `http://v4-alpha.getbootstrap.com/layout/responsive-utilities/`.

That brings to a close the most important parts of the template that you need to be aware of. The remainder of the code in the starter template should be straightforward and easy to understand.

Normalizing and Rebooting

As I mentioned earlier, Bootstrap uses `normalize.css` as the base CSS reset. With the addition of the Reboot reset, Bootstrap extends Normalize and allows for styling to only be done using CSS classes. This is a much safer pattern to follow, as it's much easier to deal with CSS specificity if you are NOT using CSS IDs for styling purposes. The CSS reset code is baked right into `bootstrap.min.css` so there is no need to include any further CSS files for the reset.

Taking the starter template further

Although we have our template set up, one of the main problems with static websites is when things change. If your project grew to 50, 100, or 500 pages and you wanted to possibly update to a new version of Bootstrap, you might be looking at having to update all of those files. This is extremely painful, to put it mildly. Now we enter static site generators.

Using a static site generator

One of the hottest trends right now in web development is the use of static site generators. What exactly does that mean? Instead of having several static files that require updating every time something changes globally, you can use a series of base templates then load your body content into them. This is sometimes called includes or partials. This way, you only have one or two layout files that include the header and footer code.

Then, when something changes, you only have to update a few files instead of 500. Once your website is complete, you then generate a version that is plain HTML, CSS, and JavaScript, and deploy it to your server. This is what I would call creating your own frontend web development environment. This is also how most people work on larger projects nowadays to keep them manageable.

Converting the base template to a generator

Why don't we integrate the basic template into a generator so I can show you what I'm talking about? My generator of choice is called **Harp.js** and you can install it over at `http://harpjs.com/`.

Before we get too far ahead of ourselves, we need to install **Node.js**. Harp runs off Node.js so it's a dependency you'll need to use. If this feels too advanced for you, feel free to skip ahead to `Chapter 2`, *Using Bootstrap Build Tools*. This section is totally optional. Head to the following URL to install Node.js if you don't already have it on your computer: `https://nodejs.org/download/`.

Follow the instructions on the Node.js website and, once you've finished installing it, run the following command in a command-line application such as Terminal or Cygwin:

```
$ node -v
```

This should spit out the version number of Node.js that you just installed and will also confirm that the installation worked. You should see something like this:

```
$ v0.10.33
```

Perfect, now let's move on to installing Harp.

Installing Harp.js

If you closed your command-line app, open it back up. If you are on a Mac, run the following command to install Harp:

```
$ sudo npm install -g harp
```

If you happen to be on a Windows machine, you'll need to enter a slightly different command, which is as follows:

```
$ npm install -g harp
```

After the installation completes, run the following command to get the Harp version number, which will also confirm that the installation was successful:

```
$ harp version
```

Adding Sass in Harp

I should also mention that most static site generators will also have built-in CSS preprocessors. This avoids you having to compile your Sass code somewhere else when working on your project. Harp includes both Sass and Less, so this will save you some time in upcoming chapters when we cover Sass in more detail.

Setting up the project

Before we convert our template to a Harp template, we need to set up the project structure. Create a new folder on your computer for the project then create the following subdirectories:

- css
- js
- `img` (if you plan on using images)
- partial
- fonts

Inserting the CSS

If you're storing the CSS files locally, copy `bootstrap.min.css` from your original project and add that into the new `/css` folder. In a future chapter, I'll show you how to code a custom Bootstrap theme. That file would also be included within this directory.

Inserting the JavaScript

The same pattern for the CSS will also apply to the JavaScript files. If you are storing `jquery.min.js` and `bootstrap.min.js` locally, then copy them into the new `/js` directory.

Other directories

The /img directory is optional and only applies if you plan to use images in your project. Ignore the /partial directory for now and I'll cover that a bit later. In the /fonts directory, you should drop in the Glyphicons icon set that comes with Bootstrap. If you downloaded Bootstrap, go back to the downloaded package and locate the font files. Copy them into this directory. Now that we have the project structure set up, we can start to break the basic page template down into a few different pieces.

Setting up the layout

In the root of your new Harp project, create a new file called `_layout.ejs`. **EJS** stands for **Embeddable JavaScript** and it's a type of template file that allows us to do more than just standard HTML. Within that file, copy and paste the code from our basic starter template. After you've inserted the code, we're going to make one change:

1. Locate the following line in the template and cut and paste it into a new file. Save the file and call it `index.ejs`:

   ```
   <h1>Hello, world!</h1>
   ```

2. Return to the layout file and insert the following line of code immediately after the `<body>` tag:

   ```
   <%- yield %>
   ```

3. Save both files then let me explain what is happening. The yield tag is a variable. Any page template such as `index.ejs` that lives in the same directory as the layout will be loaded in wherever you place the yield in the layout. So the `Hello, world!` line we inserted in the `index.ejs` file will load in here once you compile and launch your project.

Are you starting to see the advantage to this method? You could then go on and create other page templates so that all use this layout. In the future, if you need to make a change to the `<head>` of the layout, you only have to edit the one template file and it will be compiled into all of your final HTML files.

Compiling your project

Now that the template files are ready, we need to compile the project before we can preview it in the browser. Head back to your command-line app and make sure you are in the root of your project directory. Once there, run the following command to compile the project:

```
$ harp compile
```

Assuming you see no errors, your project was compiled successfully and can now be previewed in the browser. Before we move onto that step, though, take a look at your project directory and you'll see a `/www` folder. On compiling, Harp creates this directory and inserts the plain HTML, CSS, and JavaScript files. Assuming the website looks good when you preview, you then deploy the contents of the `/www` directory to your web server. More on deployment shortly.

Previewing your project

Harp has a built-in node web server that you can use to preview your project locally before deploying it. Open up your command-line app and run the following command from the root of your Harp project:

```
$ harp server
```

After doing so, you should see a message in the Terminal telling you that the server is successfully running. Open a web browser and navigate to the following URL to preview your project: `http://localhost:9000`.

Your project will load up in the browser and you should see the `Hello, world!` message that was inserted on compile. This is only a fraction of what you can do with Harp. To learn more about how Harp works, visit their website at `https://harpjs.com/`.

Deploying your project

If you're looking for a simple way to quickly deploy your project for testing, there is a tool called **Surge** from the same people that developed Harp. Surge is a free deployment solution; visit their website to learn more at `http://surge.sh/`.

Installing Surge

To install Surge, you'll need to open up your Terminal again. Once you have done this, run the following command:

```
$ npm install --global surge
```

This will install Surge and make it available anywhere on your computer.

Using Surge to deploy your project

To deploy your new project, navigate back to the root directory in the Terminal then run the following command:

```
$ surge
```

You'll now be prompted to log in or create a new account. Surge is free but you need to register an account to use it. You'll also notice in the Terminal that there is an autogenerated URL. This is the URL you can use to view your project live on the Internet. Once you've finished registering or logging in, visit the URL in your browser. If all went well, you should see the basic hello world page live.

Surge is a great tool if you're looking for a quick way to test your project on a live web server. If all goes well, you can then manually deploy your project to your own web server. Surge does offer a paid plan allowing for the use of a custom domain. So you could actually use it for your production deployment if that seems like a good idea.

Summary

That brings the first chapter to a close. I hope this chapter has proved to be a good introduction to Bootstrap 4 and provided you with a few advanced techniques for setting up your Bootstrap projects. In the next chapter, we'll take what we've learned here a step further by covering Bootstrap build tools. This will include a deeper explanation of how to use Harp, as well as other tools that are commonly used with Bootstrap.

2

Using Bootstrap Build Tools

In the previous chapter, we reviewed the process for setting up a basic Bootstrap template with the compiled framework files. What if you need to customize your Bootstrap build or you want to use additional development tools to make your life easier? This is possible through the use of a number of great tools. In this chapter, I'll show you how to install, set up, and use a number of build tools such as Node.js, Grunt.js, and Harp.js to extend Bootstrap and reveal the real power of the framework.

Different types of tools

When working with Bootstrap, there are really three types of tools you need to be aware of. The first two are `Node.js` and `Grunt.js`. These are build <ie>tools</ie> and they take the development framework files and build them into the final files that you want to include in the production version of your projects. You wouldn't include development files on your actual production web server, as they are tools. You want to compile your files into production-ready HTML, CSS, and JavaScript that a web server can read and a browser can translate into a website.

The second type of tool you might want to use is a static website generator such as Harp.js. I talked a little bit about Harp in the first chapter but I will review it again in a little more detail. The main advantages of using Harp are things such as variables and partials in HTML, and a reusable-template-based system for your pages that allows you to reuse code.

The final types of tool you can use with Bootstrap are CSS preprocessors. In Bootstrap 4, the only option is Sass and we'll cover that in more depth later. However, before you can really start to learn to use Sass, you need to learn how to compile it into regular CSS files. Once you do, you can also start to use things such as variables and mixins in your CSS to make your files cleaner and easier to write.

Installing Node.js

If you skipped installing Node.js in `Chapter 1`, *Introducing Bootstrap 4* then now is the time to follow along and install and configure all your build tools. Let's start by heading to its website, `https://nodejs.org`, and downloading `Node.js`:

Node is a JavaScript runtime that uses Google Chrome's V8 JavaScript engine. What that means is that Node is a JavaScript-based web server that you can run locally or in production. It includes an event-driven, non-blocking I/O model which is easy to use and lightweight. Node comes with a built-in package manager called `npm` which includes the largest ecosystem of open source libraries on the Web.

Follow the installation instructions on the Node.js website and once you're done, open up a command-line application such as Terminal or Cygwin. Run the following command:

```
$ node -v
```

This will print out the Node.js version number that you installed and will confirm that it worked. It should look something like this if successful:

```
$ v0.10.33
```

node version manager 'nvm' installed
Harp failed above v4.2.4LTS

Updating npm

Now that Node is installed, let's ensure that the latest version of `npm` is also installed. `npm` is a package manager for Node and allows you to install useful tools such as Grunt, which we'll do in our next step.

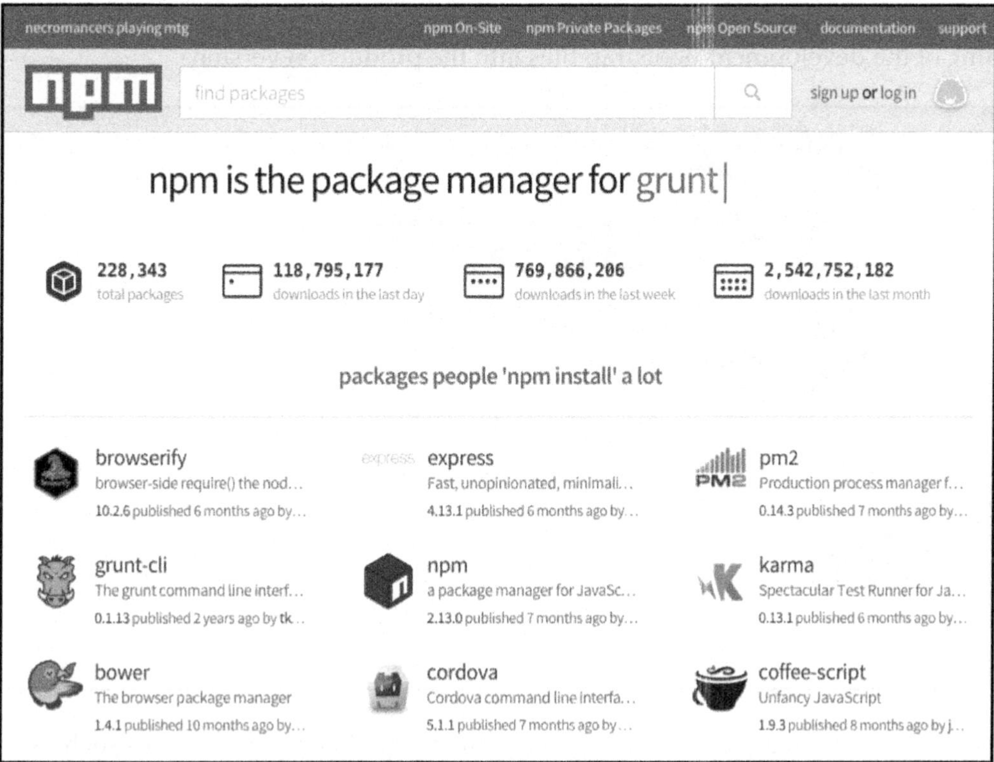

To make sure the latest version of `npm` is installed, run the following command in the Terminal:

```
npm update -g npm
```

You may need to include `sudo` before this command in some cases.

Once the update is complete, we can safely start to install the other packages we'll need for our Bootstrap development environment.

Installing Grunt

Grunt is a JavaScript task runner and it's the tool that will do the actual compiling and building of the development Bootstrap files into the production versions.

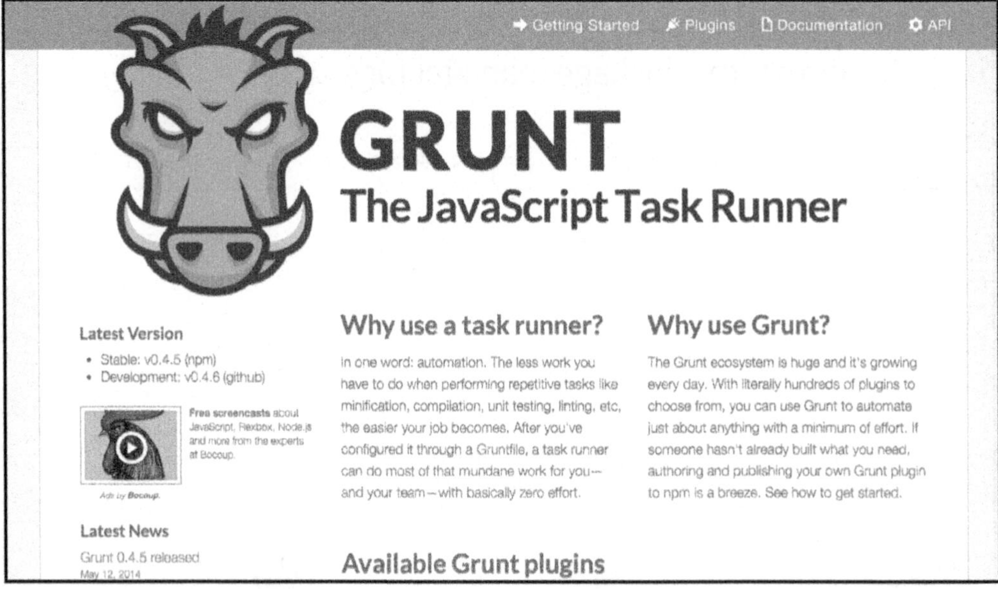

Grunt provides automation and allows you to chain together repetitive tasks such as compiling, minification, linting, and unit testing. Therefore, it's commonly used in frameworks such as Bootstrap to build the source files into production. To install Grunt, run the following command in the Terminal:

```
npm install -g grunt-cli
```

If you receive any errors, you may need to add `sudo` to the beginning of the above command. After finishing your installation, run the following command to check the Grunt version number and confirm that everything is working properly:

```
$ grunt -V
```

You should expect to see something like this printed out in the Terminal:

```
grunt-cli v0.1.13
```

Download the Bootstrap source files

To allow us to compile source files into production, we now need to download the Bootstrap source files and install them on our local machine. Head to the following URL and download the Bootstrap source files:
`http://v4-alpha.getbootstrap.com/getting-started/download/`.

Once you've download the files, unzip the package and move the directory to where you want it to live on your computer. If you just want to leave it on the desktop for now, that is fine. You can safely move the project around before or after editing it. The next thing you need to do is install the project dependencies. First, navigate to the root of the download package in the Terminal. It will likely be called something like `bootstrap-4.0.0-alpha.2`. Once you are there, run the following command to install the files:

```
$ npm install
```

If you get any type of error, try including `sudo` at the beginning of the command.

If you are using `sudo`, you'll likely be prompted for your system password. Type it in then hit *Enter* to execute the command.

Installing Ruby

Another tool you need to work with the Bootstrap source files is Ruby. Ruby is an objected-oriented programming language that was designed in the 1990s in Japan. If you are familiar with Perl, you will likely enjoy Ruby, as Perl was the main inspiration for the language.

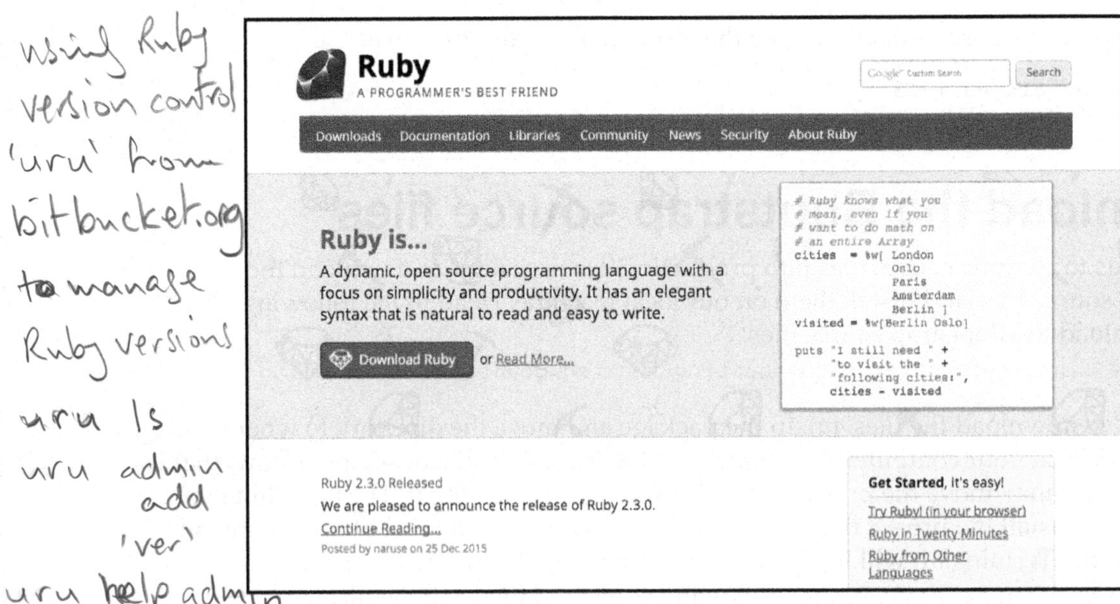

In Bootstrap, Ruby is used to run the documentation website and to compile the core Sass files into regular CSS. For the Bootstrap documentation, you can always visit `http://getbootstrap.com/`. However, in some cases, you may find yourself offline, so you might want to install a local version of the docs that you can use. Let's first start by installing Ruby before we get to the documentation.

Good news! If you're on a Mac, Ruby comes pre-installed with OS X. Run the following command to check the Ruby version number and verify that it's available:

```
$ ruby -v
```

If Ruby is installed, you should see something like this in the Terminal:

```
$ ruby 1.9.2p320 (2012-04-20 revision 35421) [x86_64-
darwin12.3.0]
```

If you're on a Windows machine, you may need to manually install Ruby. If that's the case, check out the following website to learn how to install it: `http://rubyinstaller.org/`.

Installing the Bundler gem

After Ruby is ready to roll, you need to install a Ruby gem called Bundler. In the words of the developers of Bundler: *Bundler provides a consistent environment for Ruby projects by tracking and installing the exact gems and versions that are needed.* For more info on Bundler, please visit `http://bundler.io/`.

Don't worry too much about what Bundler does. The important thing is to just install it and move on.

1. To do this, we need to run the following command in the Terminal in your Bootstrap source file root directory:

```
$ gem install bundler
```

2. Again, if you get any errors, just begin the command with `sudo`. To confirm your installation of Bundler, run the following command to view the version number as in our previous examples:

```
$ bundler -v
```

3. If all is good, you should see something like this printed out in the Terminal:

```
$ Bundler version 1.11.2
```

4. The last step you need to do is install the actual documentation bundle of files. Do this by running the following command in the Terminal from your root Bootstrap directory:

```
$ bundle install
```

5. This will install all Ruby dependencies, such as **Jekyll**, which is used for the documentation, and the Sass compiler we'll need a little later in the book. If you're a Windows user and you want to run the Jekyll documentation locally then you should check this out: `http://jekyll-windows.juthilo.com/`.

Jekyll is a database-independent static site generator that will convert plain text into a static website or blog. You can write templates in Markdown, Textile, Liquid, or HTML and CSS. On deployment, the code will be compiled into production-ready files that can be uploaded to a web server or run locally. That completes the setup for the first part of the Bootstrap build tools. Before we move onto the static site generator portion, let me show you how to run the documentation locally.

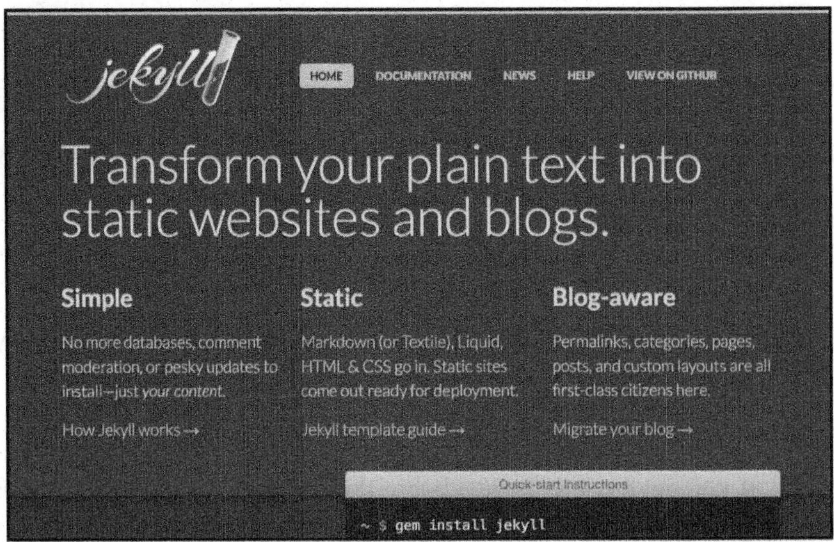

Running the documentation

Getting the documentation running locally is actually pretty easy. From the root of the Bootstrap source file directory, run the below command in the terminal:

```
bundle exec jekyll serve
```

In the Terminal, you'll see that the server is running. The next step is to open up a web browser and enter the following address:
`http://localhost:9001/`

The Bootstrap documentation website will load up and now you have a local version of the documentation! To quit out of the server, hit *Ctrl* + *C* and you will exit.

Setting up the static site generator

In `Chapter 1`, *Introducing Bootstrap 4* I gave you a quick overview of setting up Harp.js, which is a static site generator. In this chapter, I'll go into more depth on how to properly set up your website, CSS, HTML, and JavaScript files. Before I do that though, we should talk about why you might want to use Harp.js.

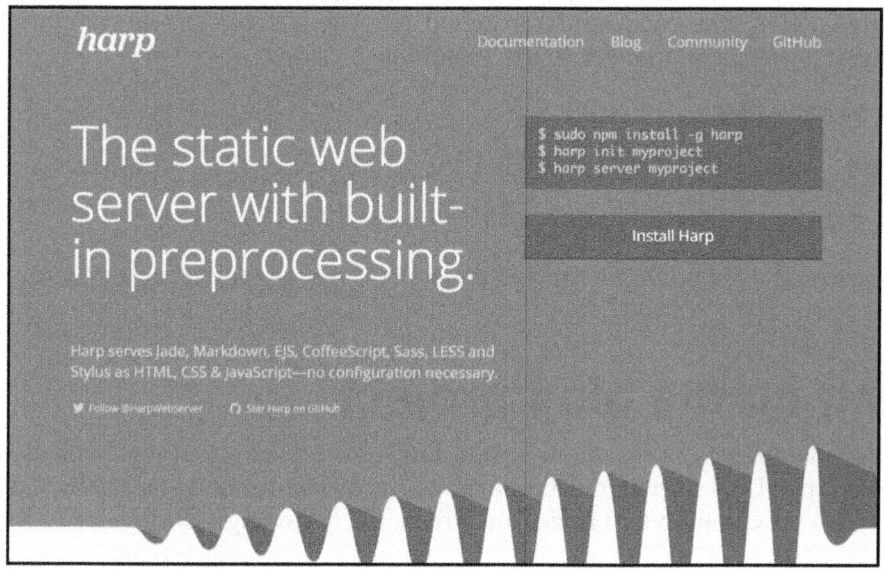

Why use Harp.js

There are a number of great arguments for using a static site generator such as Harp.js: cleaner code, modern best practices, and more. However, the best reason is that it will just make your life simple. Instead of having to update a header on all 50 pages of the website, you can simply update the header partially and then have that compiled into all your templates. You can also take advantage of using variables to insert content and configuration.

Installing Harp.js

Harp is another project that runs on Node.js so we can use `npm` to install it with the following command:

```
$ sudo npm install -g harp
```

If you did this in `Chapter 1`, *Introducing Bootstrap 4*, you can skip down to the next part of this chapter.

To confirm that Harp was successfully installed, let's use our version-checking trick by entering the following command into the Terminal:

```
$ harp version
```

If all is good, you should see something like this printed out in the Terminal:

```
$ 0.14.0
```

Harp is now installed and we can move on to setting up our project for the book.

Setting up the blog project

As I mentioned earlier, we're going to be building a blog throughout this book as we learn to use Bootstrap 4. Let's start by creating a new directory and call it something like `Bootstrap Blog`. Open up that folder and create the following sub-directories inside it:

- css
- fonts
- img
- js
- partial

css

The `css` directory will hold the Bootstrap framework's CSS file and a custom theme file which we'll build later on. Go to the Bootstrap source file directory and locate the `dist/css` folder. From there, copy `bootstrap.min.css` to our new blog project's `css` directory.

fonts

The `fonts` directory will hold either a font icon library such as Glyphicon or Font Awesome. Previously, Bootstrap shipped with Glyphicon but they have dropped it in version 4. If you wish to use it, you'll need to download the icon font set and then drop the files into this directory. You could also include a web font that you may want to use on your project in this directory. If you are looking for web fonts, a good place to start is Google Web Fonts.

img

The `img` directory will hold any images used in the blog.

js

The `js` or JavaScript directory will hold the Bootstrap framework JavaScript files. If you add any other third-party libraries, they should also be included in this directory. Go back to the Bootstrap source files one last time and locate the `dist/js` folder. From there, copy `bootstrap.min.js` to the `js` directory in the blog project.

partial

The `partial` directory will hold any reusable snippets of code that we want to use in multiple locations throughout our templates or web pages, for example, the header and footer for our project. It's important to note you can have as many partial files as you like or use none at all.

Within this folder, create two new files and name them `_header.ejs` and `footer.ejs`. For now, you can leave them blank.

EJS files

EJS stands for **Embeddable JavaScript**. This is a type of template file that allows us to use things such as partials and variables in our templates. Harp also supports Jade if you prefer that language. However, I prefer to use EJS because it is very similar to HTML and therefore really easy to learn. If you've ever used WordPress, it is very similar to using template tags to insert bits of content or components into your design.

Setting up the JSON files

Each Harp project has at least two JSON files that are used for configuring a project. JSON stands for JavaScript Object Notation and it's a lightweight format for data interchange. If that sounds complicated, don't worry about it. The actual coding of a JSON file is actually really straightforward, as I will show you now.

The first is called `_harp.json` and it's used for configuring global settings and variables that will be used across the entire blog. In this case, we're going to set up a global variable for the name of our project that will be inserted into every page template. Start by creating a new file in the root of blog project and call it `_harp.json`. Within the file, insert the following code:

```
{
   "globals": {
      "siteTitle": "Learning Bootstrap 4"
   }
}
```

Here's what's happening in this code:

- We're using the `globals` keyword so any variables under this will be available across all of our templates
- I've created a new variable called `siteTitle` which will be the title of the project
- I've inserted the name of the book, `Learning Bootstrap 4`, as the title for the project

That completes the setup of the global `_harp.json` file. In a little bit, I'll show you how to add the variable we set up to the main layout file.

Creating the data JSON file

The next thing we need to do is set up the `_data.json` file that can hold template-specific variables and settings. For our project, we'll set up one variable for each page template which will hold the name of the page. Create another file in the root of the blog project and name it `_data.json`. In that file, insert the following code:

```
{
   "index": {
      "pageTitle": "Home"
   }
}
```

Let me break down this code for you:

- `index` refers to a filename. In this case, it will be our home page. We haven't actually created this file yet but that is okay as we will in the next steps.
- I've created a variable called `pageTitle` which will refer to the title of each page template in our project

- Since this is the `index` template, I've assigned a value or name of `Home` to it

That completes the setup of the `_data.json` file for now. Later on, we'll need to update this file once we add more page templates. For now, this will give us the minimum resources that we need to get our project going.

Setting up the layout

Let's go ahead and set up the layout file for our project. The layout is a separate file that will be a wrapper for the content of all of our pages. It contains things such as the `<head>` of our page, a header partial, and a footer partial. This is one of the advantages to using a static site generator. We don't have to define this on every page so if we want to change something in our header, we only change it in the layout. On the next compile, all of the page templates' headers will be updated with the new code.

Create a new file in the root of the blog project called `_layout.ejs`. Since this is technically a type of layout file, we'll be creating it as an EJS template file. Once you've created the file, insert the following code into it:

```
<!DOCTYPE html>
<html lang="en">
  <head>
    <!-- Required meta tags always come first -->
    <meta charset="utf-8">
    <meta name="viewport" content="width=device-width, initial-scale=1,
shrink-to-fit=no">
    <meta http-equiv="x-ua-compatible" content="ie=edge">

    <title><%- pageTitle %> | <%- siteTitle %></title>

    <!-- Bootstrap CSS -->
    <link rel="stylesheet" href="css/bootstrap.min.css">
  </head>
  <body>

    <%- partial("partial/_header") %>

    <%- yield %>

    <%- partial("partial/_footer") %>

    <!-- jQuery first, then Bootstrap JS. -->
    <script
src="https://ajax.googleapis.com/ajax/libs/jquery/2.1.4/jquery.min.js"></sc
```

```
ript>
    <script src="js/bootstrap.min.js"></script>
  </body>
</html>
```

There are a few things going on here, so let me explain everything that you need to know:

- The top is your standard `<head>` section that matches the basic Bootstrap template we covered in the first chapter, with, however, a few differences.
- Note the `<title>` tag and that it includes the two variables we set up previously. One for the `pageTitle` variable which will print out **Home** if we are on the index page. The second `siteTitle` variable will always print out **Learning Bootstrap 4** as that is what we set it to in `_harp.json`.
- Skip down to the `<body>` section and you'll see some new lines of code. The first partial is for our header. This line will include a snippet of code that we'll set up later that contains the markup for our header. Since this will be the same on all pages, we only need to include it here once instead of on every page.
- The second section in the `<body>` is the `<%- yield %> tag`. This is a Harp template tag and here is where the contents of our page template files will load. In the case of our index page, any code that we enter into `index.ejs` (that we need to create still) will be loaded in at this place in the layout.
- The final line of code is a partial for the footer and works exactly the same as the header. At a minimum, you should have a header and footer partial in your projects. However, you are free to add as many partials as you like to make your project more modular.

That completes the setup of the layout. Next, let's move on to coding the header and footer partials.

Setting up the header

Let's set up our first partial by coding the header. We'll use the Bootstrap `navbar` component here for our global navigation for the blog. In the partial directory, open up the `_header.ejs` file that you created a little earlier and insert the following code:

```
<nav class="navbar navbar-light bg-faded">
  <a class="navbar-brand" href="#">Learning Bootstrap 4</a>
  <ul class="nav navbar-nav">
    <li class="nav-item active">
      <a class="nav-link" href="index.html">Home</a>
    </li>
```

```
        <li class="nav-item">
          <a class="nav-link" href="about.html">About</a>
        </li>
        <li class="nav-item">
          <a class="nav-link" href="contact.html">Contact</a>
        </li>
      </ul>
      <form class="form-inline pull-xs-right">
        <input class="form-control" type="text" placeholder="Search">
        <button class="btn btn-primary" type="submit">Search</button>
      </form>
    </nav>
```

If you're a Bootstrap 3 user, you'll likely notice that the code to render a `navbar` in version 4 is much cleaner. This will make the `navbar` much easier to use and explain. Let me break down the code for you:

- On the `<nav>` tag, we have a few classes we need to include. `.navbar` is the standard class need for this component. `.navbar-light` will render a light-colored navbar for us. There are some other color options you can check out in the Bootstrap documents. Finally, the `.bg-faded` class is optional but I like to include it as it makes the background of the `navbar` a little more subtle.
- The `.navbar-brand` class is unchanged from Bootstrap 3 and I've inserted the name of the book for this tag. Feel free to name it whatever you want.
- Next, we have our navigation list of links. The `<ul>` tag needs to have the two required classes here: `.nav` and `.navbar-nav`.
- Within the list, you'll notice three pages: `Home`, `About` and `Contact`. These are going to be the pages we'll build out through later chapters so please fill them in now.

Note the `.active` class on the index page link. This is optional and you may not want to include it in this manner as this is a global navigation.

- Finally, I've included a search form and used the `.pull-xs-right` to align it to the right of the `navbar`. If you're familiar with Bootstrap 3, this class used to simply be called `.pull-right`. In Bootstrap 4, you have more control of the alignment based on the viewport size of your device. If you always want the search bar to be aligned to the right then use the `-xs` value in the class.

Save the file and that will complete the setup of the header partial. Let's move on to setting up the footer.

Setting up the footer

The footer partial works exactly like the header. Open up the `_footer.ejs` file in the partial directory that we created earlier and paste in the following code:

```
<!-- footer //-->
<div class="container">
   <div class="row">
      <div class="col-lg-12">
         Learning Bootstrap 4 2016
      </div>
   </div>
</div>
```

The `footer` content is going to be quite basic for our blog. Here's a breakdown of the code:

- I'm using the `.container` class to wrap the entire `footer`, which will set a max width of 1140 px for the layout. The `navbar` wasn't placed into a container so it will stretch to the full width of the page. The `.container` class will also set a left and right padding of .9375rem to the block. It's important to note that Bootstrap 4 uses REMs for the main unit of measure. EMs has been deprecated with the upgrade from version 3. If you're interested in learning more about REMs, you should read this blog post: `http://snook.ca/archives/html_and_css/font-size-with-rem`.
- It's also important to note that the column classes have NOT changed from Bootstrap 3 to 4. This is actually a good thing if you are porting over a project, as it will make the migration process much easier. I've set the width of the footer to be the full width of the container by using the `.col-lg-12` class.
- Finally I've entered some simple content for the footer, which is the book name and the year of writing. Feel free to change this up to whatever you want.
- Save the file and the footer setup will be complete.

We're getting closer to having our Harp development environment set up. The last thing we need to do is set up our index page template and then we can compile and view our project.

Creating our first page template

For our first page template, we're going to create our `Home` or `index` page. In the root of the blog project, create a new file called `index.ejs`. Note this file is not prepended with an underscore like the previous files. With Harp, any file that has the underscore will be compiled into another and ignored when the files are copied into the production directory. For example, you don't want the compiler to spit out `layout.html` because it's fairly useless with the content of the `Home` page. You only want to get `index.html`, which you can deploy to your web server. The basic thing you need to remember is to *not* include an underscore at the beginning of your page template files. Once you've created the file, insert the following code:

```
<div class="container">
  <div class="row">
    <div class="col-lg-12">
      <h1>hello world!</h1>
    </div>
  </div>
</div>
```

To get us started, I'm going to keep this really simple. Here's a quick breakdown of what is happening:

- I've created another `.container` which will hold the content for the `Home` page
- Within the container, there is a full-width column. In that column, I've inserted an `<h1>` with a `hello world!` message

That will be it for now. Later on, we'll build this page out further. Save the file and close it. We've now completed setting up all the basic files for our Harp development environment. The last step is to compile the project and test it out.

Compiling your project

When we compile a project in Harp, it will find all the different partial, layout, and template files and combine them into regular HTML, CSS, and JavaScript files. We haven't used any Sass yet but, as with the template files, you can have multiple Sass files that are compiled into a single CSS file that can be used on a production web server. To compile your project, navigate to the root of the blog project in the Terminal. Once you are there, run the following command:

```
$ harp compile
```

If everything worked, a new blank line in the terminal will appear. This is good! If the compiler spits out an error, read what it has to say and make the appropriate changes to your template files. A couple of common errors that you might run into are the following:

- Syntax errors in `_harp.json` or `_data.json`
- Syntax errors for variable or partial names in `_layout.ejs`
- If you have created additional page templates in the root of your project, and *not* included them in `_data.json`, the compile will fail

Once your compile is successful, head back to the root of the blog project and notice that there is a new `www` directory. This directory holds all the compiled HTML, CSS, and JavaScript files for your project. When you are ready to deploy your project to a production web server, you would copy these files up with FTP or using another means of file transfer. Every time you run the harp compile command in your project, these files will be updated with any new or edited code.

Running your project

Harp has a built-in web server that is backed by `Node.js`. This means you don't need a web hosting account or web server to actually test your project. With a simple command, you can fire up the built-in server and view your project locally. This is also really great if you are working on a project somewhere with no Internet connection. It will allow you to continue building your projects Internet-free. To run the server, head back to the Terminal and make sure you are still in the root directory of your blog project. From there, enter the following command:

```
$ harp server
```

In the Terminal, you should see a message that the server is running. You are now free to visit the project in a browser.

Viewing your project

Now that the project is up and running on the web server, simply navigate to the following URL to view it: `http://localhost:9000`.

By default, Harp runs on port `9000` but you can specify a different port by modifying the last command. Go back to the terminal and quit the server by hitting *Ctrl* + *C*. Now enter the following command:

```
$ harp server  --port 9001
```

Using this command, you can invoke any port you would like to use. Head back to the web browser again and change the URL slightly to read `http://localhost:9001`.

Your project should load for you and look something like this:

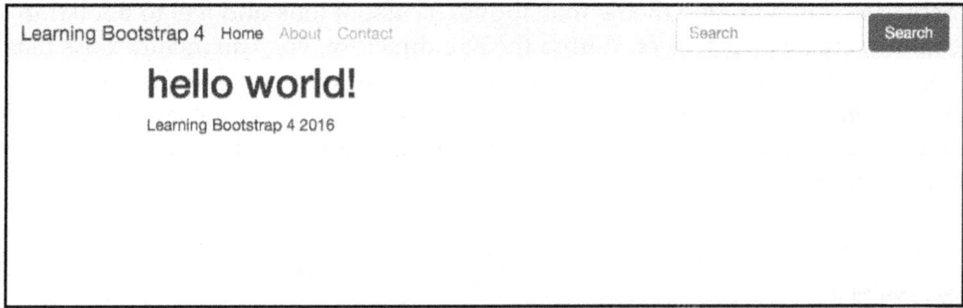

It might not be much to look at right now but it works! Your project is successfully set up and running. In future chapters, we'll add to this page and build some more using additional Bootstrap 4 components.

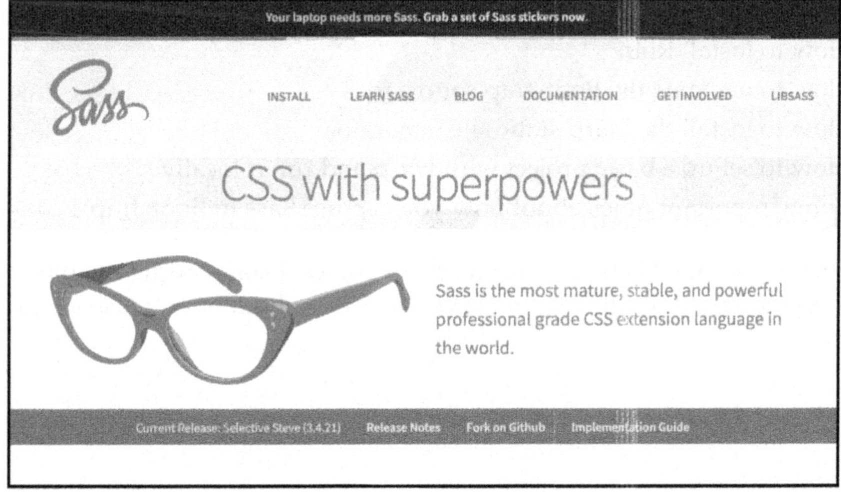

A note about Sass

When building a project with Bootstrap 4, there are two ways you can work with Sass. The first would be by editing the actual Bootstrap framework files and then recompiling them using Grunt. This is useful if you'd like to use something such as Flexbox for your grid layout. I'll discuss this in greater depth in the next chapter. The other way you might want to use Sass is to craft a unique theme that applies a custom look and feel to Bootstrap. This is done in the actual Harp project. Within the `css` directory, you can include Sass files; when you compile your Harp project, they will be converted to regular CSS, as Harp has a built-in Sass compiler. Then it is just a simple exercise of including those additional files in your layout template. I'll also get into that a little later in the book but I wanted to point out the difference now.

Summary

That brings the second chapter to a close. We've covered how to use a number of Bootstrap build tools. Let's review what we learned:

- How to install and run `Node.js` and `npm`
- How to install Grunt
- How to install Ruby
- How to navigate the Bootstrap source files
- How to install the Harp static site generator
- How to set up a basic project with Harp and run it locally
- Some important notes about how you can use Sass in Bootstrap 4

Now that our environment is set up and ready to go, we'll start coding the blog in the next chapter. To get us started, we'll jump right into learning about how to use a Flexbox layout in Bootstrap.

3
Jumping into Flexbox

Alright, now that we have finished setting up all the Bootstrap build tools, let's jump into an actual great new feature of Bootstrap 4. The latest version of the framework comes with CSS Flexbox support. The goal of the Flexbox layout module is to create a more effective way of designing a layout for a website or web application. The grid of boxes is aligned in a way that distributes them across their container even if their size is unknown. This is where the "Flex" in Flexbox comes from.

The motivation for a flexible box arose from a web design for mobiles. A way to have a section grow or shrink to best fill the available space was needed when building responsive web applications or websites. Flexbox is the opposite of block layouts that are either vertically or horizontally driven. It's important to note that Flexbox is generally best suited for use when designing web applications. The traditional grid method still works best for larger websites.

In our blog project, we're going to use Flexbox to create a homepage. There will be several rows of blocks, each being a post. I'll show you a few ways to lay the blocks out and different ways you can customize the contents of each block, all using the new Flexbox layout in Bootstrap.

Flexbox basics and terminology

Before we go too far, we should define a few Flexbox basics and some terminology that I'll use throughout the chapter. Every Flexbox layout is dependent on an outer container. As we move through the chapter, I'll refer to this container as the **parent**. Within the parent container there will always be a collection of boxes or blocks. I'll refer to these boxes as **children** or **child** elements of the parent. Why don't we start by talking a little bit more about why you would want to use Flexbox? The main purpose of Flexbox is to allow for the dynamic resizing of child boxes within their parent container.

This works for the resizing of both width and height properties on-the-fly. Many designers and developers prefer this technique as it allows for easier layouts with less code:

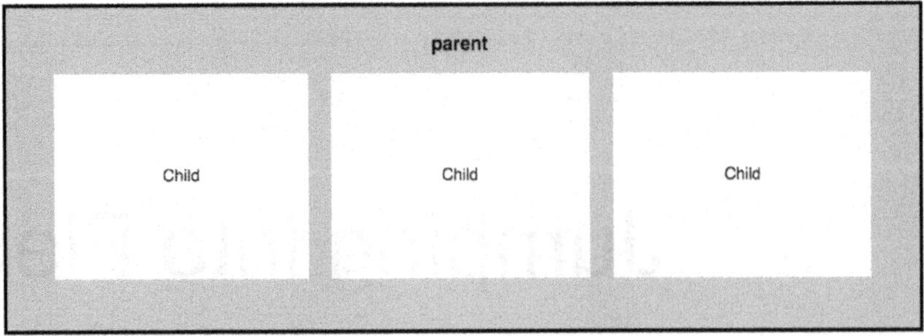

Ordering your Flexbox

Flexbox is a really powerful module as it comes with several properties that you can customize. Let's quickly go over some more basics before we fully take the plunge and use Flexbox in Bootstrap. Let's start by talking about the order of child boxes. By default, they will appear in the order that you insert them in the HTML file. Consider the following code:

```
<div class="parent">
   <div class="child">
   1
   </div>
   <div class="child">
   2
   </div>
   <div class="child">
   3
   </div>
</div>
```

A proper CSS will produce a layout that looks like this:

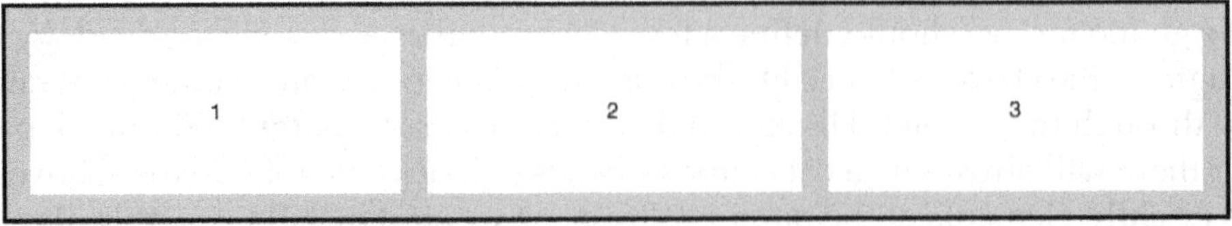

Here's the CSS to produce this layout if you are following along at home:

```
.parent {
  display: flex;
  background: #ccc;
  padding: 10px;
  font-family: helvetica;
}

.child {
  padding: 10px;
  margin: 10px;
  background: #fff;
  flex-grow: 1;
  text-align:center;
  height: 100px;
  line-height: 100px;
}
```

Now using an `order` property we can reorder the children using some CSS. Let's put the third box at the beginning. If you are reordering some blocks, you need to define the position for each one; you can't simply enter the value for a single block. Add the following CSS to your style sheet:

```
.child:nth-of-type(1) {
  order: 2;
}
.child:nth-of-type(2) {
  order: 3;
}
.child:nth-of-type(3) {
  order: 1;
}
```

I'm using the `nth-of-type` pseudo selector to target each of the three boxes. I've then used the `order` property to set the third box to the first position. I've also adjusted the other two boxes to move them over one space. Save the file and your boxes should now look like this:

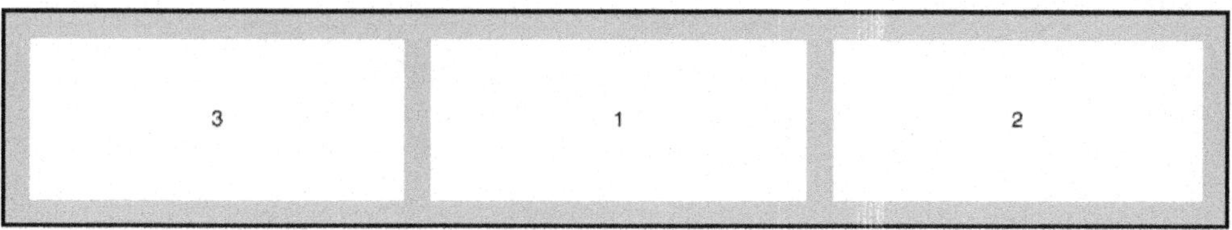

As you can see, the third box has moved to the first position. It's as easy as that to rearrange blocks on boxes on a page. I think you'll likely see how this could be useful for coding up a web application dashboard.

Stretching your child sections to fit the parent container

Another important Flexbox feature is the ability to stretch the width of the child boxes to fit the full-width of the containing parent. If you look at the preceding CSS you'll notice a `flex-grow` property on the `.child` class. The property is set to 1 which means that the child boxes will stretch to equally fill their parent. You could also do something where one box is set to a different value, using the `nth-of-type` selector, and then it would be wider than the others. Here's the code to create equal-width columns as that is what you'll likely do in most cases:

```
.child {
   flex-grow: 1;
}
```

Changing the direction of the boxes

By default in Flexbox, the child boxes will be in a row going left to right. If you like, you can change the direction using the `flex-direction` property. Let's try out a few different directions. First let's review our base HTML code again:

```
<div class="parent">
   <div class="child">
     1
   </div>
   <div class="child">
     2
   </div>
   <div class="child">
     3
   </div>
</div>
```

Here's the base CSS we wrote a little earlier. However, this time we'll add the `flex-direction` property (with a value of `row-reverse`)to the `.parent` class. This will reverse the order of the boxes:

```
.parent {
  display: flex;
  flex-direction: row-reverse;
  background: #ccc;
  padding: 10px;
}

.child {
  padding: 10px;
  margin: 10px;
  background: #fff;
  flex-grow: 1;
  text-align:center;
  height: 100px;
  line-height: 100px;
}
```

If you save the file and view it in a browser it should now look like this:

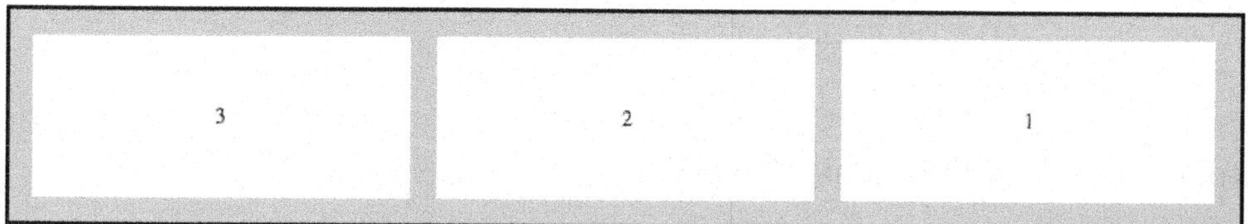

What if we wanted to order the boxes vertically so they were stacked on top of each other in descending order? We can do that by changing the `flex-direction` property to `column`:

```
.parent {
   ...
   flex-direction: column;
}
```

That configuration will produce a grid that looks like this:

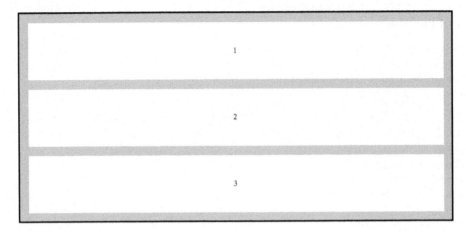

Finally there is one more direction we can try. Let's do the same vertically stacked grid but this time we'll reverse it. We do that by switching the `flex-direction` property to `column-reverse`:

```
.parent {
    ...
    flex-direction: column-reverse;
}
```

That will produce a grid that looks like this:

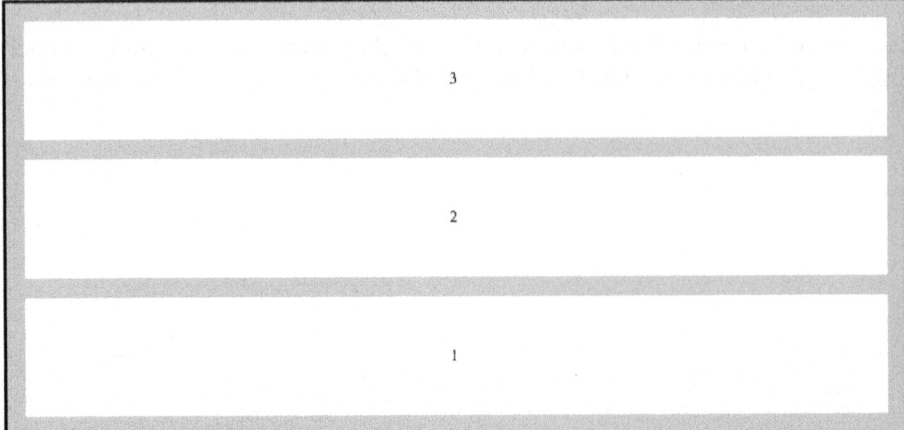

Wrapping your Flexbox

By default all of your child boxes will try to fit onto one line. If you have a layout with several boxes, this may not be the look you want. If this is the case, you can use the `flex-wrap` property to wrap the child boxes as needed. Let's add more boxes to our original code with the following HTML:

```
<div class="parent">
    <div class="child">
    1
    </div>
    <div class="child">
    2
    </div>
    <div class="child">
    3
    </div>
    <div class="child">
    4
    </div>
    <div class="child">
    5
    </div>
    <div class="child">
    6
    </div>
    <div class="child">
    7
    </div>
    <div class="child">
    8
    </div>
    <div class="child">
    9
    </div>
</div>
```

We now have nine boxes in our parent container. That should give us enough to work with to create a nice wrapping effect. Before we see what this looks like, we need to add some more CSS. Add the following properties to your CSS file:

```
.parent {
    ...
    flex-wrap: wrap;
}
```

```
.child {
    ...
    min-width: 100px;
}
```

I've added two new properties to achieve the layout we want. Let me break-down what is happening:

- I've added the `flex-wrap` property to the `.parent` class and set the value to `wrap`. This will wrap the boxes when it's appropriate.
- On the `.child` class I added a `min-width` of `100px`. I've done this so we can have some control on when the child boxes will break. If we don't add this, the width of the columns may get too thin.

Once you've added those properties to the existing code, save the file and test it. Your layout should now look something like this:

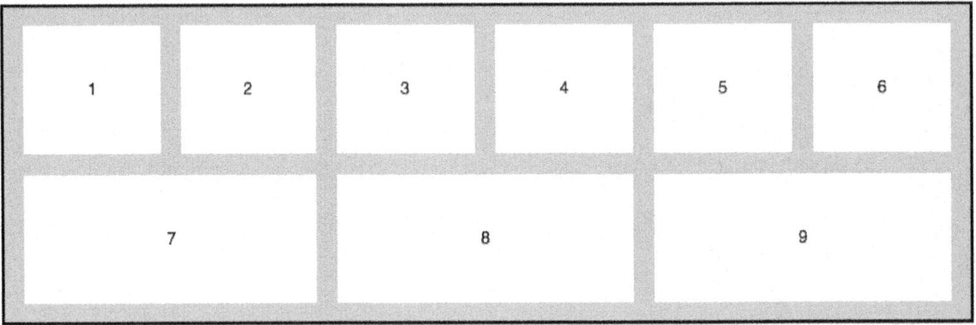

As you can see, we now have a two-row layout with six boxes on top and three below. Remember we added the `flex-grow` property previously, so the second row is stretching or growing to fit. If you want your boxes to always be equal you should use an even number, in this case 12. You could also remove the `flex-grow` property; then all the boxes would be the same width but they would not fill the layout the same way.

Creating equal-height columns

One of the best features of Flexbox is the ability to easily create equal height columns. In a regular horizontal layout, if your content is not the exact same length, each column will be a different height. This can be problematic for a web application layout because you usually want your boxes to be more uniform. Let's check out some regular layout code and what it looks like in the browser:

```
<div class="parent">
   <div class="child">
   Lorem ipsum dolor sit amet, consectetur adipiscing elit, sed do eiusmod
tempor incididunt ut labore et dolore magna aliqua. Ut enim ad minim
veniam, quis nostrud exercitation ullamco laboris nisi ut aliquip ex ea
commodo consequat.
   </div>
   <div class="child">
   Lorem ipsum dolor sit amet, consectetur adipiscing elit, sed do eiusmod
tempor incididunt ut labore et dolore magna aliqua. Ut enim ad minim
veniam, quis nostrud exercitation ullamco laboris nisi ut aliquip ex ea
commodo consequat. Lorem ipsum dolor sit amet, consectetur adipiscing elit,
sed do eiusmod tempor incididunt ut labore et dolore magna aliqua. Ut enim
ad minim veniam, quis nostrud exercitation ullamco laboris nisi ut aliquip
ex ea commodo consequat.
   </div>
   <div class="child">
   Lorem ipsum dolor sit amet, consectetur adipiscing elit, sed do eiusmod
tempor incididunt ut labore et dolore magna aliqua. Ut enim ad minim
veniam, quis nostrud exercitation ullamco laboris nisi ut aliquip ex ea
commodo consequat. Lorem ipsum dolor sit amet, consectetur adipiscing elit,
sed do eiusmod tempor incididunt ut labore et dolore magna aliqua. Ut enim
ad minim veniam, quis nostrud exercitation ullamco laboris nisi ut aliquip
ex ea commodo consequat. Lorem ipsum dolor sit amet, consectetur adipiscing
elit, sed do eiusmod tempor incididunt ut labore et dolore magna aliqua. Ut
enim ad minim veniam, quis nostrud exercitation ullamco laboris nisi ut
aliquip ex ea commodo consequat. Lorem ipsum dolor sit amet, consectetur
adipiscing elit, sed do eiusmod tempor incididunt ut labore et dolore magna
aliqua. Ut enim ad minim veniam, quis nostrud exercitation ullamco laboris
nisi ut aliquip ex ea commodo consequat. Lorem ipsum dolor sit amet,
consectetur adipiscing elit, sed do eiusmod tempor incididunt ut labore et
dolore magna aliqua. Ut enim ad minim veniam, quis nostrud exercitation
ullamco laboris nisi ut aliquip ex ea commodo consequat.
   </div>
</div>
```

I've created three columns with different amounts of text in each of them. Let's add some basic styling to these columns:

```
.parent {
  width: 100%;
  background: #ccc;
  font-family: helvetica;
  padding: 5%;
  float: left;
}

.child {
```

```
  padding: 2%;
  background: white;
  width: 25%;
  display: inline-block;
  float: left;
}
```

I've created a similar look and feel for this regular layout like our Flexbox. Let's see what this looks like if we view it in a browser:

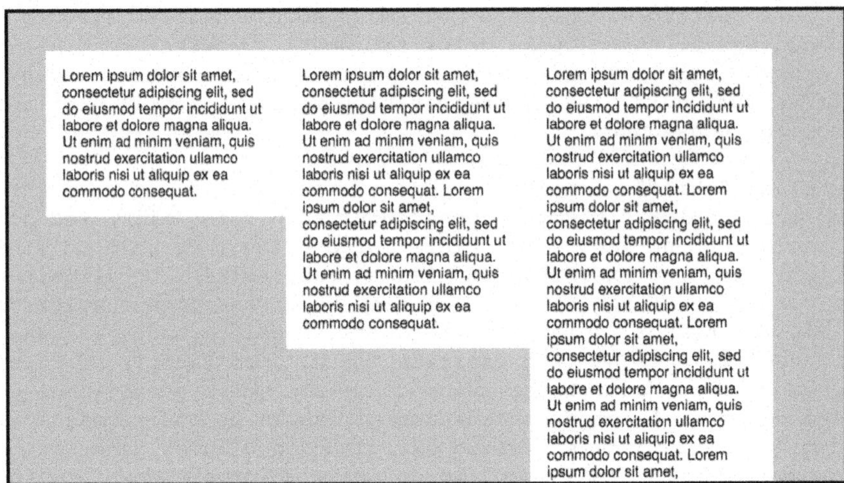

That doesn't look very good does it? What would be better is if the two smaller columns stretched vertically to match the height of the longest column. The good news is this is really easy to do with Flexbox. Leave the HTML as it is but let's go and change our CSS to use a Flexbox approach:

```
.parent {
  display: flex;
  background: #ccc;
  font-family: helvetica;
  padding: 5%;
}

.child {
  padding: 2%;
  background: white;
  flex-grow: 1;
  min-width: 200px;
}
```

The preceding code is actually very similar to one of the first examples. Therefore, an equal height column comes standard right out of the Flexbox. I have added a `min-width` of `200px` to each column so that the text is readable. With the preceding CSS our layout will now look like this:

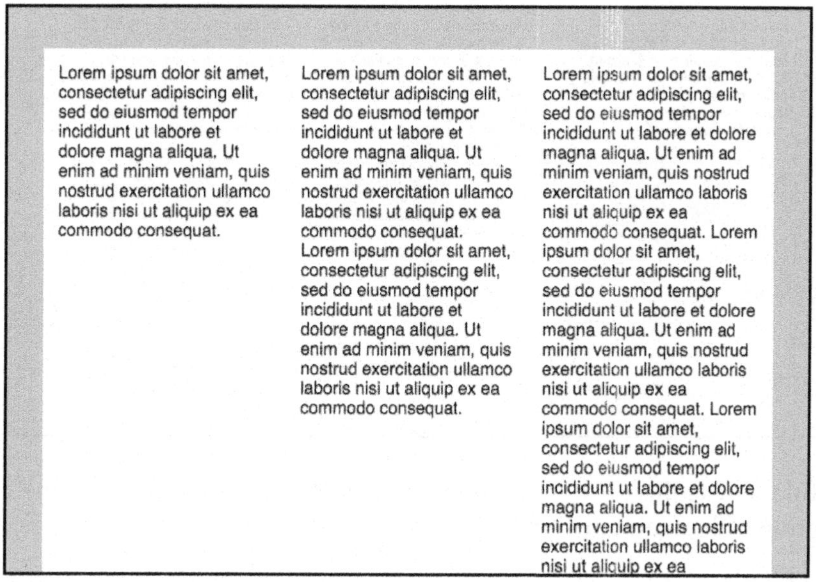

Perfect! Now the white background of each column has extended vertically to match the height of the tallest child. This looks much better and will allow for nicer horizontal alignment if you add additional rows of content. What's happening here is that the `align-items` property is defaulting to the `stretch` value. This value is what stretches the height of the columns to fit. There are some additional alignment values you can also try out. To continue, let's try out the `flex-start` value. Add the following CSS to the `.parent` class:

```
.parent {
    ...
    align-items: flex-start;
}
```

This configuration will actually undo the equal height columns and appear like a regular grid. Here's the image to refresh your memory:

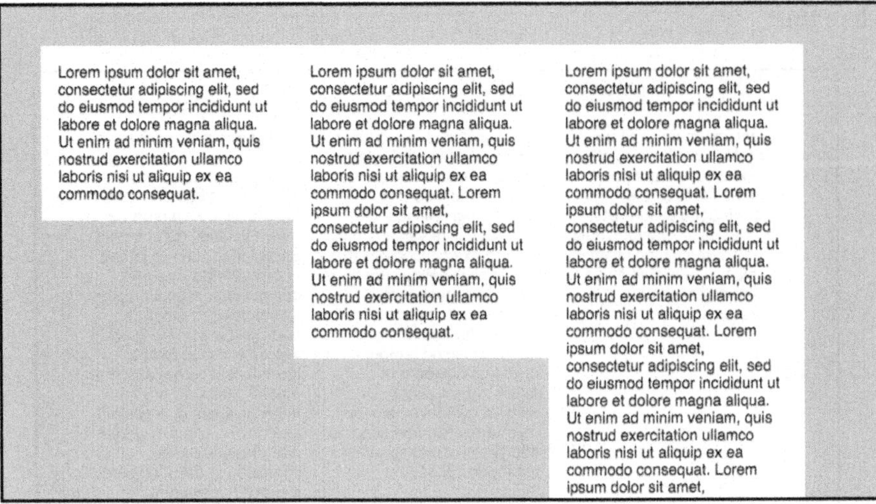

A more useful value is the `flex-end` option, which will align the boxes to the bottom of the browser window. Change your CSS to:

```
.parent {
    ...
    align-items: flex-end;
}
```

This setup will produce a grid that looks like this:

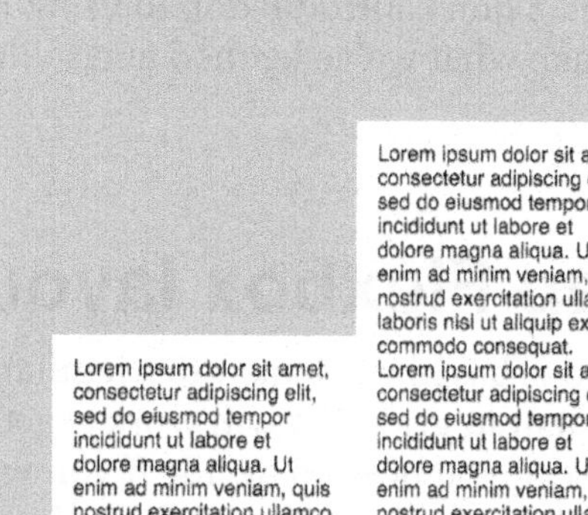

If you'd like to center your columns vertically in the layout, you can do that with the `center` value:

```
.parent {
    ...
    align-items: center;
}
```

If you go for this setup, your grid will look like this:

This is a just a taste of the properties you can use to customize the Flexbox grid. As I mentioned previously, I just wanted to give you a quick introduction to using Flexbox and some of the terminology that is needed. Let's take what we've learned and build on that by building a Flexbox grid in Bootstrap.

Setting up the Bootstrap Flexbox layout grid

Whether your are using Flexbox or not, the grid is based on Bootstrap's regular row and column classes. If you are familiar with the Bootstrap grid, this will work exactly as you expect it to. Before you start any Bootstrap project, you need to decide if you want to use a Flexbox or regular grid. Unfortunately, you can't use both at the same time in a Bootstrap project. Since the focus of this chapter is on Flexbox, we'll be using the appropriate grid configuration. By default Bootstrap is set up to use the regular grid. Therefore, we are going to need to edit the source files to activate the Flexbox grid. Let's start by downloading the source files again from `http://v4-alpha.getbootstrap.com/`.

Once you've downloaded the ZIP file, expand it and rename it so you don't get confused. Call it something like `Flexbox Bootstrap`. Next we'll need to edit a file and recompile the source files to apply the changes.

Updating the Sass variable

To use the Flexbox grid, we need to edit a Sass variable in the `_variables.scss` file. The way Sass variables work is that you set a single value in the `_variables.scss` file. When you run the built-in compiler, that value is written into every component of the Bootstrap framework where it is needed. You can then grab the compiled `bootstrap.min.css` file and it will have all the required code you need to use the Flexbox grid:

1. In your new source file directory, using the Terminal, navigate to:

```
$ scss/_variables.scss
```

2. Open the file in a text editor such as Sublime Text 2 or Notepad and find the following line of code:

```
$enable-flex: false !default;
```

3. Change the `false` value to `true`. The line of code should now read:

```
$enable-flex: true !default;
```

4. Save the file and close it. Before this change is applied, we need to recompile the source files. Since we downloaded a new version of the source files, we'll need to reinstall the project dependencies. Navigate to the root of the new Flexbox source files in the Terminal and run the following command:

```
$ npm install
```

5. This will likely take a couple minutes and you can follow the progress in the Terminal. Once it's done we need to compile the project. To do this we use Grunt. To run the compiler, simply enter the following command into the Terminal:

```
$ grunt
```

Again this will take a minute or two and you can follow the progress in the Terminal. Once it completes, the source files will have been compiled into the `/dist` directory. If it isn't clear, the production files that you want to use in your actual project will be compiled into the `/dist` directory.

Before we move onto our project, it would be a good idea to confirm that everything worked. Go back to your text editor and open the `dist/css/bootstrap.css` file from the root of your source files.

This is the un-minified version of the compiled Bootstrap CSS framework file. Once it's open do a quick find (*cmd* + *f* on Mac or *Ctrl* + *f* on Windows) and search for `flex`. If everything worked, it should quickly find an instance of `flex` in the file. This confirms that your compile worked.

Setting up a Flexbox project

A Flexbox project is structured exactly like a regular one. You just have to be sure to replace the `bootstrap.min.css` file in the `/css` directory with the new Flexbox version. Copy the project we made in the last chapter and paste it wherever you want on your computer. Rename the project to something like `Flexbox project`. Now open up that project and navigate to the `/css` directory. In a new window, open up the Flexbox sources files directory and navigate to the `/dist/css/` directory. Copy the `bootstrap.min.css` file from `/dist/css` into the `/css` directory in your new `Flexbox project`. You'll be prompted to overwrite the file and you should choose **Yes**. That's it, your new Flexbox project is ready to roll.

It would be a good idea to keep the Flexbox source files somewhere on your computer. In future projects, you can simply copy the compiled Flexbox version of the Bootstrap CSS over, saving you the trouble of having to recompile the source files each time you want a Flexbox layout.

Adding a custom theme

Before we code our first Flexbox grid, we need to add a custom CSS theme to our project. We're going to do this to add any custom look and feel styles on top of Bootstrap. In Bootstrap you never want to edit the actual framework CSS. You should use the cascading power of CSS to insert a theme for additional custom CSS or to overwrite existing Bootstrap styles. In a later chapter, I'll go into more depth on custom themes but for now let's set up a basic one that we can use for our Flexbox grid. First, let's start by creating a new file in the `/css` directory of our project called `theme.css`. For now, the file can be blank; just make sure you create it and save it.

Next we need to update our `_layout.ejs` file to include the theme file in our page. Open up `_layout.ejs` in a text editor and make sure it matches the following code:

```
<!DOCTYPE html>
<html lang="en">
  <head>
    <!-- Required meta tags always come first -->
    <meta charset="utf-8">
    <meta name="viewport" content="width=device-width, initial-scale=1,
shrink-to-fit=no">
    <meta http-equiv="x-ua-compatible" content="ie=edge">

    <title><%- pageTitle %> | <%- siteTitle %></title>

    <!-- Bootstrap CSS -->
    <link rel="stylesheet" href="css/bootstrap.min.css">
    <link rel="stylesheet" href="css/theme.css">
  </head>
  <body>

    <%- partial("partial/_header") %>

    <%- yield %>

    <%- partial("partial/_footer") %>

    <!-- jQuery first, then Bootstrap JS. -->
    <script
```

```
src="https://ajax.googleapis.com/ajax/libs/jquery/2.1.4/jquery.min.js"></sc
ript>
    <script src="js/bootstrap.min.js"></script>
  </body>
</html>
```

I've added one line of code to the template that loads in `theme.css`:

```
<link rel="stylesheet" href="css/theme.css">
```

Note that this line of code is after `bootstrap.min.css`. This is important as our theme needs to be loaded last so that we can overwrite Bootstrap default styles if we want to. Our template is now up-to-date and we are ready to start with our first grid. Feel free to keep `theme.css` open as we'll be adding some styles to it in the next step.

Creating a basic three-column grid

Now that we've set up our project, let's go ahead and start doing some Bootstrap coding. The good news is that the Bootstrap column classes used with the Flexbox grid are exactly the same as the ones used in a regular grid. There is no need to learn any new class names. In your project folder, create a new file and name it `flexbox.ejs`.

Before you go any further, you need to add an instance for this page to `_data.json`. Otherwise your `harp compile` command will fail. Open up `_data.json` and add the following code:

```
{
   "index": {
      "pageTitle": "Home"
   },
   "flexbox": {
      "pageTitle": "Flexbox"
   }
}
```

I've added a second entry for `flexbox.ejs` and given it this page title: Flexbox. Now we can safely start working on `flexbox.ejs` and the compile will work. Let's start with a simple three-column grid. Enter the following HTML code into `flexbox.ejs`:

```
<div class="container">
  <div class="row">
    <div class="col-md-4">Lorem ipsum dolor sit amet, consectetur
adipiscing elit. Nullam eget ornare lacus. Nulla sed vulputate mauris. Nunc
```

```
nec urna vel sapien mattis consectetur sit amet eu tellus.</div>
    <div class="col-md-4">Lorem ipsum dolor sit amet, consectetur
adipiscing elit. Nullam eget ornare lacus. Nulla sed vulputate mauris. Nunc
nec urna vel sapien mattis consectetur sit amet eu tellus. Suspendisse
tempus, justo sed posuere maximus, velit purus dictum lacus, nec vulputate
arcu neque et elit. Aliquam viverra vitae est eu suscipit. Donec nec neque
eu sapien blandit pretium et quis est.</div>
    <div class="col-md-4">Lorem ipsum dolor sit amet, consectetur
adipiscing elit. Nullam eget ornare lacus. Nulla sed vulputate mauris. Nunc
nec urna vel sapien mattis consectetur sit amet eu tellus. Suspendisse
tempus, justo sed posuere maximus, velit purus dictum lacus, nec vulputate
arcu neque et elit. Aliquam viverra vitae est eu suscipit. Donec nec neque
eu sapien blandit pretium et quis est. Sed malesuada sit amet mi eget
pulvinar. Mauris posuere ac elit in dapibus. Duis ut nunc at diam volutpat
ultrices non sit amet nulla. Aenean non diam tellus.</div>
  </div>
</div>
```

Let me breakdown what is happening here:

- Like in the earlier example, I've created three equal columns. Each one has a different amount of text in it.
- I'm using the `col-md-4` column class, as I want the three-column horizontal layout to be used for medium-size devices and upwards. Smaller devices will default to a single column width layout.
- I've also added a `.child` class to each of the column `<div>`s so that I can style them.

Now let's add a little CSS to `theme.css` so we can more easily see what is going on:

```
.child {
   background: #ccc;
   padding: 20px;
}
```

Here's what is happening with the `.child` class:

- I've added a light gray background color so we can easily see the child box.
- I've added some padding. Note that you can add padding to a Flexbox grid without worrying about breaking the grid. In a regular layout, this would break your box model and add extra width to the layout.

Here's what the finished layout should look like:

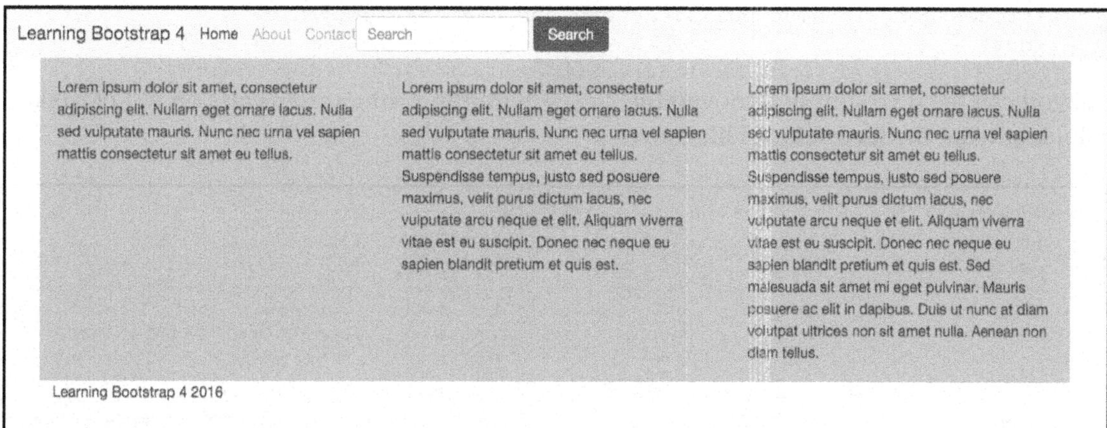

As you can see the light gray background has stretched to fit the height of the tallest column. An equal height column with almost no effort is awesome! You'll also notice that there is some padding on each column but our layout is not broken.

You may have noticed that I used the regular `.container` class to wrap this entire page layout. What if we want the layout to stretch the entire width of the browser?

Creating full-width layouts

Creating a full-width layout with no horizontal padding is actually really easy. Just remove the container class. The HTML for that type of layout would look like this:

```
<div class="row">
  <div class="col-md-4 child">Lorem ipsum dolor sit amet, consectetur
adipiscing elit. Nullam eget ornare lacus. Nulla sed vulputate mauris. Nunc
nec urna vel sapien mattis consectetur sit amet eu tellus.</div>
  <div class="col-md-4 child">Lorem ipsum dolor sit amet, consectetur
adipiscing elit. Nullam eget ornare lacus. Nulla sed vulputate mauris. Nunc
nec urna vel sapien mattis consectetur sit amet eu tellus. Suspendisse
tempus, justo sed posuere maximus, velit purus dictum lacus, nec vulputate
arcu neque et elit. Aliquam viverra vitae est eu suscipit. Donec nec neque
eu sapien blandit pretium et quis est.</div>
  <div class="col-md-4 child">Lorem ipsum dolor sit amet, consectetur
adipiscing elit. Nullam eget ornare lacus. Nulla sed vulputate mauris. Nunc
nec urna vel sapien mattis consectetur sit amet eu tellus. Suspendisse
tempus, justo sed posuere maximus, velit purus dictum lacus, nec vulputate
arcu neque et elit. Aliquam viverra vitae est eu suscipit. Donec nec neque
```

```
eu sapien blandit pretium et quis est. Sed malesuada sit amet mi eget
pulvinar. Mauris posuere ac elit in dapibus. Duis ut nunc at diam volutpat
ultrices non sit amet nulla. Aenean non diam tellus.</div>
</div>
```

As you can see, I've simply removed the `<div>` with the `.container` class on it. Let's take a look at what the layout looks like now:

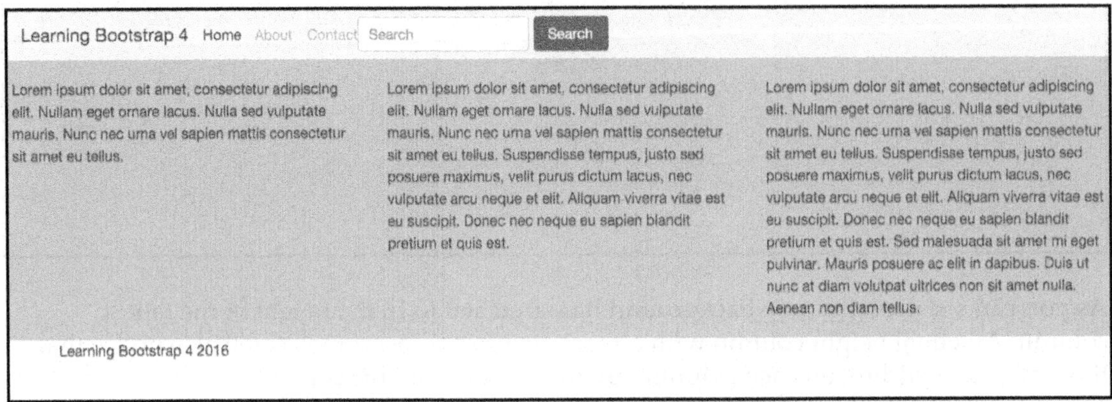

There we go, the columns are stretching right to the edges of the browser now. We've easily created a full-width layout that has equal height columns. Let's improve on this design by making each column an actual blog post and we'll also add more rows of posts.

Designing a single blog post

Let's start by designing the layout and content for a single blog post. At the very least, a blog post should have: a title, post-meta, description, and a read more link. Open up the `flexbox.ejs` file and replace the first column's code with this new code:

```
<div class="col-md-4 child">
  <h3><a href="#">Blog Post Title</a></h3>
  <p><small>Posted by <a href="#">Admin</a> on January 1, 2016</small></p>
  <p>Lorem ipsum dolor sit amet, consectetur adipiscing elit. Nullam eget
ornare lacus. Nulla sed vulputate mauris. Nunc nec urna vel sapien mattis
consectetur sit amet eu tellus.</p>
  <p><a href="#">Read More</a></p>
</div>
```

Let me breakdown what is happening here:

- I've added an <h3> tag with a link for the post title
- I've added some post-meta and wrapped it in a <small> tag so it is subtle
- I've left our description and added a read more link at the bottom

Now go ahead and copy and paste this code into the other two columns. If you want to play around with the length of the description text, feel free. For this example I'm going to keep it the same. When you're done, the entire page code should look like this. Note, I added the container <div> back in:

```
<div class="container">
  <div class="row">
    <div class="col-md-4 child">
      <h3><a href="#">Blog Post Title</a></h3>
      <p><small>Posted by <a href="#">Admin</a> on January 1,
2016</small></p>
      <p>Lorem ipsum dolor sit amet, consectetur adipiscing elit. Nullam
eget ornare lacus. Nulla sed vulputate mauris. Nunc nec urna vel sapien
mattis consectetur sit amet eu tellus.</p>
      <p><a href="#">Read More</a></p>
    </div>
    <div class="col-md-4 child">
      <h3><a href="#">Blog Post Title</a></h3>
      <p><small>Posted by <a href="#">Admin</a> on January 1,
2016</small></p>
      <p>Lorem ipsum dolor sit amet, consectetur adipiscing elit. Nullam
eget ornare lacus. Nulla sed vulputate mauris. Nunc nec urna vel sapien
mattis consectetur sit amet eu tellus.</p>
      <p><a href="#">Read More</a></p>
    </div>
    <div class="col-md-4 child">
      <h3><a href="#">Blog Post Title</a></h3>
      <p><small>Posted by <a href="#">Admin</a> on January 1,
2016</small></p>
      <p>Lorem ipsum dolor sit amet, consectetur adipiscing elit. Nullam
eget ornare lacus. Nulla sed vulputate mauris. Nunc nec urna vel sapien
mattis consectetur sit amet eu tellus.</p>
      <p><a href="#">Read More</a></p>
    </div>
  </div>
</div>
```

Save your file, do a harp compile if you haven't done so for in a while. Then do a harp server to launch the web server and head to `http://localhost:9000` to preview the page. It should look like this:

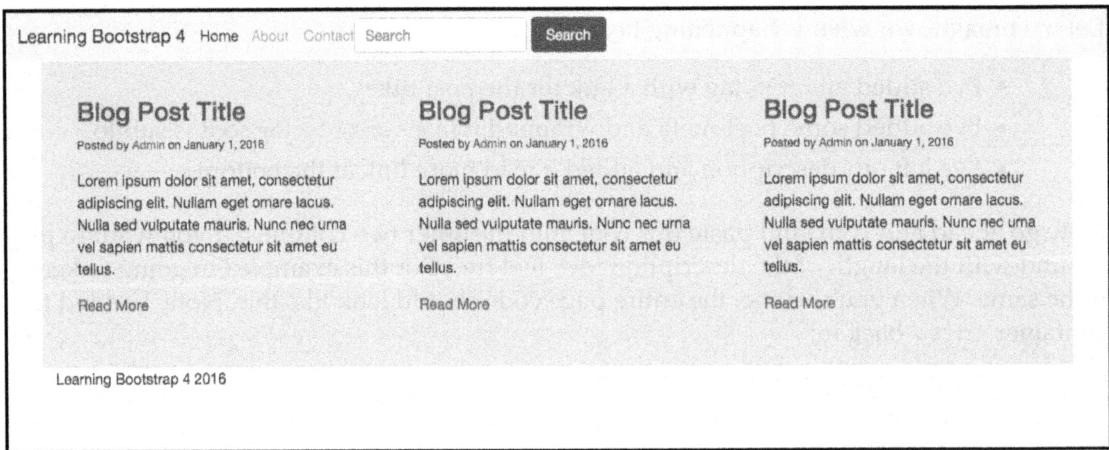

Great, now we have a decent-looking blog homepage. However, we need to add more posts to fill this out. Let's go ahead and add more column <div>s inside the same row. Since this is Flexbox, we don't need to start a new <div> with a row class for each row of posts. Let's add three more posts in then see what it looks like:

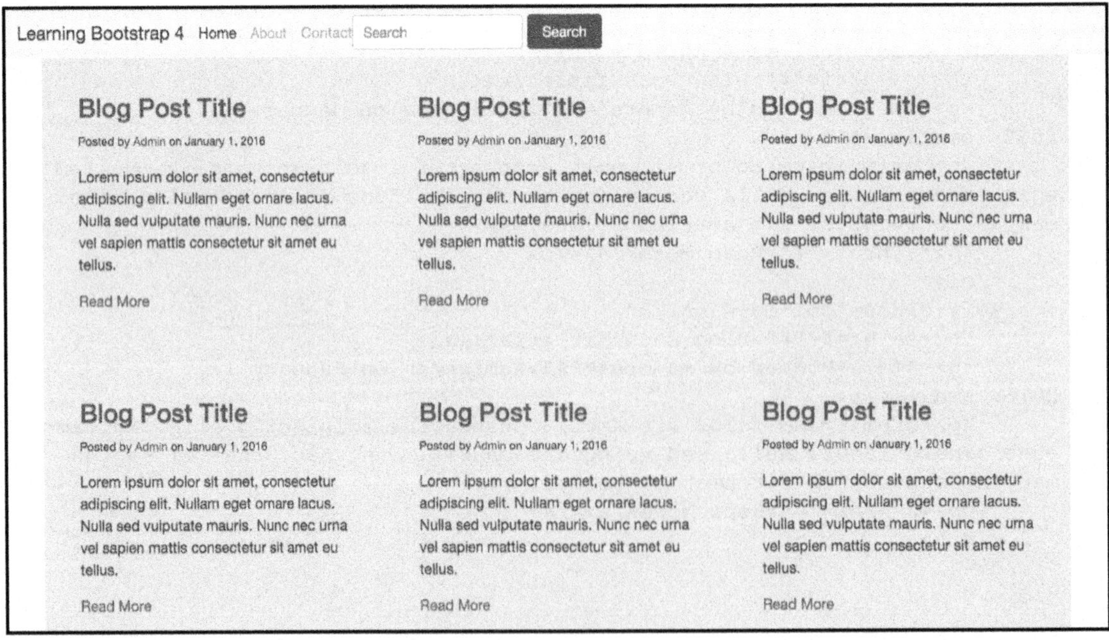

Perfect. Now our homepage is starting to take shape. Continue adding more posts until you have a number that you are happy with. At this point you should have a decent understanding of the Flexbox grid.

Summary

We started by reviewing the basic functionality of the Flexbox module and the terminology that goes along with it. Next, I showed you how to activate the Flexbox grid in Bootstrap by editing the Sass variable and recompiling the source files. Finally we got our hands dirty by learning how to build a blog homepage and feed using the Bootstrap Flexbox grid. In the next chapter, we'll move further into layouts and how you can set up your pages with Bootstrap.

4 Working with Layouts

The core of any Bootstrap website is the layout or grid component. Without a grid, a website is pretty much useless. One of the biggest layout challenges we face as web developers nowadays is dealing with a large array of screen resolutions, from desktop to tablets, mobile phones, and even Apple watches. It is not easy to lay out a website and we rely on responsive web design and media queries to take a mobile-first approach. Perhaps the best feature of the Bootstrap layout grid is that it's mobile-first and built using media queries. This takes the hardest part out of constructing a grid and lets us concentrate on the actual design of our projects. Before we start to layout the next part of our blog project, let's review the lay out grid basics in Bootstrap 4.

In this chapter, we are going to discuss the following listed topics briefly:

- Working with containers
- Adding columns to your layout
- Creating a simple three-column layout
- Coding the blog home page
- Using responsive utility classes

Working with containers

The base of any Bootstrap layout is a container class. There are two types of containers you can choose to use. The first is `.container-fluid`, which is a full-width box and will stretch the layout to fit the entire width of the browser window.

There is some left and right padding added so the content doesn't bump right up against the browser edge:

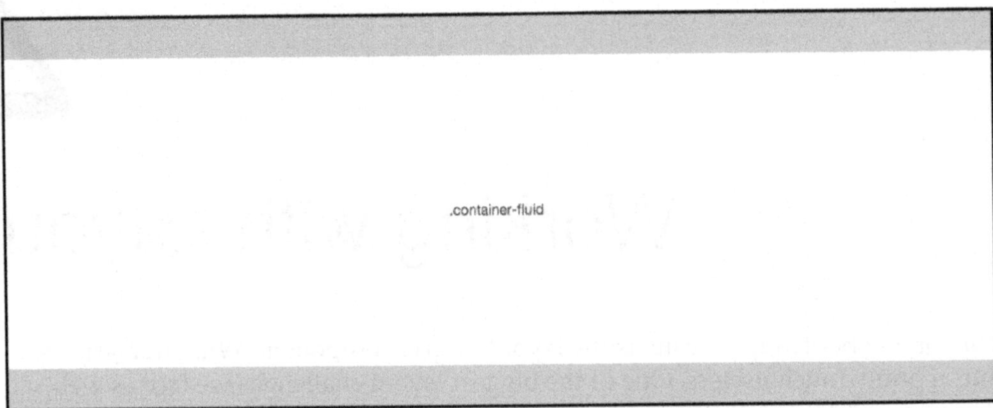

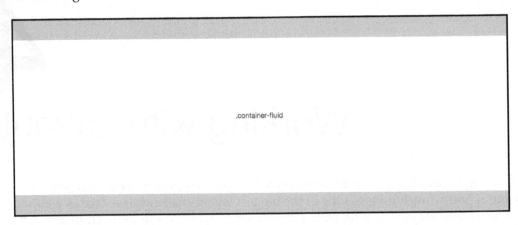

The second option is the basic `.container` class, which will have a fixed width based on the size of your device's viewport. There are five different sizes in Bootstrap, with the following width values:

- Extra small <544px
- Small >544px
- Medium >768px
- Large >992px
- Extra large >1140px

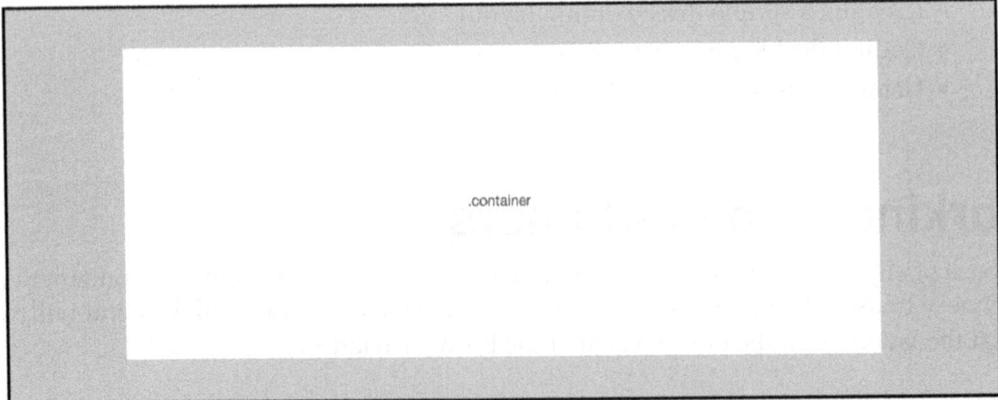

Let's take a look at the markup for both container types. I'll start with the basic `.container` class:

```
<div class="container">
  ...
</div>
```

That's pretty easy. Now let's look at the code for the fluid container:

```
<div class="container-fluid">
  ...
</div>
```

Again, that is straightforward and is all that you need to know about using the container classes in Bootstrap 4.

Creating a layout without a container

Now, in some cases, you may not want to use a container and that is totally fine. An example of this would be if you want a full width layout but you don't want the default left and right padding. You may have an image banner that you want to stretch to the full width of the browser with no padding. In this case, just remove the `<div>` with the `container` class on it.

Using multiple containers on a single page

It is perfectly fine to use multiple containers on a single page template. The containers are CSS classes, so they are reusable. You may want to do this on longer page layouts, perhaps a landing page design, where you have multiple large regions. Another example is using a container to wrap your footer. If you are using a template system like Harp, you'll want to create a footer partial. You can make the footer component more self contained by giving it its own container. Then you don't have to worry about closing a container `<div>` in the footer that was opened in a page template or even the header. I would recommend using multiple containers to make your designs more modular and easier to manage by multiple users. Let's take a quick look at how you would structure a basic page with multiple containers:

```
<div class="container">
  <!-- header code goes here, harp partial name would be _header.ejs //-->
</div>

<div class="container">
```

```
   <!-- template code goes here, harp file name would be index.ejs //-->
</div>

<div class="container">
   <!-- footer code goes here, harp partial name would be _footer.ejs //-->
</div>
```

We have three separate files there and using a container class for each makes each section more modular. You also don't have to worry about opening a `<div>` in one file then closing it in another. This is a good way to avoid orphan closing `</div>` tags.

Inserting rows into your layout

The next step in creating a layout is to insert at least a single row of columns. Each container class can have one or more rows nested inside of it. A row defines a collection of horizontal columns that can be broken up to twelve times. The magic number when it comes to columns in Bootstrap is twelve, and you can sub-divide them any way you like. Before we get into columns though, let's review the markup for rows. First let's look at an example of a container with a single row:

```
<div class="container">
   <div class="row">
      <!-- insert column code here //-->
   </div>
</div>
```

As you can see, this is an easy next step in setting up your layout. Like I mentioned, you can have as many rows within a container as you like. Here's how you would code a five-row layout:

```
<div class="container">
   <div class="row">
      <!-- insert column code here //-->
   </div>
   <div class="row">
      <!-- insert column code here //-->
   </div>
   <div class="row">
      <!-- insert column code here //-->
   </div>
   <div class="row">
      <!-- insert column code here //-->
   </div>
   <div class="row">
      <!-- insert column code here //-->
```

```
    </div>
</div>
```

Like the container class, rows are also a CSS class, so they can be reused as many times as you like on a single page template.

You should never include actual contents inside a row `<div>`. All content should be included with column `<div>`s.

Adding columns to your layout

Before we jump into actually adding the columns, let's talk a little bit about the different column classes you have at your disposal with Bootstrap. In Bootstrap 3 there were four different column class widths to choose from: extra small, small, medium, and large. With Bootstrap 4, they have also introduced a new extra large column class. This is likely to allow for extra large monitors, like you would find on an iMac. Let's go over the fine points of each column class in Bootstrap 4.

Extra small

The smallest of the grid classes uses the naming pattern `.col-xs-#`, where `-#` is equal to a number from 1 to 12. Remember, in Bootstrap, your row must be divided into a number of columns that adds up to 12. A couple of examples of this would be `.col-xs-6` or `.col-xs-3`. The extra smallcolumn class is for targeting mobile devices that have a `max-width` of 544 pixels.

Small

The smallcolumn class uses the syntax pattern `.col-sm-#`, and some examples of that would be `.col-sm-4` or `.col-sm-6`. It is targeted for devices with a resolution greater than 544 pixels but smaller than 720 pixels.

Medium

The mediumcolumn class uses a similar naming pattern of `.col-md-#` and some examples would be `.col-md-3` or `.col-md-12`. This column class is for devices greater than 720 pixels and smaller than 940 pixels.

Large

The largecolumn class again uses the naming pattern of `.col-lg-#` and some examples would be `.col-lg-6` or `.col-lg-2`. This column class targets devices that are larger than 940 pixels but smaller than 1140 pixels.

Extra large

The final and new column class is extra large and the syntax for it is `.col-xl-#` with examples being `.col-xl-1` or `.col-xl-10`. This column class option is for all resolutions greater than or equal to 1140 pixels.

Choosing a column class

This is a good question. With all of the class options, it can be hard to decide which ones to use. If you are building a mobile app, then you would likely want to stick to the extra small or small column classes. For a tablet, you might want to use medium. If the primary user for your application will be on a desktop computer, then use the large or extra large classes. But what if you are building a responsive website and you need to target multiple devices? If that is the case, I usually recommend using either the medium or large column classes. Then you can adjust to use larger or smaller classes where necessary if you have a component that needs some extra attention for specific resolutions.

Creating a simple three-column layout

Let's assume that we are building a simple responsive website and we need a three-column layout for our template. Here's what your markup should look like:

```
<div class="container">
   <div class="row">
      <div class="col-md-4">
         <!-- column 1 //-->
      </div>
      <div class="col-md-4">
         <!-- column 2 //-->
      </div>
      <div class="col-md-4">
         <!-- column 3 //-->
      </div>
   </div>
</div>
```

As you can see, I've inserted three `<div>`s inside my row `<div>`, each with a class of `.col-md-4`. For devices that have a resolution of 768 pixels or greater, you'll see a three-column layout like this:

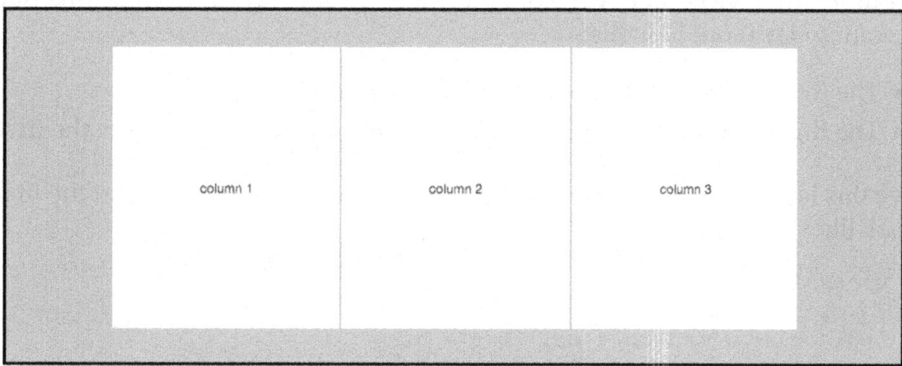

Now, if you were to view this same layout on a device with resolution smaller than 768 pixels, each column's width would change to 100% and the columns would be stacked on top of each other. That variation of the layout for smaller screens would look like this:

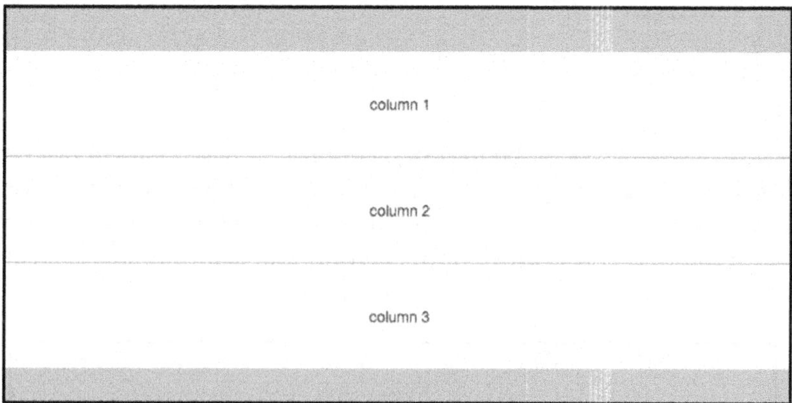

That's all well and good, but what if we wanted to have a different layout for the columns on smaller devices that didn't set them all to 100% width? That can be done by mixing column classes.

Mixing column classes for different devices

Adding additional classes to each of our column <div>s will allow us to target the grid layout for different devices. Let's consider our three-column layout from before, but this time, we want to lay it out like this:

- The first two columns should be 50% of the layout
- The third column should stretch 100% of the layout and be below the first two

To achieve this layout, we'll mix some different column classes. Here's what the markup should look like:

```
<div class="container">
   <div class="row">
      <div class="col-md-4 col-xs-6">
         <!-- column 1 //-->
      </div>
      <div class="col-md-4 col-xs-6">
         <!-- column 2 //-->
      </div>
      <div class="col-md-4 col-xs-12">
         <!-- column 3 //-->
      </div>
   </div>
</div>
```

I've added the `.col-xs-6` class to the first two column <div>s. Now, if our device resolution is less than 768 pixels, the first two columns will be set to a width of 50%. For the third column, I've used the `.col-xs-12` class, which will wrap the third column onto a new line and set it to 100% of the width of the layout. The resulting layout will look like this on smaller devices:

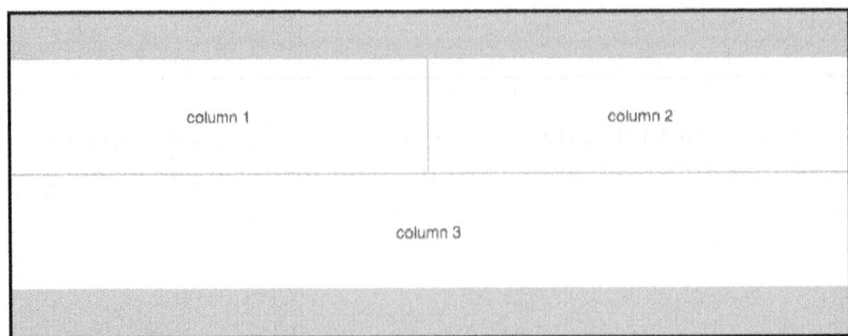

This will only apply to devices with a layout of less than 768 pixels. If you were to view this grid, using the latest code, on a larger device, it will still appear as three equal columns laid out horizontally.

What if I want to offset a column?

Perhaps your layout requires you to offset some columns and leave some horizontal blank space before your content starts. This can easily be used with Bootstrap's offset grid classes. The naming convention is similar to the regular column classes, but we need to add the offset keyword, like this: `.col-lg-offset-#`. A couple examples of this would be `.col-lg-offset-3` or `.col-md-offset-6`. Let's take our three-column grid from before but remove the first column. However, we want the second and third columns to remain where they are in the layout. This will require us to use the offset grid class. Here's what your markup should look like:

```
<div class="container">
   <div class="row">
      <div class="col-md-4 col-md-offset-4">
         <!-- column 2 //-->
      </div>
      <div class="col-md-4">
         <!-- column 3 //-->
      </div>
   </div>
</div>
```

Note how I removed the first column `<div>`. I also added the class `.col-md-offset-4` to the second column's `<div>`. Once you've done this, your layout should appear like this.

There you go; you've successfully offset your column by removing the first column and then sliding over the other two columns:

That concludes the basics of the Bootstrap grid that you'll need to know for the remainder of this chapter. Now that you have a good understanding of how the grid works, let's move onto coding up our blog home page layout using the grid classes.

Coding the blog home page

Now that you have a good grasp of how to use the Bootstrap 4 grid, we're going to code up our blog home page. This page will include a feed of posts, a sidebar, and a newsletter sign-up form section at the bottom of the page. Let's start by taking the code we wrote in `Chapter 2`, *Using Bootstrap Build Tools* for our `hello world!` template and duplicating the entire directory. Rename the folder `Chapter 4: Working with Layouts` or `Bootstrap Layout`.

Remember, we are using the regular grid moving forward, not the Flexbox grid. Make sure you are using the default build of `bootstrap.min.css`. If you carry out a simple duplication of the second chapter's code then you'll have the right file configuration.

Writing the index.ejs template

Good news! Since we set up our Harp project in `Chapter 2`, *Using Bootstrap Build Tools*, we can reuse a bunch of that code now for our blog home page. There's no need to make any updates to the JSON files and header or footer partials. The only file we need to make changes to is `index.ejs`. Open the file up in a text editor and paste the following code to get started:

```
<div class="container">
  <!-- page title //-->
  <div class="row m-t-3">
    <div class="col-md-12">
      <h1>Blog</h1>
    </div>
  </div>
  <!-- page body //-->
  <div class="row m-t-3">
    <div class="col-md-8">
      <!-- blog posts //-->
    </div>
    <div class="col-md-4">
      <!-- sidebar //-->
    </div>
```

```
  </div>
  <!-- mailing list //-->
  <div class="row m-t-3">
    <div class="col-md-12">
      <!-- form //-->
    </div>
  </div>
</div>
```

There are a few different things going on here so let me break them all down for you:

- I don't want a full width layout, so I've decided to use the `.container` class to wrap my templates layout.
- I've created three different rows, one for our page title, one for the page content (blog feed and sidebar), and one for the mailing list section.
- There are some classes on the row `<div>`s that we haven't seen before, like `m-t-3`. I'll cover what those do in the next section.
- Since I want my blog to be readable on devices of all sizes, I decided to use the medium-sized column classes.
- The page title column is set to `.col-md-12`, so it will stretch to 100% of the layout width.
- I've divided the second row, which holds most of our page content, into a two-column grid. The first column will take up 2/3 of the layout width with the `col-md-8` class. The second column, our sidebar, will take up 1/3 of the layout width with the `col-md-4` class.
- Finally, the third row will hold the mailing list and it is also using the `col-md-12` class and will stretch to fill the entire width of the layout.

The basic layout of the grid for our blog home page is now complete. However, let's revisit those new CSS classes from our layout that I added to the row `<div>`s.

Using spacing CSS classes

One of the new utilities that has been added in Bootstrap 4 is spacing classes. These are great as they add an easy, modular way to add extra vertical spacing to your layouts without having to write custom CSS classes for each region. Spacing classes can be applied to both the CSS `margin` and `padding` properties. The basic pattern for defining the class is as follows:

```
{property}-{sides}-{size}
```

Let's break down how this works in more detail:

- `property` is equal to either `margin` or `padding`.
- `sides` is equal to the side of a box you want to add either `margin` or `padding` to. This is written using a single letter: `t` for top, `b` for bottom, `l` for left, and `r` for right.
- `size` is equal to the amount of margin or padding you want to add. The scale is 0 to 3. Setting the size value to 0 will actually remove any existing margin or padding on an element.

To better understand this concept, let's construct a few spacer classes. Let's say that we want to add some top margin to a row with a size value of 1. Our class would look like this:

```
.m-t-1
```

Applied to the actual row, `<div>`, the class would look like this:

```
<div class="row m-t-1">
```

For a second example, let's say we want to add some left padding to a div with a value of 2. That combination would look like this when combined with a row `<div>`:

```
<div class="row p-l-2">
```

Are you starting to see how easy it is to add some spacing around your layout and components?

Spacing classes can be used on any type of element, not just the Bootstrap grid.

Now that you understand how these classes work, let's take a look at our blog home page template again. In that case, our `<div>`s looks like this:

```
<div class="row m-t-3">
```

On three sections of the template, I've decided to use these classes and they are all top margin with a size value of three. It's a good idea to try and keep these consistent as it will result in a visually appealing layout when you are done. It also makes it a little easier to do the math when you are setting up your page. Now that we've gone over the entire home page layout, we need to test it.

Testing out the blog home page layout

Let's test it out in the browser to make sure it's looking the way we want. Before we can do that we'll need to compile our code with Harp. Open the Terminal back up and navigate to the project directory for this chapter's code that we created. Run the `harp compile` command, here it is again in case you forgot:

```
$ harp compile
```

That should run without any errors; then, we can start-up the web server to view our page. Here's the command again to run the web server:

```
$ harp server
```

Now that the server has launched, head to a web browser and enter `http://localhost:9000` in the URL bar to bring up the blog home page. Here's what your page should look like:

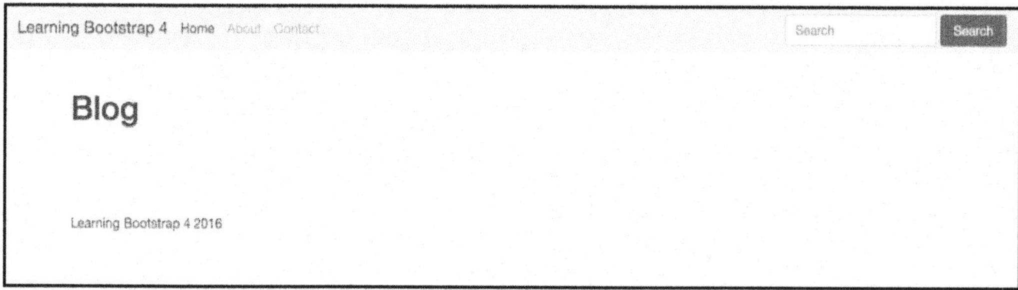

Uh oh, that doesn't look quite right. You can see the page title but we can't see any of our columns. Oh yeah! We need to fill in some content so the columns are revealed. Let's add in some dummy text for demo purposes. In later chapters, I'll get into coding the actual components we want to see on this page. This chapter is just about setting up our layout.

Adding some content

Head back to `index.ejs` in your text editor and let's add some dummy text. Go to the first column of the main content area first and enter something like this:

```
<div class="col-md-8">
      <p>Pellentesque habitant morbi tristique senectus et netus et
malesuada fames ac turpis egestas. Vestibulum tortor quam, feugiat vitae,
ultricies eget, tempor sit amet, ante. Donec eu libero sit amet quam
egestas semper. Aenean ultricies mi vitae est. Mauris placerat eleifend
```

```
leo. Quisque sit amet est et sapien ullamcorper pharetra. Vestibulum erat
wisi, condimentum sed, commodo vitae, ornare sit amet, wisi. Aenean
fermentum, elit eget tincidunt condimentum, eros ipsum rutrum orci,
sagittis tempus lacus enim ac dui. Donec non enim in turpis pulvinar
facilisis. Ut felis. Praesent dapibus, neque id cursus faucibus, tortor
neque egestas augue, eu vulputate magna eros eu erat. Aliquam erat
volutpat. Nam dui mi, tincidunt quis, accumsan porttitor, facilisis luctus,
metus</p>
</div>
```

If you're looking for a quick way to get filler text in HTML format, visit `http://html-ipsum.com/`.

Next, go to the sidebar column `<div>` and add the same paragraph of text, like so:

```
<div class="col-md-4">
      <p>Pellentesque habitant morbi tristique senectus et netus et
malesuada fames ac turpis egestas. Vestibulum tortor quam, feugiat vitae,
ultricies eget, tempor sit amet, ante. Donec eu libero sit amet quam
egestas semper. Aenean ultricies mi vitae est. Mauris placerat eleifend
leo. Quisque sit amet est et sapien ullamcorper pharetra. Vestibulum erat
wisi, condimentum sed, commodo vitae, ornare sit amet, wisi. Aenean
fermentum, elit eget tincidunt condimentum, eros ipsum rutrum orci,
sagittis tempus lacus enim ac dui. Donec non enim in turpis pulvinar
facilisis. Ut felis. Praesent dapibus, neque id cursus faucibus, tortor
neque egestas augue, eu vulputate magna eros eu erat. Aliquam erat
volutpat. Nam dui mi, tincidunt quis, accumsan porttitor, facilisis luctus,
metus</p>
</div>
```

Finally, drop down to the mailing list `<div>` and add the same paragraph of content again. It should look like this:

```
<div class="col-md-12">
      <p>Pellentesque habitant morbi tristique senectus et netus et
malesuada fames ac turpis egestas. Vestibulum tortor quam, feugiat vitae,
ultricies eget, tempor sit amet, ante. Donec eu libero sit amet quam
egestas semper. Aenean ultricies mi vitae est. Mauris placerat eleifend
leo. Quisque sit amet est et sapien ullamcorper pharetra. Vestibulum erat
wisi, condimentum sed, commodo vitae, ornare sit amet, wisi. Aenean
fermentum, elit eget tincidunt condimentum, eros ipsum rutrum orci,
sagittis tempus lacus enim ac dui. Donec non enim in turpis pulvinar
facilisis. Ut felis. Praesent dapibus, neque id cursus faucibus, tortor
neque egestas augue, eu vulputate magna eros eu erat. Aliquam erat
volutpat. Nam dui mi, tincidunt quis, accumsan porttitor, facilisis luctus,
metus</p>
</div>
```

Now that we've added some actual content to our page body, let's recompile the project and launch the web server again:

With Harp, you don't actually have to recompile after every little change you make. You can also make changes to your files while the server is running and they will be picked up by the browser. It's a good habit to compile regularly in case you run into an error on compile. This will make it easier to troubleshoot potential problems.

Once the server is up and running, return to your browser and refresh the page. Now your layout should look like this:

Blog

Pellentesque habitant morbi tristique senectus et netus et malesuada fames ac turpis egestas. Vestibulum tortor quam, feugiat vitae, ultricies eget, tempor sit amet, ante. Donec eu libero sit amet quam egestas semper. Aenean ultricies mi vitae est. Mauris placerat eleifend leo. Quisque sit amet est et sapien ullamcorper pharetra. Vestibulum erat wisi, condimentum sed, commodo vitae, ornare sit amet, wisi. Aenean fermentum, elit eget tincidunt condimentum, eros ipsum rutrum orci, sagittis tempus lacus enim ac dui. Donec non enim in turpis pulvinar facilisis. Ut felis. Praesent dapibus, neque id cursus faucibus, tortor neque egestas augue, eu vulputate magna eros eu erat. Aliquam erat volutpat. Nam dui mi, tincidunt quis, accumsan porttitor, facilisis luctus, metus

Pellentesque habitant morbi tristique senectus et netus et malesuada fames ac turpis egestas. Vestibulum tortor quam, feugiat vitae, ultricies eget, tempor sit amet, ante. Donec eu libero sit amet quam egestas semper. Aenean ultricies mi vitae est. Mauris placerat eleifend leo. Quisque sit amet est et sapien ullamcorper pharetra. Vestibulum erat wisi, condimentum sed, commodo vitae, ornare sit amet, wisi. Aenean fermentum, elit eget tincidunt condimentum, eros ipsum rutrum orci, sagittis tempus lacus enim ac dui. Donec non enim in turpis pulvinar facilisis. Ut felis. Praesent dapibus, neque id cursus faucibus, tortor neque egestas augue, eu vulputate magna eros eu erat. Aliquam erat volutpat. Nam dui mi, tincidunt quis, accumsan porttitor, facilisis luctus, metus

Pellentesque habitant morbi tristique senectus et netus et malesuada fames ac turpis egestas. Vestibulum tortor quam, feugiat vitae, ultricies eget, tempor sit amet, ante. Donec eu libero sit amet quam egestas semper. Aenean ultricies mi vitae est. Mauris placerat eleifend leo. Quisque sit amet est et sapien ullamcorper pharetra. Vestibulum erat wisi, condimentum sed, commodo vitae, ornare sit amet, wisi. Aenean fermentum, elit eget tincidunt condimentum, eros ipsum rutrum orci, sagittis tempus lacus enim ac dui. Donec non enim in turpis pulvinar facilisis. Ut felis. Praesent dapibus, neque id cursus faucibus, tortor neque egestas augue, eu vulputate magna eros eu erat. Aliquam erat volutpat. Nam dui mi, tincidunt quis, accumsan porttitor, facilisis luctus, metus

Learning Bootstrap 4 2016

Yay! We can now see our columns and the dummy text that we just added. The page may not be much to look at right now, but what's important is to verify that your columns are laid out correctly.

What about mobile devices?

We need to consider what will happen to our layout on mobile devices and smaller screen resolutions. I used the medium grid layout class, so any device that is smaller than 720 pixels will have an adjusted layout. Resize your browser window, making it smaller to trigger the media query, and you'll see that all of the columns will be resized to 100% width of the container. Here's what it looks like:

I'm going to keep our blog layout pretty minimal so I'm okay with this layout. In this format, the sidebar will slide in under the main blog feed of posts. I'm actually not that crazy about this design, so I'm just going to hide the sidebar altogether when you view the blog on a smaller device.

Using responsive utility classes

Responsive utility classes will allow you to selectively hide `<div>`s or components based on the screen resolution size. This is great for creating a mobile-first web application, because in many cases you'll want to hide some components that don't work well on a phone or tablet. Mobile application design generally means a simpler, more minimal experience some using responsive utility classes will allow you to achieve this. Open up `index.ejs` in a text editor and go down to the sidebar `<div>`, then add the `.hidden-md-down` class to your code:

```
<div class="col-md-4 hidden-md-down">
```

Adding this class will hide the `<div>` from the browser when your screen resolution is smaller than 720 pixels. Make sure your column class, in this case `-md`, matches the hidden class. Now, if you shrink your web browser down again, you'll notice that the sidebar `<div>` will disappear.

There are a number of responsive utility classes you can use in your projects. There is a `-down` version for each of the column class names. You can also use a `-up` version if you wish to hide something when viewing at a larger resolution. Some examples of that class are `.hidden-lg-up` or `.hidden-xl-up`. To learn more about responsive utility classes, check out the page in the Bootstrap docs at `http://v4-alpha.getbootstrap.com/layout/responsive-utilities/`.

That completes the layout of the grid for our blog home page. Before we move onto learning about content classes in Bootstrap 4, let's set up the layout grid for the other pages we'll be building for the blog.

Coding the additional blog project page grids

Before we create new templates for our contact and single blog post pages, we need to update some of the Harp project files. Let's update those files, then we'll move onto the page templates.

Updating _data.json for our new pages

Remember a couple chapters back we learned how to code the `_data.json` file and we created a variable for the page title of each of our templates? We need to update this file for our two new pages by providing the `pageTitle` variable value for each of them. Open up `_data.json` in a text editor; you can find the file in the root of your blog project directory.

Once you have the file open, insert the following code. The entire file should read as follows:

```
{
   "index": {
      "pageTitle": "Home"
   },
   "contact": {
      "pageTitle": "Contact"
   },
   "blog-post": {
      "pageTitle": "Blog Post"
   }
}
```

Originally, we only included the `index` file. I've added two more entries, one for the contact page and one for the blog-post page. I've entered a value for each page's `pageTitle` variable. It's as simple as that. Save the JSON file and then you can close it.

Creating the new page templates

Now that `_data.json` has been updated, we need to create the actual page template EJS files like we did with index. In your text editor, create two new files and save them as `contact.ejs` and `blog-post.ejs`. For now, just leave them blank and we'll start to fill them in the next steps. The templates are now set up and ready to be coded. For now, both of our new pages will use the same `_layout.ejs` file as the index file, so there is no need to create any more layouts. Let's start by coding the contact page template.

Coding the contact page template

Open up the `contact.ejs` file you just created in your text editor. Let's start the template by setting up our page title. Enter the following code into the file:

```
<div class="container">
  <!-- page title //-->
  <div class="row m-t-3">
    <div class="col-lg-12">
      <h1>Contact</h1>
    </div>
  </div>
</div>
```

Let's breakdown what's happening here in the code:

- I've opened up the file with a `<div>` with a `.container` class on it.
- Next I added `.row` `<div>` and I've added the same `m-t-3` spacing classes so it matches the blog home page.
- I've added a column `<div>` with a class of `.col-md-12`. Since this is our page title, we want it to stretch to the width of our layout.
- Finally, I've added an `<h1>` tag with our contact page title.

Adding the contact page body

Next let's insert our grid layout for the body of the contact page. Following the page title code, insert the following grid code:

```
<!-- page body //-->
  <div class="row m-t-3">
    <div class="col-md-12">
      <p>Pellentesque habitant morbi tristique senectus et netus et
malesuada fames ac turpis egestas. Vestibulum tortor quam, feugiat vitae,
ultricies eget, tempor sit amet, ante. Donec eu libero sit amet quam
egestas semper. Aenean ultricies mi vitae est. Mauris placerat eleifend
leo. Quisque sit amet est et sapien ullamcorper pharetra. Vestibulum erat
wisi, condimentum sed, commodo vitae, ornare sit amet, wisi. Aenean
fermentum, elit eget tincidunt condimentum, eros ipsum rutrum orci,
sagittis tempus lacus enim ac dui. Donec non enim in turpis pulvinar
facilisis. Ut felis. Praesent dapibus, neque id cursus faucibus, tortor
neque egestas augue, eu vulputate magna eros eu erat. Aliquam erat
volutpat. Nam dui mi, tincidunt quis, accumsan porttitor, facilisis luctus,
metus</p>
    </div>
  </div>
```

Let's review the code for the page body:

- I've opened up another row `<div>` for the page body. It also has the same `m-t-3` spacing class on it for consistent vertical spacing.
- I've used the `col-md-12` column class again because the contact page layout will fill the whole width of our container.
- I've added some filler text for now so that we can verify that the page is laid out properly.

Before we finish, let's add one more row for our mailing list section. I'd like this to be available on every page of our blog. The grid code for this section will be identical to the markup we did for the page body. Here's what it looks like, for reference:

```
<!-- mailing list //-->
<div class="row m-t-3">
  <div class="col-md-12">
   <p>Pellentesque habitant morbi tristique senectus et netus et malesuada
fames ac turpis egestas. Vestibulum tortor quam, feugiat vitae, ultricies
eget, tempor sit amet, ante. Donec eu libero sit amet quam egestas semper.
Aenean ultricies mi vitae est. Mauris placerat eleifend leo. Quisque sit
amet est et sapien ullamcorper pharetra. Vestibulum erat wisi, condimentum
sed, commodo vitae, ornare sit amet, wisi. Aenean fermentum, elit eget
tincidunt condimentum, eros ipsum rutrum orci, sagittis tempus lacus enim
ac dui. Donec non enim in turpis pulvinar facilisis. Ut felis. Praesent
dapibus, neque id cursus faucibus, tortor neque egestas augue, eu vulputate
magna eros eu erat. Aliquam erat volutpat. Nam dui mi, tincidunt quis,
accumsan porttitor, facilisis luctus, metus</p>
  </div>
</div>
```

Since this code is identical to the page body, I won't bother breaking it down again. Our layout for the contact page is now complete. Make sure you save the file and let's test it before we move onto the blog post page.

Open your Terminal back up and navigate to the root directory of the blog project. Once there, run the `harp compile` command and then the Harp server command to launch the local web server. Open your web browser and enter the following URL to preview your page: `http://localhost:9000/contact.html.`

Your contact page should load up and you should see a page title and two rows of filler text. Here's what it should look like:

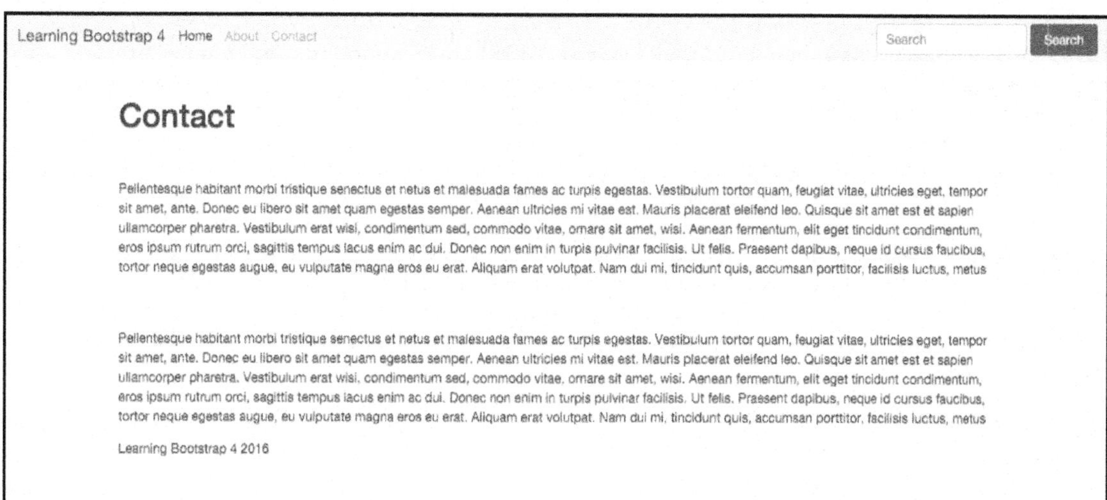

Our contact page grid is now complete. Before we move onto creating the blog post template, let's take a look at all the code for the contact template:

```
<div class="container">
  <!-- page title //-->
  <div class="row m-t-3">
    <div class="col-md-12">
      <h1>Contact</h1>
    </div>
  </div>
  <!-- page body //-->
  <div class="row m-t-3">
    <div class="col-md-12">
      <p>Pellentesque habitant morbi tristique senectus et netus et
malesuada fames ac turpis egestas. Vestibulum tortor quam, feugiat vitae,
ultricies eget, tempor sit amet, ante. Donec eu libero sit amet quam
egestas semper. Aenean ultricies mi vitae est. Mauris placerat eleifend
leo. Quisque sit amet est et sapien ullamcorper pharetra. Vestibulum erat
wisi, condimentum sed, commodo vitae, ornare sit amet, wisi. Aenean
fermentum, elit eget tincidunt condimentum, eros ipsum rutrum orci,
sagittis tempus lacus enim ac dui. Donec non enim in turpis pulvinar
facilisis. Ut felis. Praesent dapibus, neque id cursus faucibus, tortor
neque egestas augue, eu vulputate magna eros eu erat. Aliquam erat
volutpat. Nam dui mi, tincidunt quis, accumsan porttitor, facilisis luctus,
metus</p>
    </div>
  </div>
  <!-- mailing list //-->
  <div class="row m-t-3">
```

```
    <div class="col-md-12">
      <p>Pellentesque habitant morbi tristique senectus et netus et
malesuada fames ac turpis egestas. Vestibulum tortor quam, feugiat vitae,
ultricies eget, tempor sit amet, ante. Donec eu libero sit amet quam
egestas semper. Aenean ultricies mi vitae est. Mauris placerat eleifend
leo. Quisque sit amet est et sapien ullamcorper pharetra. Vestibulum erat
wisi, condimentum sed, commodo vitae, ornare sit amet, wisi. Aenean
fermentum, elit eget tincidunt condimentum, eros ipsum rutrum orci,
sagittis tempus lacus enim ac dui. Donec non enim in turpis pulvinar
facilisis. Ut felis. Praesent dapibus, neque id cursus faucibus, tortor
neque egestas augue, eu vulputate magna eros eu erat. Aliquam erat
volutpat. Nam dui mi, tincidunt quis, accumsan porttitor, facilisis luctus,
metus</p>
    </div>
  </div>
</div>
```

Coding the blog post template

Head back to your text editor and open the file `blog-post.ejs` that you previously created. Like our contact page template, let's start by first setting up the page title section of code. Enter the following code into the blog post template file:

```
<div class="container">
  <!-- page title //-->
  <div class="row m-t-2 m-b-2">
    <div class="col-lg-12">
      <h1>Post Title</h1>
    </div>
  </div>
</div>
```

As you can see, this code is almost identical to the contact page. There are two small differences that I will point out for you:

- I've changed up the spacing classes on the row `<div>`. In a future chapter, we are going to add some different components around the page title, so I've altered the vertical spacing to allow for them. I'm using the same margin top spacer but I've only set it to a value of 2. I've added a second margin bottom spacer with a value of 2 with the `.m-b-2` class. Switching the `-t` to a `-b` will apply a bottom margin instead a of top margin.
- I've changed the page title to `Post Title` in the `<h1>` tag.

Adding the blog post feature

The body of our blog post will have some different elements compared to the blog home template. After the page title, I'm going to insert a feature section that will be used for an image or carousel in a future chapter. For now, let's just lay in the grid column and some filler text for testing purposes. Enter the following code after the page title section:

```
<!-- feature //-->
<div class="row">
  <div class="col-md-12">
    <p>Pellentesque habitant morbi tristique senectus et netus et malesuada
fames ac turpis egestas. Vestibulum tortor quam, feugiat vitae, ultricies
eget, tempor sit amet, ante. Donec eu libero sit amet quam egestas semper.
Aenean ultricies mi vitae est. Mauris placerat eleifend leo. Quisque sit
amet est et sapien ullamcorper pharetra. Vestibulum erat wisi, condimentum
sed, commodo vitae, ornare sit amet, wisi. Aenean fermentum, elit eget
tincidunt condimentum, eros ipsum rutrum orci, sagittis tempus lacus enim
ac dui. Donec non enim in turpis pulvinar facilisis. Ut felis. Praesent
dapibus, neque id cursus faucibus, tortor neque egestas augue, eu vulputate
magna eros eu erat. Aliquam erat volutpat. Nam dui mi, tincidunt quis,
accumsan porttitor, facilisis luctus, metus</p>
  </div>
</div>
```

This is a very simple section. Notice the `row` `<div>` doesn't have a spacer class on it, since we added the bottom margin to the page title section. I've inserted a full-width `col-md-12` column class so the feature can stretch to the width of the layout.

Adding the blog post body

Now that we've added the blog post feature section, let's add the actual body part of the template. This section will use the same layout as our blog home page. It will be a two-column layout, the first being 2/3 wide, and the sidebar being 1/3 of the layout. Insert the following code after the feature section:

```
<!-- page body //-->
<div class="row m-t-2">
  <div class="col-md-8">
      <p>Pellentesque habitant morbi tristique senectus et netus et
malesuada fames ac turpis egestas. Vestibulum tortor quam, feugiat vitae,
ultricies eget, tempor sit amet, ante. Donec eu libero sit amet quam
egestas semper. Aenean ultricies mi vitae est. Mauris placerat eleifend
leo. Quisque sit amet est et sapien ullamcorper pharetra. Vestibulum erat
wisi, condimentum sed, commodo vitae, ornare sit amet, wisi. Aenean
fermentum, elit eget tincidunt condimentum, eros ipsum rutrum orci,
```

```
sagittis tempus lacus enim ac dui. Donec non enim in turpis pulvinar
facilisis. Ut felis. Praesent dapibus, neque id cursus faucibus, tortor
neque egestas augue, eu vulputate magna eros eu erat. Aliquam erat
volutpat. Nam dui mi, tincidunt quis, accumsan porttitor, facilisis luctus,
metus</p>
   </div>
   <!-- sidebar //-->
   <div class="col-md-4 hidden-md-down">
    <p>sidebar</p>
    <p>Pellentesque habitant morbi tristique senectus et netus et malesuada
fames ac turpis egestas. Vestibulum tortor quam, feugiat vitae, ultricies
eget, tempor sit amet, ante. Donec eu libero sit amet quam egestas semper.
Aenean ultricies mi vitae est. Mauris placerat eleifend leo. Quisque sit
amet est et sapien ullamcorper pharetra. Vestibulum erat wisi, condimentum
sed, commodo vitae, ornare sit amet, wisi. Aenean fermentum, elit eget
tincidunt condimentum, eros ipsum rutrum orci, sagittis tempus lacus enim
ac dui. Donec non enim in turpis pulvinar facilisis. Ut felis. Praesent
dapibus, neque id cursus faucibus, tortor neque egestas augue, eu vulputate
magna eros eu erat. Aliquam erat volutpat. Nam dui mi, tincidunt quis,
accumsan porttitor, facilisis luctus, metus</p>
  </div>
</div>
```

Let's break down what's happening here in the code:

- The row `<div>` has a `m-t-2` spacer class added on to provide some vertical spacing
- I'm using the same `col-md-8` and `col-md-4` column classes to set up the layout
- I've also used the `hidden-md-4` class on the sidebar `<div>` so that this section will not be visible on smaller resolution devices
- Finally, I added some temporary filler text for testing purposes

Converting the mailing list section to a partial

As I mentioned earlier, I would like the mailing list section to appear on all pages of the blog. Since this is the case, it would make more sense to make this chunk of code a partial that can be included in each template. It saves us having to reinsert this snippet in every one of our page templates.

From your text editor, create a new file called `_mailing-list.ejs` and save it to the `partial` directory in the root of your blog project. Once the file is saved, insert the following code into it:

```
<div class="row m-t-3">
  <div class="col-md-12">
    <p>Pellentesque habitant morbi tristique senectus et netus et malesuada
fames ac turpis egestas. Vestibulum tortor quam, feugiat vitae, ultricies
eget, tempor sit amet, ante. Donec eu libero sit amet quam egestas semper.
Aenean ultricies mi vitae est. Mauris placerat eleifend leo. Quisque sit
amet est et sapien ullamcorper pharetra. Vestibulum erat wisi, condimentum
sed, commodo vitae, ornare sit amet, wisi. Aenean fermentum, elit eget
tincidunt condimentum, eros ipsum rutrum orci, sagittis tempus lacus enim
ac dui. Donec non enim in turpis pulvinar facilisis. Ut felis. Praesent
dapibus, neque id cursus faucibus, tortor neque egestas augue, eu vulputate
magna eros eu erat. Aliquam erat volutpat. Nam dui mi, tincidunt quis,
accumsan porttitor, facilisis luctus, metus</p>
  </div>
</div>
```

Now go back to the blog post template file and insert the following line of code where the mailing list section should appear:

```
<%- partial("partial/_mailing-list") %>
```

Remember to do the same thing for the index and contact template. Delete the hardcoded mailing list and replace it with the preceding partial line.

That concludes the setup of the blog post template. Let's test it out before we move onto the next chapter, to make sure the new mailing list partial is working properly. Return to the Terminal and compile your project from the root directory. Run the Harp server command, then visit the following URL: `http://localhost:9000/blog-post.html`.

If all went as planned, your blog post page should look like this:

Learning Bootstrap 4 Home About Contact Search Search

Post Title

Pellentesque habitant morbi tristique senectus et netus et malesuada fames ac turpis egestas. Vestibulum tortor quam, feugiat vitae, ultricies eget, tempor sit amet, ante. Donec eu libero sit amet quam egestas semper. Aenean ultricies mi vitae est. Mauris placerat eleifend leo. Quisque sit amet est et sapien ullamcorper pharetra. Vestibulum erat wisi, condimentum sed, commodo vitae, ornare sit amet, wisi. Aenean fermentum, elit eget tincidunt condimentum, eros ipsum rutrum orci, sagittis tempus lacus enim ac dui. Donec non enim in turpis pulvinar facilisis. Ut felis. Praesent dapibus, neque id cursus faucibus, tortor neque egestas augue, eu vulputate magna eros eu erat. Aliquam erat volutpat. Nam dui mi, tincidunt quis, accumsan porttitor, facilisis luctus, metus

Pellentesque habitant morbi tristique senectus et netus et malesuada fames ac turpis egestas. Vestibulum tortor quam, feugiat vitae, ultricies eget, tempor sit amet, ante. Donec eu libero sit amet quam egestas semper. Aenean ultricies mi vitae est. Mauris placerat eleifend leo. Quisque sit amet est et sapien ullamcorper pharetra. Vestibulum erat wisi, condimentum sed, commodo vitae, ornare sit amet, wisi. Aenean fermentum, elit eget tincidunt condimentum, eros ipsum rutrum orci, sagittis tempus lacus enim ac dui. Donec non enim in turpis pulvinar facilisis. Ut felis. Praesent dapibus, neque id cursus faucibus, tortor neque egestas augue, eu vulputate magna eros eu erat. Aliquam erat volutpat. Nam dui mi, tincidunt quis, accumsan porttitor, facilisis luctus, metus

sidebar

Pellentesque habitant morbi tristique senectus et netus et malesuada fames ac turpis egestas. Vestibulum tortor quam, feugiat vitae, ultricies eget, tempor sit amet, ante. Donec eu libero sit amet quam egestas semper. Aenean ultricies mi vitae est. Mauris placerat eleifend leo. Quisque sit amet est et sapien ullamcorper pharetra. Vestibulum erat wisi, condimentum sed, commodo vitae, ornare sit amet, wisi. Aenean fermentum, elit eget tincidunt condimentum, eros ipsum rutrum orci, sagittis tempus lacus enim ac dui. Donec non enim in turpis pulvinar facilisis. Ut felis. Praesent dapibus, neque id cursus faucibus, tortor neque egestas augue, eu vulputate magna eros eu erat. Aliquam erat volutpat. Nam dui mi, tincidunt quis, accumsan porttitor, facilisis luctus, metus

Pellentesque habitant morbi tristique senectus et netus et malesuada fames ac turpis egestas. Vestibulum tortor quam, feugiat vitae, ultricies eget, tempor sit amet, ante. Donec eu libero sit amet quam egestas semper. Aenean ultricies mi vitae est. Mauris placerat eleifend leo. Quisque sit amet est et sapien ullamcorper pharetra. Vestibulum erat wisi, condimentum sed, commodo vitae, ornare sit amet, wisi. Aenean fermentum, elit eget tincidunt condimentum, eros ipsum rutrum orci, sagittis tempus lacus enim ac dui. Donec non enim in turpis pulvinar facilisis. Ut felis. Praesent dapibus, neque id cursus faucibus, tortor neque egestas augue, eu vulputate magna eros eu erat. Aliquam erat volutpat. Nam dui mi, tincidunt quis, accumsan porttitor, facilisis luctus, metus

Learning Bootstrap 4 2016

Make sure you don't forget to test the index and contact page templates in your browser to make sure the mailing list partial is working properly. That concludes the design layout for the blog post template. All of our templates are now ready to go, but before we move onto the next chapter on content components, let's review what we've learned.

Summary

This chapter has been a detailed explanation of the Bootstrap layout grid, how to use it, and how to build a sample project. We started out by learning the basics of the Bootstrap container, container-fluid, and row classes. Next, we moved onto learning the differences between all the Bootstrap column classes. Following the columns, we covered some more advanced topics, like offsetting columns, spacing, and responsive utilities. Once you had a solid understanding of the grid, we coded up the remaining page layouts that we'll need for the rest of the book. Now that we have everything set up, we'll start to drop some real content into the blog using Bootstrap content classes.

5
Working with Content

Content components in Bootstrap 4 are reserved for the most commonly used HTML elements such as images, tables, typography, and more. In this chapter, I'll teach you how to use all the building blocks of HTML that you'll need to build any type of website or web application. We'll start with a quick overview of each component and then we'll build it into our blog project. Bootstrap 4 comes with a brand new CSS reset called Reboot. It builds on top of `Normalize.css` to make your site look even better out of the box. Before we jump in, let's review some Reboot basics when dealing with content components in Bootstrap 4.

Reboot defaults and basics

Let's start this chapter by reviewing the basics of Reboot when using content components in Bootstrap. One of the main changes for content components in Bootstrap 4 is the switch from `em` to `rem` units of measure. `rem` is short for **root em** and is a little bit different from a regular `em` unit. `em` is a relative unit to the font-size of the parent element it is contained within. This can cause a compounding issue in your code that can be difficult to deal with when you have a highly nested set of selectors. The `rem` unit is not relative to its parent, it is relative to the root or HTML element. This makes it much easier to determine the actual size of text or other content components that will appear on the screen.

The `box-sizing` property is globally set to `border-box` on every element. This is good because it ensures that the declared width of an element doesn't exceed its size due to excess margins or padding.

The base `font-size` for Bootstrap 4 is `16px` and it is declared on the `html` element. On the `body` element, the `font-size` is set to `1rem` for easy responsive type-scaling when using media queries.

There are also global `font-family` and `line-height` values set on the `body` tag for consistency through all components. By default, the `background-color` is set to `#fff` or white on the `body` selector.

Headings and paragraphs

There are no major changes to the styles for headings and paragraphs in Bootstrap 4. All heading elements have been reset to have their `top-margin` removed. Headings have a `margin-bottom` value of `0.5rem`, while paragraphs have a `margin-bottom` value of `1rem`.

Lists

The list component comes in three variations: `<ul>`, `<ol>`, and `<dl>`. Each list type has had its `top-margin` removed and has a `bottom-margin` of `1rem`. If you are nesting lists inside one another, there is no `bottom-margin` at all.

Preformatted text

This typography style is used for displaying blocks of code on a website using the `<pre>` tag. Like the previous components, its `top-margin` has been removed and it has a `bottom margin` of `1rem`.

Tables

The table component has been adjusted slightly to ensure consistent text alignment in all cells. The styles for the `<caption>` tag have also been adjusted a bit for better legibility.

Forms

The form component is much simpler in Bootstrap 4. Much of the default styling has been removed to make the component easier to use and customize. Here are some of the highlights you should be aware of:

- Most of the styles have been removed on the `<fieldset>` tag. The borders, padding, and margin are no longer there.
- The `<legend>` tag has been simplified and is much more minimal in look now.

- The `<label>` tag is now set to `display: inline-block` to allow margins to be added.
- Default margins have been removed from the following tags: `<input>`, `<select>`, `<textarea>`, and `<button>`.
- `<textarea>`s can now only be resized vertically. They can't be resized horizontally, which often breaks page layouts.

That covers the key elements you need to be aware of with Reboot. If you're interested in learning more, please check out the docs at `http://v4-alpha.getbootstrap.com/content/reboot/`.

Now that we've reviewed the Reboot CSS reset, it's time to actually start covering the content components and adding them to our blog project.

Content classes in Bootstrap 4 are not that different from version 3. If you are fluent in Bootstrap 3, you may want to jump ahead to the next chapter at this point.

Learning to use typography

In Bootstrap 4, there are no major changes with the core typographic HTML tags. Header tags and their supporting CSS classes still work as they always have. However, there are some new utility classes you can use with some type tags to provide further variations for things like headers and titles. Later on in the book we'll be using a number of type tags and styles in our blog project. A couple of quick examples would be header tags for page and post titles, and lists for a number of different components. Let's start by reviewing the new display heading classes in Bootstrap 4.

Using display headings

Regular header tags work great in the flow of a page and are key for setting up the hierarchy of an article. For a landing page or other display-type templates, you may require additional header styles. This is where you can use the new display heading classes to create slightly larger titles with some different styling. There are four different levels of display headings you can use and the markups to render them are as follows:

```
<h1 class="display-1">Display 1</h1>
<h1 class="display-2">Display 2</h1>
<h1 class="display-3">Display 3</h1>
```

```
<h1 class="display-4">Display 4</h1>
```

Keep in mind you can apply these classes to any header tag you like. `display-1` will be the largest and the headers will shrink as you increase their size. For example, `display-4` would be the smallest of the options. Here's what the headers will look like when rendered in the browser:

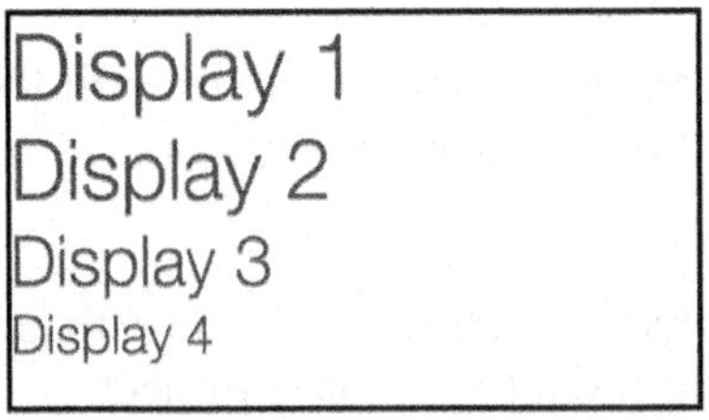

Display 1
Display 2
Display 3
Display 4

Keep in mind, you can apply these classes to any header tag you like. `display-1` will be the largest and the headers will shrink as you increase their size. For example, `display-4` would be the smallest of the options.

Customizing headings

You may want to add some additional context to your headers and you can easily do this with some included Bootstrap 4 utility classes. By using a contextual text class, you can tag on a description to a heading like this:

```
<h3>
  This is the main title
  <small class="text-muted">this is a description</small>
</h3>
```

As you can see, I've added a class of `text-muted` to a <small> tag that is nested within my header tag. This will style the descriptive part of the text a bit differently, which creates a nice looking effect:

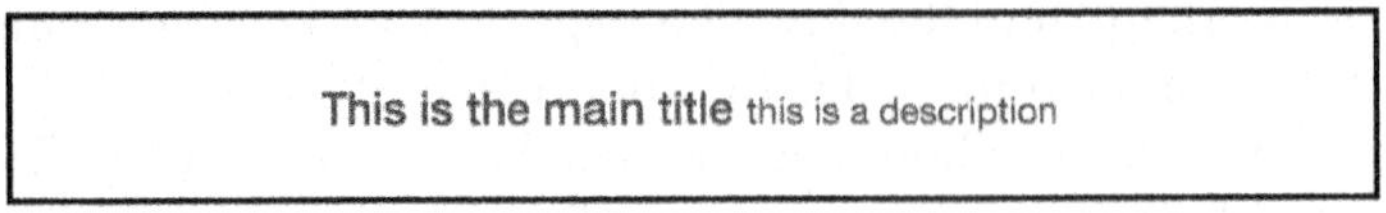

This is the main title this is a description

Using the lead class

Another utility text class that has been added to Bootstrap 4 is the lead class. This class is used if you want to make a paragraph of text stand out. It will increase the font size by 25% and set the font-weight of the text to light or 300. It's easy to add, as the following code shows:

```
<p class="lead">
here's some text with the .lead class to make this paragraph look a bit
different and standout.
</p>
```

The output of the preceding code will look like this:

here's some text with the .lead class to make this paragraph look a bit different and standout.

As you can see, this gives the text a unique look. This would be good to use as the first paragraph in a blog post or perhaps to call out some text at the top of a landing page.

Working with lists

Bootstrap 4 comes with a number of list options out of the box. These CSS classes can be applied to the <ul>, <ol>, or <dl> tags to generate some styling. Let's start with the unstyled list.

Coding an unstyled list

In some cases, you may want to remove the default bullets or numbers that come with ordered or unordered lists. This can be useful when creating a navigation, or perhaps you just want to create a list of items without bullet points. You can do this by using the list-unstyled class on the wrapping list tag. Here's an example of a basic unstyled, unordered list:

```
<ul class="list-unstyled">
  <li>item</li>
  <li>item</li>
  <li>item</li>
  <li>item</li>
  <li>item</li>
</ul>
```

This will produce a list with no bullet points that will look like this:

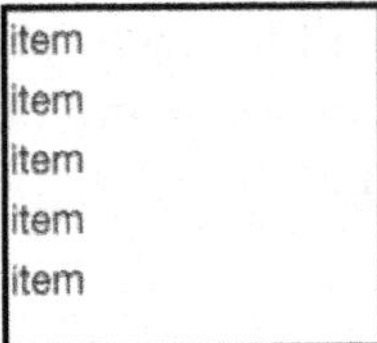

We can also nest additional lists inside if we want to create multi-level, indented lists. However, keep in mind that the `list-unstyled` class will only work on the first level of your list. Any nested additional lists will have their bullets or numbers. The code for this variation would look something like this:

```
<ul class="list-unstyled">
  <li>item
    <ul>
      <li>child item</li>
      <li>child item</li>
      <li>child item</li>
      <li>child item</li>
     </ul>
  </li>
  <li>item</li>
  <li>item</li>
  <li>item</li>
  <li>item</li>
</ul>
```

The preceding variation will look like the following output:

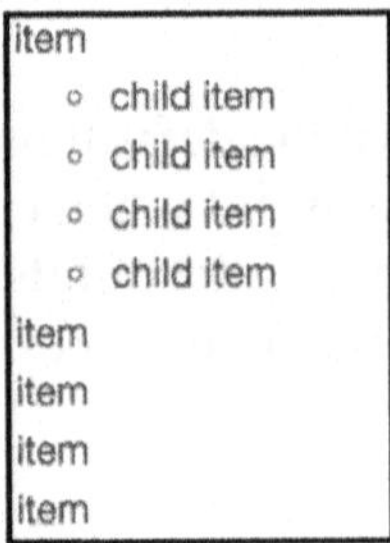

Now, if we check out this code sample in a browser, you'll notice you will see the bullet points for the child list that is nested within the parent.

Creating inline lists

The unstyled list is probably the one you will use the most. The next most useful class is list-inline, which will line up each <li> in a horizontal line. This is very useful for creating navigations or sub-navigations in a website or application. The code for this list is almost the same as the last, but we change the class name to list-inline. We also need to add a class of list-inline-item to each <li> tag. This is a new change for Bootstrap 4, so make sure you don't miss it in the following code:

```
<ul class="list-inline">
  <li class="list-inline-item">item</li>
  <li class="list-inline-item">item</li>
  <li class="list-inline-item">item</li>
  <li class="list-inline-item">item</li>
  <li class="list-inline-item">item</li>
</ul>
```

As I mentioned, the code is similar to the unstyled list, with a few changes. Here's what it will look like when rendered in the browser:

item item item item item

I think you can see how this would be a lightweight way to set up a horizontal navigation for your project. Let's move onto the last list type, which is a description list.

Using description lists

A description list allows you to create a horizontal display for terms and descriptions. Let's take a look at a basic list's code and then break it down:

```
<dl class="dl-horizontal">
  <dt class="col-sm-3">term 1</dt>
  <dd class="col-sm-9">this is a description</dd>

  <dt class="col-sm-3">term 2</dt>
  <dd class="col-sm-9">this is a different description</dd>

  <dt class="col-sm-3 text-truncate">this is a really long term name</dt>
  <dd class="col-sm-9">this is one last description</dd>
</dl>
```

There are a few things going on here that you need to be aware of, so let me break them all down for you:

- First you start a description list using the `<dl>` tag. It requires a class of `dl-horizontal` to trigger the list component styles.
- Each row is made up of a `<dt>` and `<dd>` tag. `<dt>` stands for term, while `<dd>` stands for description. Each tag should take a column class and is flexible, depending on how you want to lay out your list.
- On the third row, you'll notice a class called `text-truncate`. This class will truncate really long terms or text so they don't run outside the width of the column. This is a good technique to use for long chunks of text.

Now that I've explained all the code for the description list, let's see what this sample should look like in the browser:

term 1	this is a description
term 2	this is a different description
this is a really l...	this is one last description

That completes the typography styles that you need to know about in Bootstrap 4. Next, let me teach you what you can do with images in Bootstrap.

How to style images

Bootstrap allows you to do a few useful things with images through the use of CSS classes. These things include: making images responsive, converting images to shapes, and aligning images. In the next section, I'll show you how to apply all these techniques to your images.

Making images responsive

Bootstrap 4 comes with a new responsive image class that is super-handy when developing websites or web-based applications. When applying the class `img-fluid` to an `<img>` tag, it will automatically set the `max-width` of the image to `100%` and the `height` to `auto`. The result will be an image that scales with the size of the device viewport. Here's what the code looks like:

```
<img src="myimage.jpg" class="fluid-image" alt="Responsive Image">
```

It's as easy as adding that class to the image to trigger the responsive controls. A word of advice: I would recommend making your images a little bit bigger than the maximum size you think you will need. That way, the image will look good on all screen sizes.

Using image shapes

Bootstrap allows you to apply three different shape styles to images:

- `img-rounded` will add round corners to your image
- `img-circle` will crop your image into a circle
- `img-thumbnail` will add round corners and a border to make the image look like a thumbnail

As with the responsive images, all you need to do is add a single CSS class to the `<img>` tag to apply these styles. The reason you would want to use these classes is to avoid having to actually create these variations in an app such as Photoshop. It's much easier to apply this simple image formatting using code. Here's the code for each variation:

```
<img src="myimage.jpg" class="img-rounded" alt="Image Rounded">

<img src="myimage.jpg" class="img-circle" alt="Image Circle">

<img src="myimage.jpg" class="img-thumbnail" alt="Image Thumbnail">
```

Once you've coded that up, it should look like this in the browser:

I'm using one of my own images here; you'll need to swap in an image in your code.

Aligning images with CSS

The final Bootstrap classes you can apply to images are the alignment classes. They will allow you to align your image to the left, right, or center of your layout. Like the previous examples, you only need to add a single CSS class to the `<img>` tag to apply the alignment you want. With left and right alignment, you can also provide a column size within the class name. The best policy would be to use the same size as the column the image is contained within. Therefore, if your image is displayed in a column with a class of `col-xs-4`, then use the `-xs` unit in the alignment class name. Here's what the left and right alignment code looks like using the extra small size:

```
<img src="myimage.jpg" class="pull-xs-left" alt="Left Aligned Image">
```

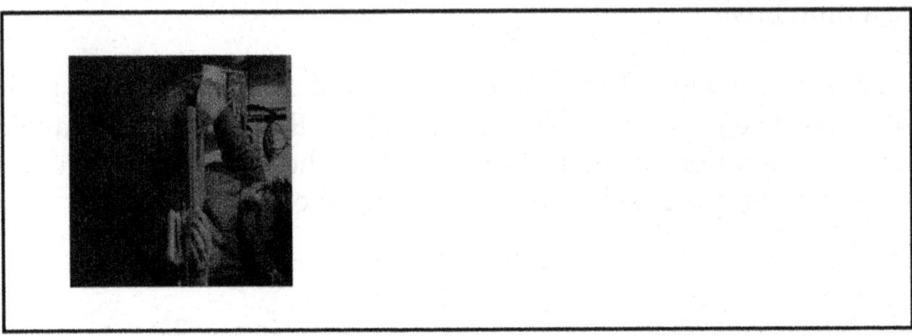

```
<img src="myimage.jpg" class="pull-xs-right" alt="Right Aligned Image">
```

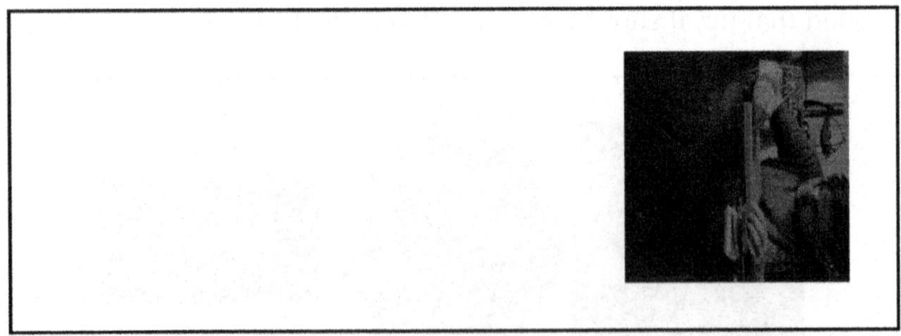

The final image alignment class you can use is to center the image in the layout. The class name for this is a little bit different, as you can see here:

```
<img src="myimage.jpg" class="center-block" alt="Center Aligned Image">
```

That concludes the section on image classes that you can use in your Bootstrap layouts. Next we will look at writing and rendering tables using Bootstrap 4.

Coding tables

Tables in Bootstrap 4 are largely unchanged from the previous version of the framework. However, there are a few new things, like inverse color table options and responsive tables. Let's start with the basics and we will build in the new features as we go.

Setting up the basic table

The basic table structure in Bootstrap takes advantage of almost all the available HTML table tags. The header is wrapped in `<thead>` and the body `<tbody>` tags. This will allow additional styling as we get into the inverse table layout. For now, let's see how we put together a basic table in Bootstrap:

```
<table class="table">
<thead>
  <tr>
    <th>first name</th>
    <th>last name</th>
    <th>twitter</th>
  </tr>
</thead>
<tbody>
  <tr>
    <td>john</td>
    <td>smtih</td>
    <td>@jsmtih</td>
  </tr>
  <tr>
    <td>steve</td>
```

```
      <td>stevens</td>
      <td>@stevens</td>
    </tr>
    <tr>
      <td>mike</td>
      <td>michaels</td>
      <td>@mandm</td>
    </tr>
  </tbody>
  </table>
```

As you can see, the syntax is fairly straightforward. The only class being applied is the root `table` class on the `<table>` tag. This needs to be applied to any table variation you are using in Bootstrap. This will produce a table that looks like the following in the browser:

first name	last name	twitter
john	smtih	@jsmtih
steve	stevens	@stevens
mike	michaels	@mandm

As you can see, the syntax is fairly straightforward. The only class being applied is the root `table` class on the `<table>` tag. This needs to be applied to any table variation you are using in Bootstrap.

Inversing a table

Let me quickly show you one of the new table classes in Bootstrap 4. If we add the class `table-inverse` to the `<table>` tag, the table colors will flip to be a dark background with light text. Here's the code you need to change:

```
<table class="table table-inverse">
  ...
</table>
```

This slight variation in code will produce a table that looks like this:

first name	last name	twitter
john	smtih	@jsmtih
steve	stevens	@stevens
mike	michaels	@mandm

That's a pretty handy trick to know if you need to get a quick variation of the basic table styles going.

Inversing the table header

Perhaps you don't want to inverse the entire table? If that is the case, you can use the `thead-inverse` class on the `<thead>` tag to only inverse that row:

```
<table class="table">
<thead class="thead-inverse">
  ...
</thead>
  ...
</table>
```

If this variation is applied, then your table will look like this:

first name	last name	twitter
john	smtih	@jsmtih
steve	stevens	@stevens
mike	michaels	@mandm

If you're looking for a more subtle design for your project, this approach may be more appealing to you.

Adding striped rows

Although not new to Bootstrap 4, the `table-striped` class is one that I use all the time. Applying this class to the `<table>` tag will add zebra striping to your table, starting with the first row in the body and applying a light grey background color on all the odd numbered rows:

```
<table class="table table-striped">
```

Using this class will produce a table that looks like this:

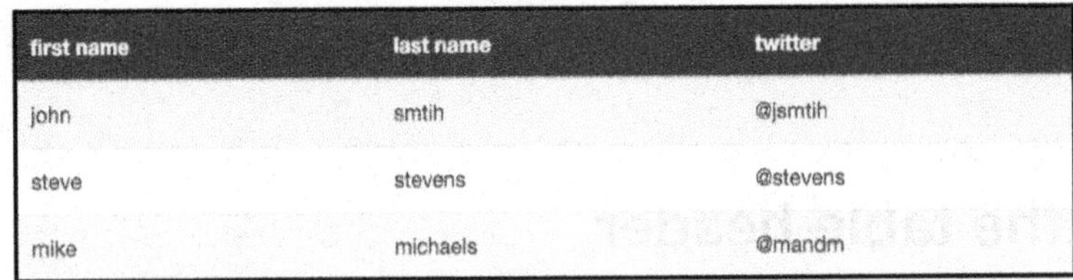

first name	last name	twitter
john	smtih	@jsmtih
steve	stevens	@stevens
mike	michaels	@mandm

Now our table is starting to come together. With a few classes, we can get an attractive-looking layout. Let's see what else we can do with tables.

Adding borders to a table

Another style that is regularly used is to add borders to your table. This can be done in the same way as stripes. Just change or add another class to the `<table>` tab called `table-bordered`. For this example, I'll remove the stripes and add the borders:

```
<table class="table table-bordered">
```

Now that we've added the borders and taken away the stripes, our table should look like this:

```
<table class="table table-bordered table-striped">
```

first name	last name	twitter
john	smtih	@jsmtih
steve	stevens	@stevens
mike	michaels	@mandm

It's important to know that you can combine the table classes and use more than one. What if you wanted a table with stripes and borders? You can do that easily, by including both of the corresponding classes.

Adding a hover state to rows

It's possible and easy to add a hover state to each of your table rows. To do so, you just need to add the table-hover class to the <table> tag. When used, if you hover over a row in the table, its background color will change to indicate a state change:

```
<table class="table table-hover">
```

Here I've removed the other table classes to show you the basic hover table option. When viewed in the browser, the table should look like the following when a row is hovered over with the mouse:

first name	last name	twitter
john	smtih	@jsmtih
steve	stevens	@stevens
mike	michaels	@mandm

In some cases you may require a table with smaller text and compressed height. This can be done by adding the table-sm class to the <table> tag. This will make the look of the table more compact when viewing it:

```
<table class="table table-sm">
```

If you choose to use this class, your table should look like this:

first name	last name	twitter
john	smtih	@jsmtih
steve	stevens	@stevens
mike	michaels	@mandm

Creating smaller tables

That concludes the core table variations that you can apply through a simple CSS class. Before we move on, there are a couple more important points on tables that we should go over.

Color-coating table rows

In some cases, you may want to color the background of a table row in a different color. This can easily be achieved through the use of some included contextual classes. There are five different color variations you can choose from:

- `table-active` is the hover color, light grey by default
- `table-success` is green for a positive action
- `table-info` is blue for an informational highlight
- `table-warning` is yellow to call out something that needs attention
- `table-danger` is red for a negative or error action

The preceding classes can be applied to either a `<tr>` or `<td>` tag. If I apply all of these color variations to a single table, they look like this:

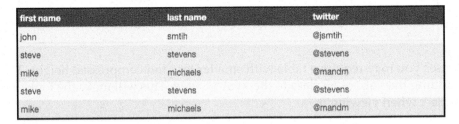

first name	last name	twitter
john	smtih	@jsmtih
steve	stevens	@stevens
mike	michaels	@mandm
steve	stevens	@stevens
mike	michaels	@mandm

As you can see, these classes can be useful for validation or just highlighting a particular row that needs to stand out more.

Making tables responsive

Adding responsiveness to tables has never been very easy to do with CSS. Thankfully, Bootstrap 4 comes with some support built right in that you can easily take advantage of. To make a table responsive, you simply need to wrap a `<div>` around your `<table>` that has a class of `table-responsive` on it:

```
<div class="table-responsive">
  <table class="table">
    ...
  </table>
</div>
```

If you view the table on a viewport that is smaller than 768px, then the table cells will scroll horizontally, so they can all be viewed. If the viewport is larger, you will see no difference in the table compared to a regular one.

Summary

With tables finished off, that brings this chapter to a close. I hope this has been a good introduction to content components in Bootstrap, as well as a good review of what's new for these types of components in Bootstrap 4. To review, we learned about: Reboot, typography, images, and tables. In the next chapter, we'll start to jump into some more complicated components and build them into our blog project.

6
Playing with Components

The real power of Bootstrap lies in the components contained within the framework. In this chapter, we'll go through a number of new and existing components. I'll show you how to use them and then we'll insert them into our sample blog project so you can see them in practice. Let's get right into it by covering one of the most commonly used components, which are buttons.

Using the button component

Buttons are one of the most commonly used components in Bootstrap. In version 4 of Bootstrap, some of the new options for the button component include an outlined variation, toggle states, and button groups with checkboxes and radios. Before we get into that, let's review the basic button options and configuration. Here's a few general points to keep in mind when using buttons:

- No matter what type of button you are creating, it will require the `.btn` CSS class to be included at a minimum
- The `.btn` class can be attached to a number of HTML tags, such as `<button>`, `<a>`, and `<input>`, to render a button
- There are different CSS classes for creating different size and color buttons

Basic button examples

Before we move on to more advanced configuration, let's cover the basics of creating Bootstrap buttons. If you aren't new to Bootstrap, you may want to skip this section. Bootstrap comes with six different button color options out of the box. Here's a breakdown of their names and when to use them:

- **Primary**: The main button used on your website. It is blue by default.
- **Secondary**: The alternate or secondary button used in your website. It is white by default.
- **Success**: Used for positive-based actions. It is green by default.
- **Info**: Used for informational buttons. It is a light blue by default.
- **Warning**: Used for warning-based actions. It is yellow by default.
- **Danger**: Used for error-based actions. It is red by default.

Now that I've explained all the button variations, let's check out the code for a button:

```
<button type="button" class="btn btn-primary">Primary</button>
```

As you can see, I'm using the `<button>` tag and I've added a couple of CSS classes to it. The first is the `.btn` class, which I mentioned you need to include on all buttons. The second is the `.btn-primary` class, which indicates that you want to use the **Primary** button variation. If you want to use a different button style, you simply change up that second class to use the corresponding keyword. Let's take a look at the code for all of the button variations:

```
<button type="button" class="btn btn-primary">Primary</button>

<button type="button" class="btn btn-secondary">Secondary</button>

<button type="button" class="btn btn-success">Success</button>

<button type="button" class="btn btn-info">Info</button>

<button type="button" class="btn btn-warning">Warning</button>

<button type="button" class="btn btn-danger">Danger</button>

<button type="button" class="btn btn-link">Link</button>
```

It's as easy as that. Note that the last line is a **Link** button option that I haven't talked about. This variation will appear as a text link in the browser, but will act as a button when you click or hover over it. I don't often use this variation so I left it out at first. If you view this code in your browser, you should see the following buttons:

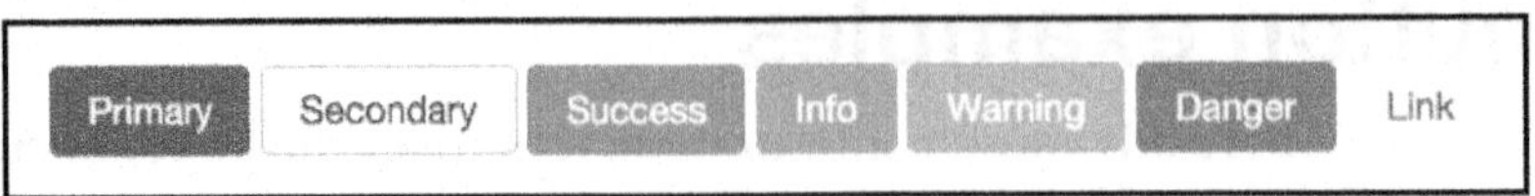

Creating outlined buttons

Starting in Bootstrap 4, they've introduced a new button variation which will produce an outlined button instead of a filled one. To apply this look and feel, you need to change up one of the button classes. Let's take a look at the following code for all variations:

```
<button type="button" class="btn btn-primary-outline">Primary</button>
<button type="button" class="btn btn-secondary-outline">Secondary</button>
<button type="button" class="btn btn-success-outline">Success</button>
<button type="button" class="btn btn-info-outline">Info</button>
<button type="button" class="btn btn-warning-outline">Warning</button>
<button type="button" class="btn btn-danger-outline">Danger</button>
```

As you can see, the class names have changed; here's how they map to each button variation:

- `btn-primary-outline`
- `btn-secondary-outline`
- `btn-success-outline`
- `btn-info-outline`
- `btn-warning-outline`
- `btn-danger-outline`

Basically, you just need to append `-outline` to the default button variation class name. Once you do, your buttons should look like this:

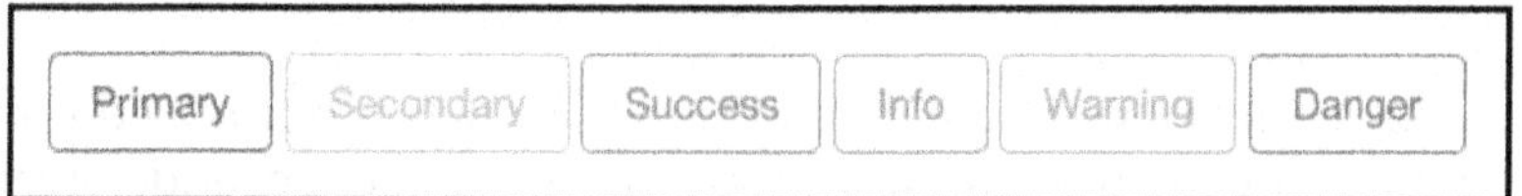

Checkbox and radio buttons

A new feature in Bootstrap 4 is the ability to convert checkboxes and radio buttons into regular buttons. This is really handy from a mobile standpoint because it is much easier to touch a button than it is to check a box or tap a radio button. If you are building a mobile app or responsive website, it would be a good idea to use this component. Let's start by taking a look at the code to generate a group of three checkboxes as a button group:

```
<div class="btn-group" data-toggle="buttons">
  <label class="btn btn-primary active">
    <input type="checkbox" checked autocomplete="off"> checkbox 1
```

```
    </label>
    <label class="btn btn-primary">
      <input type="checkbox" autocomplete="off"> checkbox 2
    </label>
    <label class="btn btn-primary">
      <input type="checkbox" autocomplete="off"> checkbox 3
    </label>
  </div>
```

Let me break down the code and explain what is going on here:

- To generate a button group with checkboxes, you need to wrap the boxes in a `<div>` with a class of `.btn-group`.
- To allow the buttons to toggle on and off, you also need to add the data attribute `data-toggle="buttons"` to the `<div>`.
- Next we need to use the button classes on the `<label>` tag to convert each checkbox into a button. Note that on the first button I'm using the `.active` class, which will make this checkbox toggled on by default. This class is totally optional.
- Your basic checkbox `<input>` tag is nested within the label.

Keep in mind since these are checkboxes, you can toggle multiple options on or off. Here's what the button group should look like when rendered in the browser:

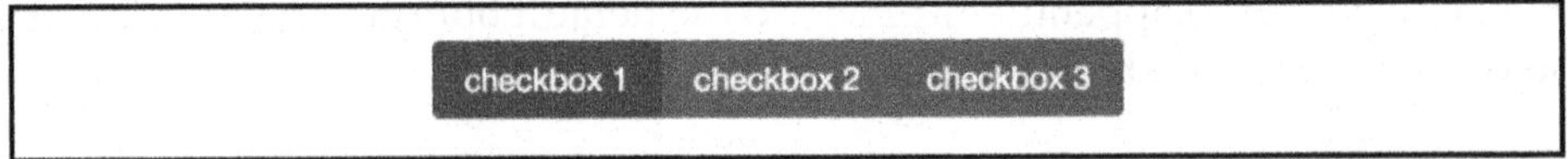

As you can see, this renders a nice-looking button group that is optimized for mobile and desktop. Also, notice how the first checkbox has a different background color as it is currently toggled on because of the `.active` class applied to that label. In the same way that we've created a button group with checkboxes, we can do the same thing with radio buttons.

Creating a radio button group

Creating a radio button group is very similar to the checkboxes. Let's start by checking out the code to generate this different variation:

```
<div class="btn-group" data-toggle="buttons">
  <label class="btn btn-primary active">
    <input type="radio" name="options" id="option1" autocomplete="off"
```

```
checked> radio 1
  </label>
  <label class="btn btn-primary">
    <input type="radio" name="options" id="option2" autocomplete="off">
radio 2
  </label>
  <label class="btn btn-primary">
    <input type="radio" name="options" id="option3" autocomplete="off">
radio 3
  </label>
</div>
```

Let me explain what's happening here with this code:

- Like the checkboxes, you need to wrap your collection of radio buttons in a `<div>` with the same class and data attribute
- The `<label>` tag and button classes also work the same way
- The only difference is that we are swapping the checkbox `<input>` type for radio buttons

Keep in mind that with radio buttons, only one can be selected at a time. In this case, the first one is selected by default, but you could easily remove that. Here's what the buttons should look like in the browser:

As you can see, the button group is rendered the same way as the checkboxes, but in this case we are using radios. This should be the expected result to optimize your group of radio buttons for mobile and desktop. Next we'll build on what we've learned about button groups, but learn how to use them in other ways.

We'll circle back later in this chapter and actually add the components to our blog project.

Using button groups

If you're new to Bootstrap, button groups are exactly as they sound. They are a group of buttons that are connected horizontally or vertically to look like a single component. Let's take a look at the code to render the most basic version of the component:

```
<div class="btn-group" role="group" aria-label="Basic example">
  <button type="button" class="btn btn-secondary">Left</button>
  <button type="button" class="btn btn-secondary">Middle</button>
  <button type="button" class="btn btn-secondary">Right</button>
</div>
```

As you can see, we have a group of regular button tags surrounded by `<div>` with a class of `.btn-group` on it. At the very least, this is all you need to do to render a button group. There are a couple of other optional attributes on the `<div>` tag, which are `role` and `aria-label`. If you need to worry about accessibility, then you should include those attributes, otherwise they are optional. One other small change in this code is I've decided to use the `.btn-secondary` class to mix things up a bit with the button styles. Let's take a look at how this will appear in the browser:

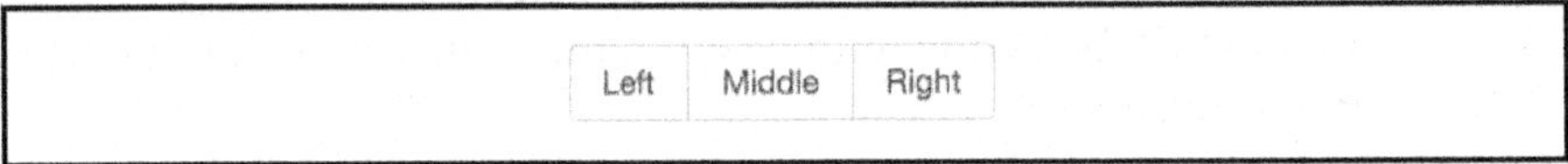

As you can see, we have a single component that is made up of three buttons. This component is commonly used for a secondary navigation, or in a form like I explained in the previous section. If you'd like to display the buttons vertically, that is also possible with a small change.

Creating vertical button groups

If you'd like to arrange the buttons in your group vertically, that is actually quite easy to do. There is no need to change any of the code on the `<button>` tags, you just need to update the CSS class name on the wrapping `<div>` tag. Here's the code you need to change:

```
<div class="btn-group-vertical">
  ...
</div>
```

If you make that alteration to your code, then the same button group will appear like this in the browser:

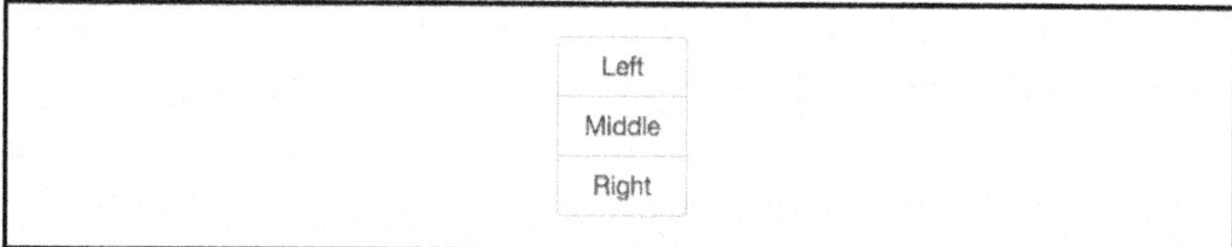

It would probably have made sense to change the left button label to the top and the right button label to the bottom. However, I left them as they are because I wanted to show you how you can simply shift the alignment of the group by changing one CSS class. That covers the basics of using the button groups component; in the next section, I'll show you how to create button drop-down menus.

Coding a button dropdown

The code to render a button as a dropdown is a little bit more complicated but still fairly easy to get up and running. You'll combine a button tag with <div> that has a nested collection of links inside it. Let's take a look at the code required to render a basic drop-down button:

```
<div class="btn-group">
  <button type="button" class="btn btn-secondary dropdown-toggle" data-toggle="dropdown" aria-haspopup="true" aria-expanded="false">
    Dropdown
  </button>
  <div class="dropdown-menu">
    <a class="dropdown-item" href="#">Link</a>
    <a class="dropdown-item" href="#">Link Two</a>
    <a class="dropdown-item" href="#">Link Three</a>
    <div class="dropdown-divider"></div>
    <a class="dropdown-item" href="#">Link Four</a>
  </div>
</div>
```

Okay, there are a few things going on here. Let's break them down one by one and explain how the dropdown works:

- The entire component needs to be wrapped in a <div> with a class of `.btn-group` on it.

- Next you insert a `<button>` tag with some button CSS classes on it. Like in the previous section, some of the other attributes are optional. However, it is a good idea to include this attribute: `aria-expanded`. This can either be set to `false` or `true` and controls whether the dropdown is open or closed on page load. In most cases, you will want to set this to `false`.
- After the `<button>` tag, insert another `<div>` tag which will hold all the links that appear in the drop-down menu list. Make sure you give this `<div>` a class of `.dropdown-menu`.
- Within the second `<div>` you insert a collection of `<a>` tags, one for each item in your list. Each `<a>` tag requires a class of `.dropdown-item` so that the proper CSS styling is applied.
- You may also want to insert a divider in your drop-down list if you have a large amount of links. This is done by inserting a third `<div>` with a class of `.dropdown-divider` on it.

As I mentioned, this component is a little more complex, but in Bootstrap 4 they have actually simplified it a bit to make it easier to use. Let's take a look at what it should look like in the browser. In the following screenshot, I've showed what the expanded version of the dropdown will look like so you can see the button and the list of links:

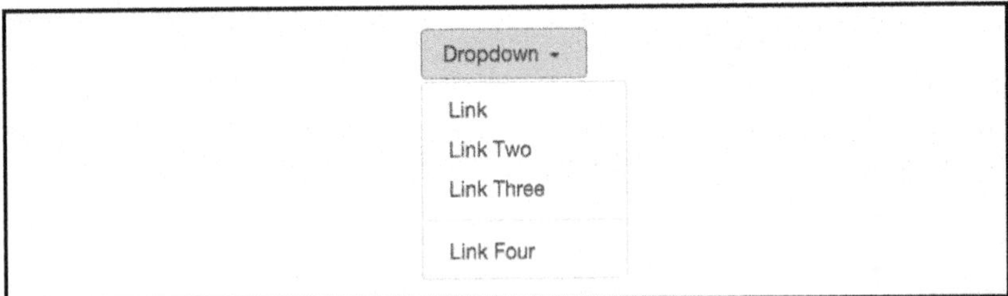

As you can see, we have a drop-down button with a list of links nested within it. Keep in mind that if you want to use this component, it does require that you include jQuery and `bootstrap.min.js` in your template. There are some other variations of this component you can easily implement, such as the pop-up menu.

Creating a pop-up menu

In some cases, you might want to have your menu pop up above the button instead of below it. You can achieve this by adding one class on the wrapping `<div>` for the component. Check out the code here:

```
<div class="btn-group dropup">
  ..
</div>
```

As you can see, I've added the class `.dropup` to the `<div>`. This will make the menu appear above the button, and it should look like this:

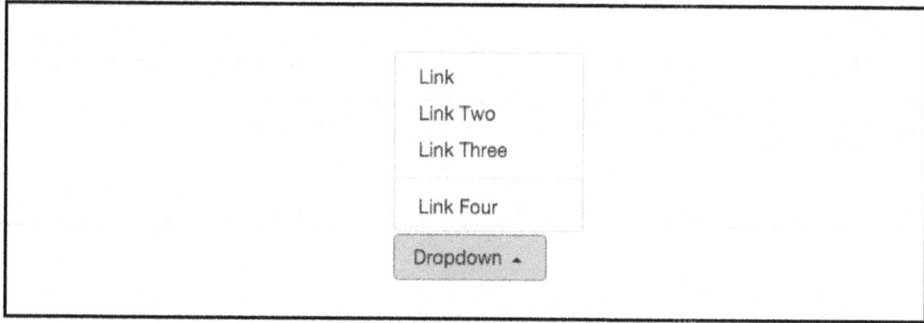

As you can see, the list appears above the button when it is expanded.

Creating different size drop-down buttons

By adding a single class to the `<button>` tag in the dropdown, you can make the trigger larger or smaller. Let's take a look at the code for the smaller and larger button variations:

```
<!-- large button //-->
<div class="btn-group">
  <button class="btn btn-secondary btn-lg dropdown-toggle" type="button"
data-toggle="dropdown" aria-haspopup="true" aria-expanded="false">
    Large button
  </button>
  <div class="dropdown-menu">
    ...
  </div>
</div>

<!-- small button //-->
<div class="btn-group">
  <button class="btn btn-secondary btn-sm dropdown-toggle" type="button"
data-toggle="dropdown" aria-haspopup="true" aria-expanded="false">
    Small button
  </button>
  <div class="dropdown-menu">
    ...
  </div>
```

```
</div>
```

If you find the button tag in the first example, you'll see I've added a class of `.btn-lg` to it. This class will increase the button size to be larger than the default. Take a look at the second chunk of code, find the `<button>` tag again, and you'll see a class of `.btn-sm` on it. This works the same way except the button will now be smaller than the default. Let's see how these buttons will render in the browser.

The `.btn-lg` and `.btn-sm` classes are not exclusive to the button drop-down component. You can use them on any button component variation you like.

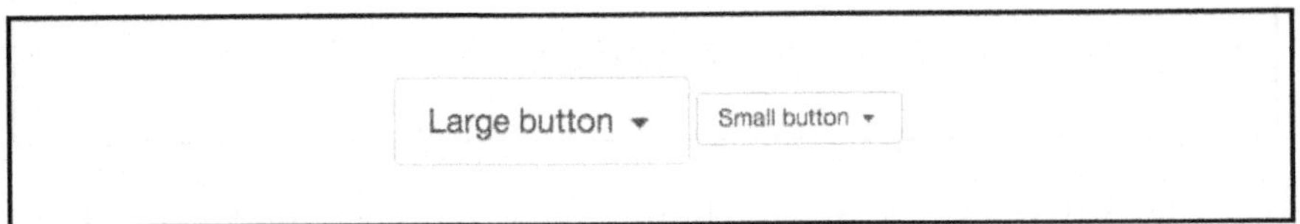

That concludes the basics of using the button drop-down component. In the next section, we'll cover a more complicated component, which is forms.

Coding forms in Bootstrap 4

If you are familiar with Bootstrap 3, then you'll notice the CSS form classes are pretty much the same in version 4. The biggest change I see in forms for the new version is that each form group uses a `<fieldset>` tag instead of `<div>`. If you are new to Bootstrap forms, a basic form group is made up of a label and an input. It can also include help text, but that is optional. Let's jump right in by creating a generic form that uses a number of core components.

Setting up a form

At the very least, a form needs to be made up of one input and one button. Let's start with the basics and create a form following those requirements. Here's the code to get you started:

```
<form>
  <fieldset class="form-group">
    <label>Text Label</label>
    <input type="text" class="form-control" placeholder="Enter Text">
```

```
    <small class="text-muted">This is some help text.</small>
  </fieldset>
  <button type="submit" class="btn btn-primary">Submit</button>
</form>
```

Let me explain what is happening here in the code:

- Every form needs to start with a `<form>` tag. However, no special classes are required on this tag.
- I've inserted a `<fieldset>` tag with a class of `.form-group` on it for our single input. This `<fieldset>` pattern will be repeated in the future when you add additional inputs.
- Within the `<fieldset>`, we have a `<label>`. Again, no special CSS classes need to be added to the `<label>`.
- After the label, you need to insert the form `<input>` tag. In this case, I'm using a text input. On this HTML tag, you need to add a class of `.form-control`. All input tags in Bootstrap will require this class. The placeholder text is optional but nice to add for usability.
- In the last line of the `<fieldset>`, I've included a `<small>` tag with a class of `.text-muted`, which will render the text small and light grey. This is the pattern you should use if you want to include some help text with your form input.
- Close the `<fieldset>` tag and then you need to add a `<button>` tag for the form `submit` button.
- Close the `<form>` and you are done.

After you've finished reviewing the code, fire up your web browser, and your form should look like this:

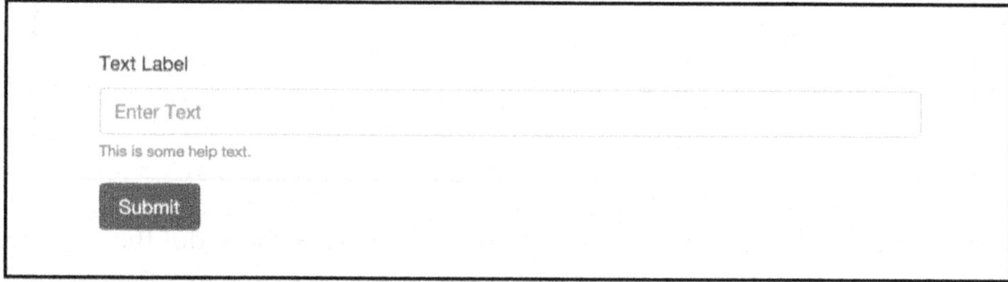

You've successfully coded your first Bootstrap 4 form. Let's continue and I'll explain how to implement other common form components using the latest version of Bootstrap.

Adding a select dropdown

Let's build on our form code by adding a select drop-down menu. Insert the following code after our text input:

```
<fieldset class="form-group">
  <label>Select dropdown</label>
  <select class="form-control">
    <option>one</option>
    <option>two</option>
    <option>three</option>
    <option>four</option>
    <option>five</option>
  </select>
</fieldset>
```

Let's break down the parts of the code you need to be aware of:

- Note that the entire `<select>` is wrapped in a `<fieldset>` with a class of `.form-group`. This pattern should repeat for each type of form input you add.
- On the `<select>` tag, there is a class of `.form-control` that needs to be added.
- Aside from that, you should code the `<select>` as you normally would, following the best HTML syntax practices.

Once you're done, if you view the form in the browser, it should now look like this:

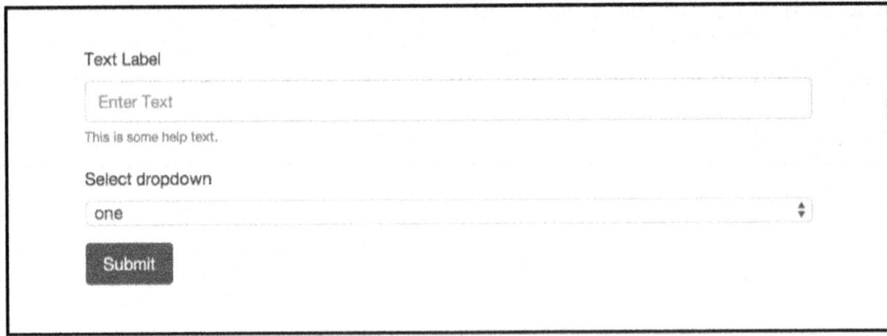

That completes the setup for `<select>` dropdowns. Next let's check out the `<textarea>` tag.

Inserting a textarea tag into your form

Moving along to the next input type, let's insert a `<textarea>` tag into our form. After the `<select>` menu, add the following code:

```
<fieldset class="form-group">
  <label>Textarea</label>
  <textarea class="form-control" rows="3"></textarea>
</fieldset>
```

Using this input is fairly simple. Like our other examples, you need to use a `<fieldset>` tag with a CSS class of `.form-group` to wrap the entire thing. On the actual `<textarea>` tag, you need to add the `.form-control` class. That's it; once you're done, your form should now look like this:

Now that the `<textarea>` is complete, let's move on to the file input form field.

Adding a file input form field

Historically, the file input form field has been a tricky one to style with CSS. I'm happy to say that in Bootstrap 4 they've created a new approach that's the best I've seen to date. Let's start by inserting the following code after the `<textarea>` in our form:

```
<fieldset class="form-group">
  <label>File input</label>
  <input type="file" class="form-control-file">
  <small class="text-muted">This is some help text. Supported file types
```

```
are: .png</small>
</fieldset>
```

Again, this form field is constructed in the same manner as the previous ones. However, there is one small change you need to be aware of with the **File input** field. On the `<input>` tag, you need to change the CSS class to `.form-control-file`. There are some specific styles being applied to clean up the look and feel of this form field. Once you're done, your form should look like this:

That completes the **File input** field which leaves us with two more basic form field inputs to go over. They are radio buttons and checkboxes. Let's learn how to add them next.

Inserting radio buttons and checkboxes to a form

These fields are pretty similar so I'm going to group them together in their own section. The code for these two fields differs a little bit from the other inputs, as I'll outline now. First, let's insert the following code after the `File input` field in our form:

```
<div class="radio">
  <label>
    <input type="radio" name="optionsRadios" id="optionsRadios1"
value="option1" checked>
    Option 1
  </label>
</div>
<div class="radio">
  <label>
    <input type="radio" name="optionsRadios" id="optionsRadios2"
value="option2">
        Option 2
  </label>
</div>

<div class="checkbox">
  <label>
    <input type="checkbox"> Checkbox
  </label>
</div>
```

Let's start by going over the radio button code first, then we'll move on to the checkbox:

- The fields don't use the `<fieldset>` tag as the wrapper. In this case, you should use a `<div>` and give it a class of either `.radio` or `.checkbox`, depending on what type you want to use.
- For these fields, the `<label>` tag will also wrap around the `<input>` tag so that everything is displayed in a horizontal line. We don't want the text label to drop down below the radio button or checkbox.
- You don't need a special class on the `<input>` for either of these fields.

As you can see, the code for these fields is a bit different from what we've learned about the other form inputs. Not to worry, as they are pretty easy to use and there aren't a bunch of CSS classes you have to memorize. One of the nicest changes with forms in Bootstrap 4 is that they require less HTML markup, so are easier to write. Finally, if you view our form in the browser, it should look like this:

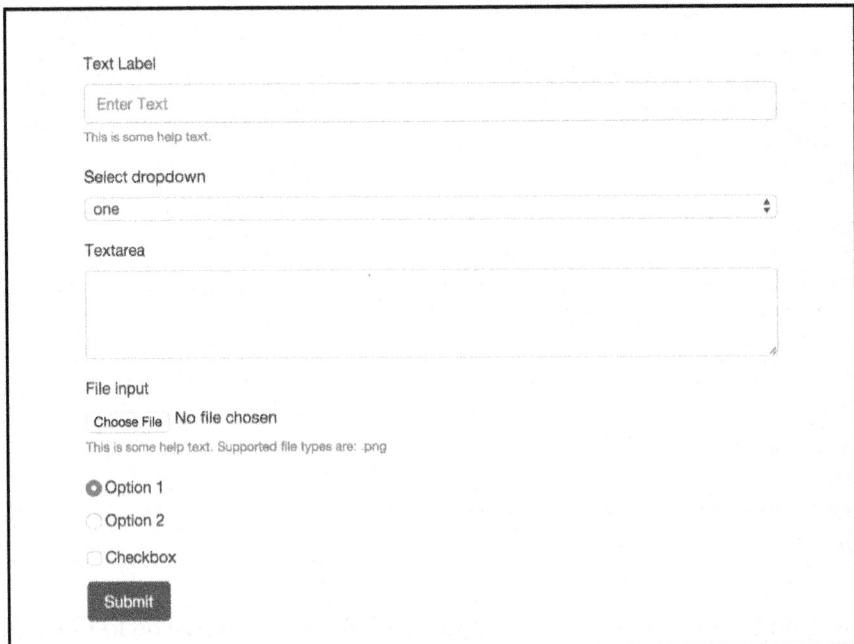

That completes the explanation of all the core form fields that you need to know how to use in Bootstrap 4. Before we move on to some more advanced form fields and variations, why don't we add a form to our blog project?

Adding a form to the blog contact page

I know, I know. I said we would wait till the end of the chapter to build components into the blog project. However, I'm thinking you might like a break from learning and actually add some of what you've learned to your project. Let's go ahead and do just that by filling in a form on the **Contact** page.

Updating your project

Let's start by opening up our project directory and finding the file named `contact.ejs`. Open up that file in your text editor and we are going to add some new form code and remove some filler code. To start, find the body section of the page that is wrapped in the following column `<div>`:

```
<div class="col-md-12">
```

Within that `<div>` is currently some filler text. Remove that text and replace it with the following form code:

```
<form>
  <fieldset class="form-group">
    <label>Email</label>
    <input type="email" class="form-control" placeholder="Enter email">
    <small class="text-muted">We'll never share your email with anyone
else.</small>
  </fieldset>
  <fieldset class="form-group">
    <label>Name</label>
    <input type="text" class="form-control" placeholder="Name">
  </fieldset>
  <fieldset class="form-group">
    <label>Message</label>
    <textarea class="form-control" rows="3"></textarea>
  </fieldset>
  <button type="submit" class="btn btn-primary">Submit</button>
</form>
```

I've coded up a basic contact form that you'll commonly see on a blog. It has e-mail, name, and message fields along with a **submit** button. Save your file and then preview your project in a browser. The **Contact** page should now look like this:

That concludes the updates to the **Contact** page for now. Later on in the book, we'll add some additional components to this page. Let's jump back into learning about forms in Bootstrap 4 by reviewing some additional form controls.

Additional form fields

Now that we've learned how to build a basic form and added one to our project, let's circle back and talk about some more advanced form fields and variations you can apply with Bootstrap 4. I'm going to start by showing you how to lay out forms in a few different ways.

Creating an inline form

Let's start by learning how to create an inline form. This is a layout you might want to use in the header of a project or perhaps for a login page. In this case, we're going to align the fields and buttons of the form vertically across the page. For this example, let's create a simple login form with the following code:

```
<form class="form-inline">
  <div class="form-group">
    <label>Name</label>
    <input type="text" class="form-control" placeholder="Mike Smith">
  </div>
  <div class="form-group">
    <label>Email</label>
    <input type="email" class="form-control" placeholder="mike@gmail.com">
  </div>
  <button type="submit" class="btn btn-primary">Login</button>
</form>
```

There are a few things going on in this form, so let me explain them for you:

- For inline forms, we need to add a CSS class named `.form-inline` to the `<form>` tag.
- You'll also notice the `<fieldset>` tags have been replaced with `<div>` tags. This is so they can be set to `display` as `inline-block`, which won't work with a fieldset.

Aside from those two differences, the form is coded up the same way as a regular one. Once you're done, your form should look like this in the browser:

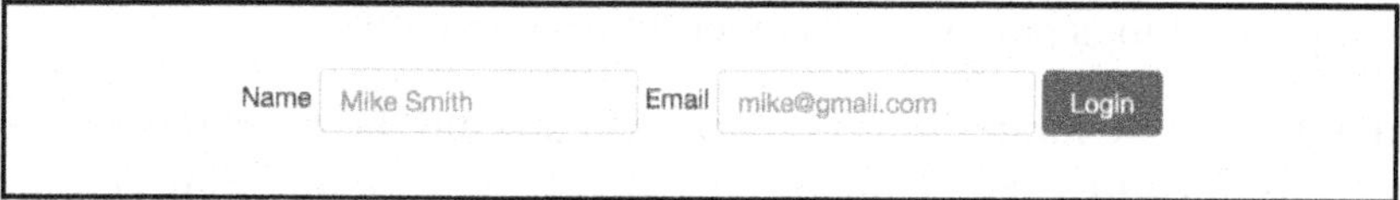

If you're like me, you might find the labels next to the text inputs kind of ugly. The good news is there is an easy way to hide them.

Hiding the labels in an inline form

The reason those labels are there is for accessibility and screen readers. We don't want to remove them altogether from the code, but we can hide them by adding a CSS class named `.sr-only`. This class stands for **screen reader only** and will therefore only show the labels if they are viewed on an accessible screen reader. Here is an example of how to add the CSS class:

```
<label class="sr-only">Name</label>
```

After you apply that CSS class to all the labels in the form, it should now appear like this in the browser:

That concludes how to make a basic inline form. However, what if you want to include other fields in an inline manner? Let's see how we can add checkboxes and radios.

Adding inline checkboxes and radio buttons

If you'd like to include checkboxes and radio buttons to an inline form you need to make some changes to your code. Let's start by going over the checkbox code. Insert the following code after the last text input in the inline form:

```
<label class="checkbox-inline">
  <input type="checkbox" value="option1"> Remember me?
</label>
```

There are a couple of things here that you need to be aware of:

- First, there is no longer a `<div>` wrapped around the checkbox
- You need to add a class named `.checkbox-inline` to the checkbox's `<label>` tag

Once you do this, save your form and it should look like this in the browser:

Now that we've added the checkbox, let's check out an example using radio buttons. Add the following code to your form after the checkbox code:

```
<label class="radio-inline">
  <input type="radio" name="inlineRadioOptions" id="inlineRadio1"
value="option1"> Yes
</label>
<label class="radio-inline">
  <input type="radio" name="inlineRadioOptions" id="inlineRadio2"
value="option2"> No
</label>
```

As you can see, the pattern here is exactly the same. The `<div>` around each radio button has been removed. Instead, there is a CSS class named `.radio-inline` that needs to be added to each radio `<label>` tag. Once you've completed this step, your form should look like this:

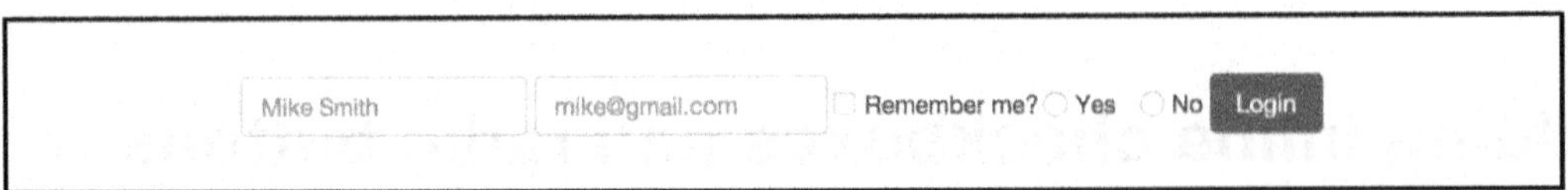

That completes everything you need to know about inline forms. Let's now move on to some more utility-type actions that you can apply to your form fields.

Changing the size of inputs

Bootstrap comes with a few handy utility CSS classes that you can use with form fields to have them appear at different sizes. Along with the default size, you can choose to display your fields in a larger or smaller size. Let's take a look at the code to render all three size variations:

```
<input class="form-control form-control-lg" type="text" placeholder="form-
control-lg">
<input class="form-control" type="text" placeholder="Default input, No
class required">
<input class="form-control form-control-sm" type="text" placeholder="form-
control-sm">
```

To use the different size inputs, you simply have to add an additional class to the tag:

- For a larger input, use the class `.form-control-lg`
- For a smaller input, use the class `.form-control-sm`
- The default input size requires no extra CSS class

Here's how each version looks in the browser:

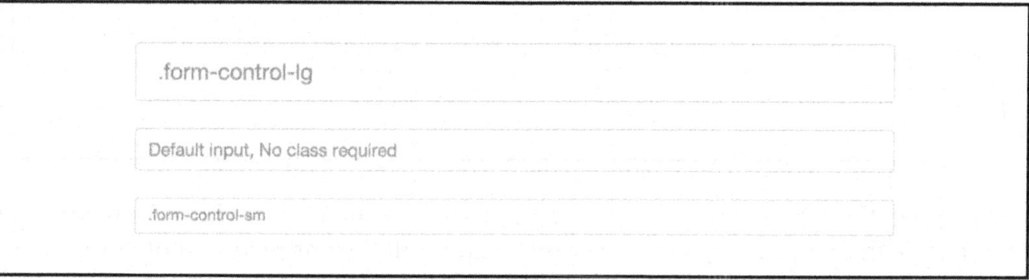

As you can see, the larger input is taller and has some additional padding. The smaller input is shorter with reduced padding. These classes only cover the vertical size of an input. Now let's learn how to control the width of inputs.

Controlling the width of form fields

Since Bootstrap is a mobile-first framework, form fields are designed to stretch to fit the width of their column. Therefore, if you are using `.col-md-12` for your column class, the field is going to stretch to the width of the layout. This may not always be what you want, you may only want the input to stretch to half of the width of the layout.

If this is the case, you need to wrap your field in a `<div>` with a column class on it to control the width. Let's check out some example code to get the point across:

```
<div class="col-md-12">
    <input type="text" class="form-control" placeholder="full width">
```

```
    </div>
    <div class="col-md-6">
        <input type="text" class="form-control" placeholder="half width">
    </div>
```

In the preceding code, I've removed some of the labels and other form code to make it easier to see what is going on. Here's a breakdown of what you need to know:

- You need to wrap your input in a `<div>` with a column class on it
- The first input will stretch to the width of the layout because of the `.col-md-12` class
- The second input will only stretch to fill 50% of the layout because of the `.col-md-6 class`

Let's take a look at how this will look in the actual browser:

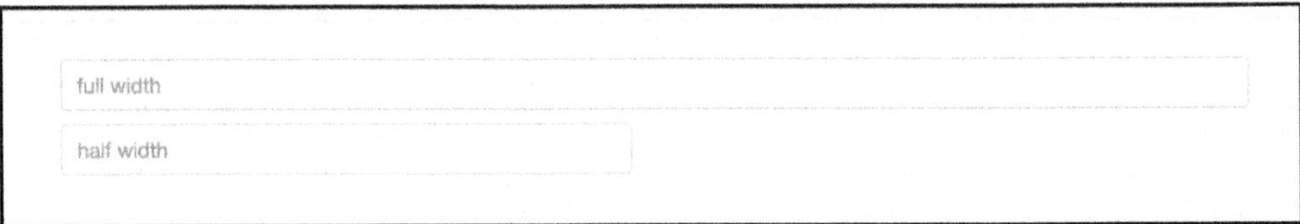

As you can see, the second input only stretches to half of the width. This is how you can control the width of inputs if you don't want them to fill the entire layout of your page. The last thing I'd like to cover when it comes to forms is validation of input fields.

Adding validation to inputs

Bootstrap 4 comes with some powerful yet easy to use validation styles for input fields. Validation styles are used to show things such as errors, warnings, and success states for form fields when you submit the actual form. Let's take a look at the code to render all three validation states:

```
<div class="form-group has-success">
  <label class="form-control-label">Input with success</label>
  <input type="text" class="form-control form-control-success">
</div>
<div class="form-group has-warning">
  <label class="form-control-label">Input with warning</label>
  <input type="text" class="form-control form-control-warning">
</div>
<div class="form-group has-danger">
```

```
    <label class="form-control-label">Input with danger</label>
    <input type="text" class="form-control form-control-danger">
  </div>
```

The markup for each validation variation is very similar to a regular input with the addition of a few CSS classes to apply the proper state look and feel. Let's go over each change you need to be aware of:

- The first input is the success state. The wrapping `<div>` needs to have a class called `.has-success` added to it.
- Each `<label>` tag needs to have a class named `.form-control-label` added to it. This is required to color the label to match the state color.
- The success input requires a class named `.form-control-success.`
- The second input is the warning state. The wrapping `<div>` needs a class named `.has-warning` added to it.
- The warning input also needs a class named `.form-control-warning` added.
- Finally, the last input is the danger or error state. The wrapping `<div>` needs to have a class named `.has-danger` added.
- The danger input also needs a class named `.form-control-danger` added.

Let's take a look at how all these validation inputs should look in the browser:

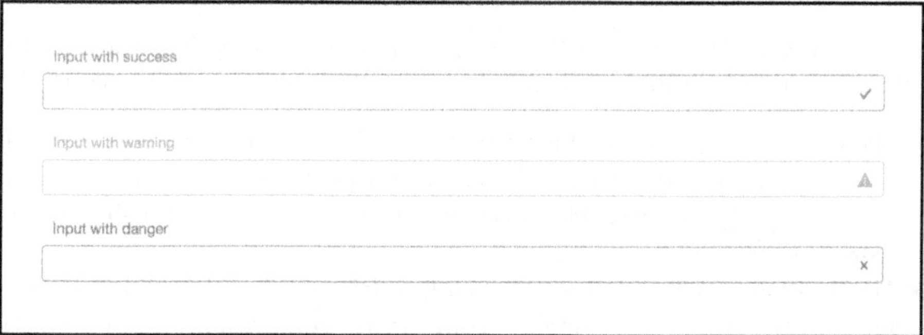

As you can see, the inputs and labels are colored to match their state. You'll also notice each input has an icon to the right edge of it. These icons are automatically added when you include the required CSS files. There is no need to actually use any images here, which is great. That concludes everything that you need to know about forms in Bootstrap 4. In the next section, I'll teach you about the **Jumbotron** component.

Using the Jumbotron component

If you're new to Bootstrap, you may be asking yourself what the heck is a Jumbotron component. Jumbotron is used to feature a block of content, usually at the top of your page. This is your standard main feature block that you'll see on a number of websites. If you require something more sophisticated than a simple page title, Jumbotron is the component you'll want to use. Let's take a quick look at the code required to create this component:

```
<div class="jumbotron">
  <h1 class="display-3">Feature title</h1>
  <p class="lead">This is a basic jumbrotron call to action</p>
  <hr class="m-y-2">
  <p>This is some further description text for your main feature</p>
  <p class="lead">
    <a class="btn btn-primary btn-lg" href="#" role="button">Learn more</a>
  </p>
</div>
```

There are some new CSS classes here that we need to review, as well as some existing ones we have already learned about. Let's break down what's happening in the code:

- The Jumbotron component is based off a `<div>` with a CSS class named `.jumbotron`. Within this `<div>`, you can pretty much use whatever text formatting tags you like. However, there are a few basics you should include to make it look good.
- The first tag you'll see is the `<h1>` with a class of `.display-3` on it. Since the Jumbotron is more of a "display" component, you'll want to beef up the size of your `<h1>` by using the optional class we learned about earlier in the book.
- Next, you'll see a simple `<p>` tag for the feature's tagline. On that tag, there is a class named `.lead`. This class increases the base font size by 25% and sets the `font-weight` to `300` which is a lighter weight. Again, this gives the Jumbotron component more of a "feature" like look and feel.
- After the tagline text, you'll see an `<hr>` tag with a class of `.m-y-2` on it. If you remember, this is a utility spacing class. The `-y` in this case will add a `margin` above and below the `<hr>` tag.

- Next we have another <p> tag with some additional descriptive text in it.
- Finally, we have a <button> wrapped in a <p> tag so that there is a conclusion to the call to action in the Jumbotron block. Note that the user of the `.btn-lg` class will produce a larger-sized button.

After you've coded up your Jumbotron component, it should look like this in the browser:

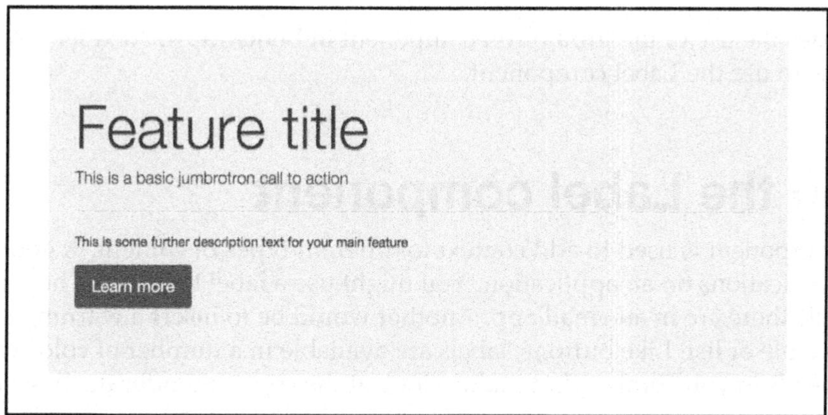

By default, the Jumbotron component will stretch to fit the width of the column it is contained within. In most cases, you'll likely want it to span the entire width of your page. However, in some cases, you might want a Jumbotron to stretch from one edge of the browser to the other without any horizontal padding on it. If this is the case, you need to add the `.jumbotron-fluid` class to the main <div> and make sure it is outside of a Bootstrap `.container`. Let's take a look at the following code to see what I mean:

```
<div class="jumbotron jumbotron-fluid">
  <div class="container">
    <h1 class="display-3">Feature title</h1>
      <p class="lead">This is a basic jumbrotron call to action</p>
  </div>
</div>
```

As you can see, the `.container` <div> is now inside of the Jumbotron <div>. This is how you remove the horizontal padding on the section. Once completed, it should look like this in the browser:

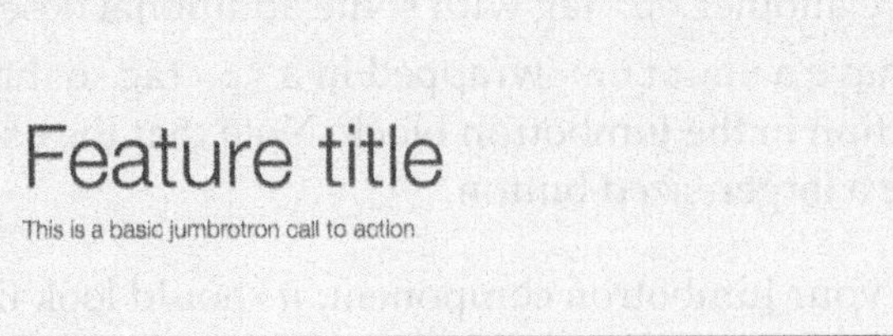

That concludes the use of the Jumbotron component in Bootstrap 4. Next let's move on to learning how to use the Label component.

Adding the Label component

The Label component is used to add context to different types of content. A good example would be notifications on an application. You might use a label to indicate how many unread emails there are in an email app. Another would be to insert a warning tag next to an item in a table or list. Like buttons, labels are available in a number of color variations to meet your needs in your project. Let's take a look at the code to render the basic label options:

```
<span class="label label-default">Default</span>
<span class="label label-primary">Primary</span>
<span class="label label-success">Success</span>
<span class="label label-info">Info</span>
<span class="label label-warning">Warning</span>
<span class="label label-danger">Danger</span>
```

You'll likely notice some similarities here with the Button component CSS classes. When using a label, you should use the `<span>` tag as your base for the component. Here are some more important facts when using this component:

- Every variation of the Label component requires the use of the `.label` class on the `<span>` tag
- The **Default** label uses the `.label-default` class and is grey
- The **Primary** label uses the `.label-primary` class and is blue
- The **Success** label uses the `.label-success` class and is green
- The **Info** label uses the `.label-info` class and is light blue
- The **Warning** label uses the `.label-warning` class and is yellow
- Finally, the **Danger** label uses the `.label-danger` class and is red

Once you've coded that up, it should look like this in your browser:

By default, labels will be rectangular with slightly rounder corners. If you'd like to display them in pill format, you can do so by adding the `.label-pill` class to the `<span>` tag. Here's an example to see what I mean:

```
<span class="label label-pill label-default">Default</span>
<span class="label label-pill label-primary">Primary</span>
<span class="label label-pill label-success">Success</span>
<span class="label label-pill label-info">Info</span>
<span class="label label-pill label-warning">Warning</span>
<span class="label label-pill label-danger">Danger</span>
```

If you add that class to your labels, they should look like this in the browser:

That concludes the Label component in Bootstrap 4. Next, I'll teach you how to use the Alerts component.

Using the Alerts component

The Alerts component in Bootstrap provides contextual messages for typical uses, such as validation and general information, that need to stand out more. Like our previous components, it comes in a few different variations depending on your needs. Let's start by looking at the basic code required to render the different alert options:

```
<div class="alert alert-success" role="alert">
  A success alert
</div>
<div class="alert alert-info" role="alert">
  An info alert
</div>
<div class="alert alert-warning" role="alert">
  A warning alert
</div>
```

```
<div class="alert alert-danger" role="alert">
  A danger alert
</div>
```

The classes used to create an alert can be added to any block element, but for demo purposes we'll implement them using `<div>` tags. Here are the key points you need to know:

- Any instance of the Alert component will require the use of the `.alert` CSS class on the `<div>` tag
- You also need a second CSS class to indicate which version of the alert you want to use
- The **Success** alert uses the class `.alert-success` and is green
- The **Info** alert uses the class `.alert-info` and is blue
- The **Warning** alert uses the class `.alert-warning` and is yellow
- The **Danger** alert uses the class `.alert-danger` and is red

Once you've set up the code for those alerts, they should look like this in the browser:

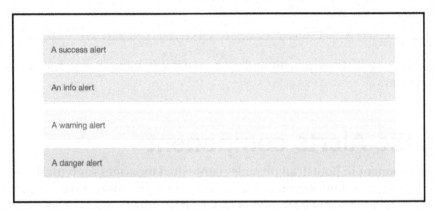

That was a basic example of using Alerts. There are some additional things you can do to extend this component such as adding a dismiss button.

Adding a dismiss button to alerts

If you want to make your alert bar dismissible, you can add a button to do this. To include the link, update the code for your bar, as follows:

```
<div class="alert alert-success" role="alert">
    <button type="button" class="close" data-dismiss="alert" aria-
label="Close">
    <span aria-hidden="true">&times;</span>
  </button>
  A success alert
</div>
```

The previous Alert bar code doesn't change, but you do need to add a button before the alert message:

- The `<button>` requires a class named `.close` to appear
- You'll also need the `data-dismiss` attribute to be included with a value of `alert`
- The `×` code will be rendered as an **X** in the browser

Once you've added the new code, your alert bar should look like this:

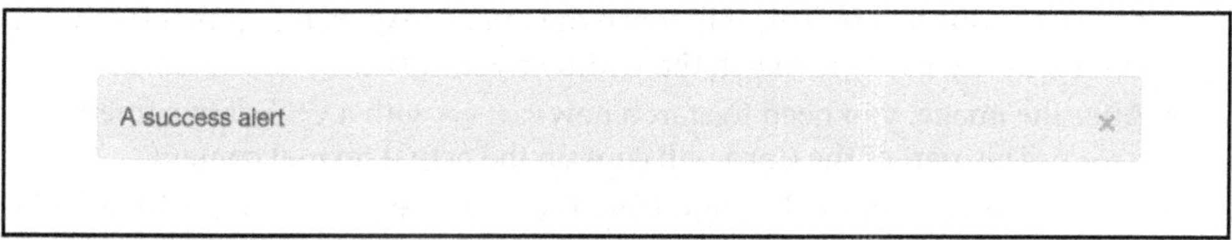

Now your alert bar has a dismissible **X** button that can be triggered to close when you implement the functionality of the component in your app or website. That completes the Alert component in Bootstrap 4. In the next section, I'll teach you about the best new component in version 4, which is Cards.

Using Cards for layout

In my opinion, the best new feature in Bootstrap 4 is the new Card component. If you're unfamiliar with Cards, they were made popular with the release of Google Material Design. They are a mobile first content container that works well for phones, tablets, and the desktop.

We'll be using the Card component heavily in our blog project so let's jump right in and start learning how to use them. Check out the following code to learn how to render a basic card:

```
<div class="card">
```

```
    <img class="card-img-top img-fluid"  src="path/to/your/image.jpg">
    <div class="card-block">
      <h4 class="card-title">Card title</h4>
      <p class="card-text">Some basic description text for your card should
  appear in this section.</p>
      <a href="#" class="btn btn-primary">Button</a>
    </div>
  </div>
```

There are a number of new CSS classes you need to be aware of here, so let's go through them one by one:

- Any instance of the Card component must use a `<div>` tag with a CSS class named `.card` on it.
- If you wish to include an image inside your card, it comes next. The image requires a class named `.card-img-top` to display the image at the top of the card. Although not required, I would also recommend adding the class `.img-fluid` to your image. This will make the image responsive so that it will automatically resize to match the width of your card.
- After the image, you need to start a new `<div>` with a CSS class named `.card-block`. This part of the Card will contain the actual textual content.
- The first thing your card should have is a title. Use an `<h4>` tag with a CSS class of `.card-title` for this section.
- Next, you can insert a paragraph of text with a `<p>` tag and a class of `.card-text`. If you choose to have multiple paragraphs, make sure each one uses that same class name.
- Finally, I've inserted a primary `<button>` so the user has something to click on to view the full piece of content.

After you've finished coding this up, it should appear like this in your browser. Note for demo purposes, I've included an image of my own so you can see how it works. You'll need to provide your own images for your projects:

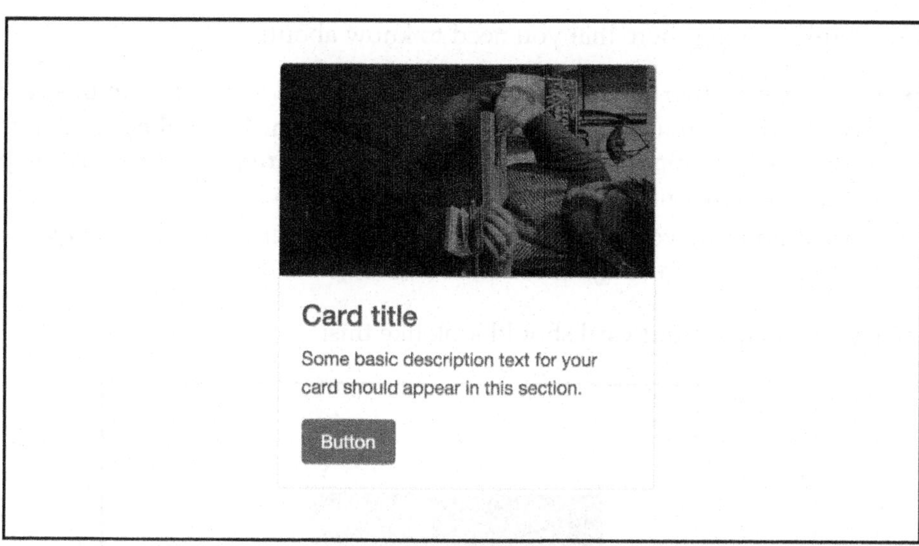

As you can see, this will render a neat-looking little content component that you can use in many different ways. Let's move on by learning some other ways that you can customize the Card component.

Moving the Card title

Perhaps you want to move the title of your card above the image? This is actually really easy to do, you simply need to move the `<title>` tag before the image in the flow of the component, like this:

```
<div class="card">
  <div class="card-block">
    <h4 class="card-title">Card title</h4>
  </div>
  <img
  class="card-img-top img-fluid"
  src="http://mattlambert.ca/img/matt-lambert.jpg">
  <div class="card-block">
    <p class="card-text">Some basic description text for your card should
appear in this section.</p>
    <a href="#" class="btn btn-primary">Button</a>
  </div>
</div>
```

There are a couple of things here that you need to know about:

- There are now two instances of `<div class="card-block">` in this card. It is perfectly fine to reuse this section within a single card. You'll notice that the header tag is wrapped inside of this `<div>`. This is required to apply the proper padding and margin around the title in the card.
- The second thing you need to note is that the header tag has been moved above the image in the Card layout.

After making this change, your card should look like this:

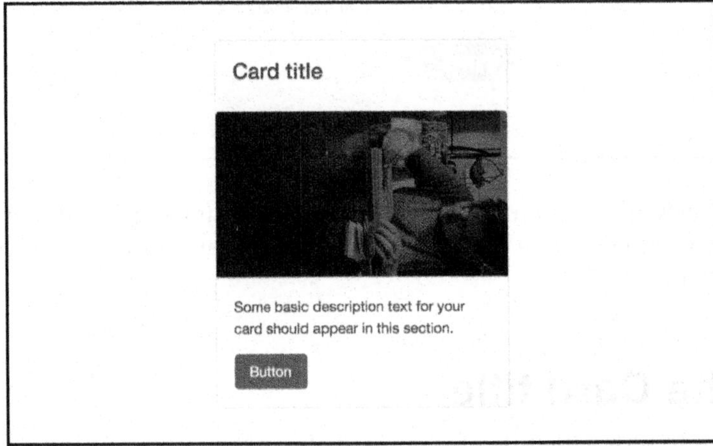

Hopefully this shows you how easy it is to work with different content in cards. Let's continue by showing some other things that you can do.

Changing text alignment in cards

By default, text and elements will always align left in a card. However, it is possible to change this quite easily. Let's create a second card and then we'll center one and right align the other. I'm going to remove the image so the code is easier to understand:

```
<div class="card">
  <div class="card-block text-xs-center">
    <h4 class="card-title">Card title</h4>
    <p class="card-text">Some basic description text for your card should
appear in this section.</p>
    <a href="#" class="btn btn-primary">Button</a>
  </div>
```

```
</div>
<div class="card">
  <div class="card-block text-xs-right">
    <h4 class="card-title">Card title</h4>
    <p class="card-text">Some basic description text for your card should
appear in this section.</p>
    <a href="#" class="btn btn-primary">Button</a>
  </div>
</div>
```

Not much has changed here, but let's go over what is different:

- First, as I mentioned, I removed the image to make the code simpler
- On the first card, I've added a class of `.text-xs-center`, which will center the text in the card
- On the second card, I added a class named `.text-xs-right`, which will right align everything

That's all you need to do. If you view this in the browser it should look like this:

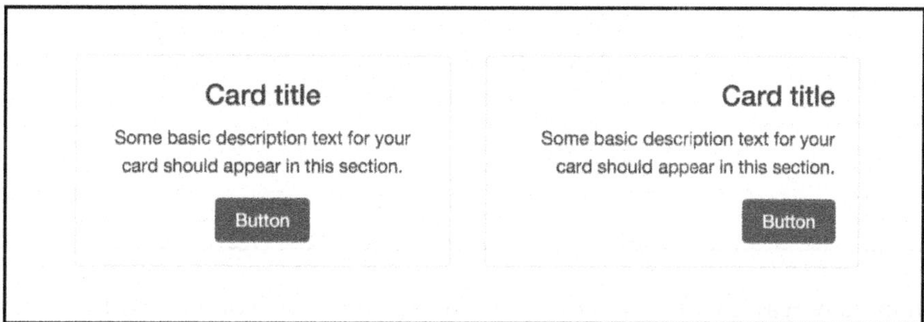

So with one additional CSS class we can easily control the alignment of the text and elements in a card. Cards are a pretty powerful component, so let's continue to learn how you can customize them.

Adding a header to a Card

If you want to add a header to your Card, this is also pretty easy to do. Check out this code sample to see it in action:

```
<div class="card">
    <div class="card-header">
    Header
  </div>
```

```
  <div class="card-block">
    <h4 class="card-title">Card title</h4>
    <p class="card-text">Some basic description text for your card should
appear in this section.</p>
    <a href="#" class="btn btn-primary">Button</a>
  </div>
</div>
```

With the addition of a new section of code, we can add a header:

- Before the `.card-block` section, insert a new `<div>` with a class named `.card-header`
- Within this new `<div>`, you can add the header title

Save your file and check it out in the browser, and it should look like this:

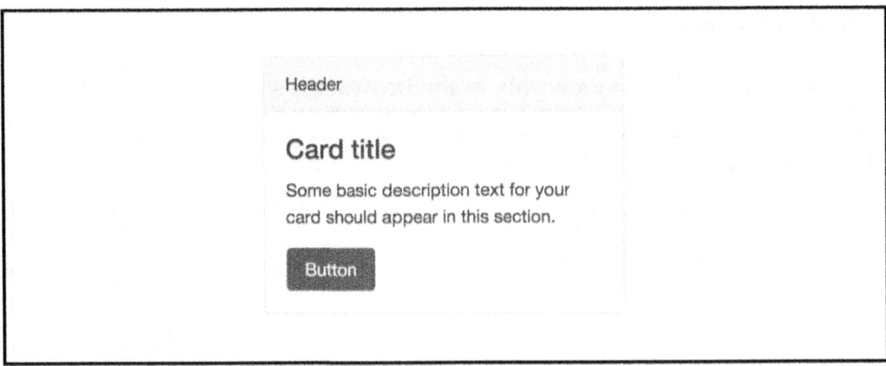

That's a super easy way to add a header section to your card. You can add a footer in the same manner. Let's add some additional code for the footer:

```
<div class="card">
    <div class="card-header">
    Header
  </div>
  <div class="card-block">
    <h4 class="card-title">Card title</h4>
    <p class="card-text">Some basic description text for your card should
appear in this section.</p>
    <a href="#" class="btn btn-primary">Button</a>
  </div>
  <div class="card-footer">
      footer
  </div>
</div>
```

The setup for the footer is very similar to the header; let's break it down:

- This time, below the `.card-block` section, insert a new `<div>` with a class named `.card-footer`
- Inside this new `<div>`, insert your footer text

Save the file again and view it in the browser, and it should look like this:

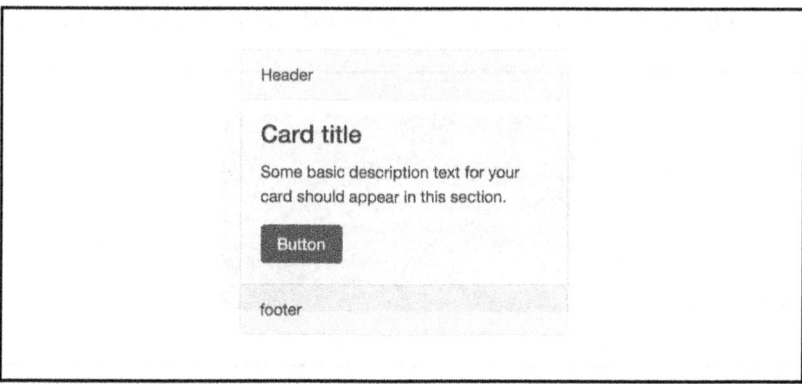

Easy as that, we've now also included a footer with our Card. Next, let's learn a way to apply a different look and feel to our Card.

Inverting the color scheme of a Card

In some cases, you may want a different look and feel for your Card to make it stand out more. There are some CSS classes included with Bootstrap that will allow you to inverse the color scheme. Let's take a look at the code to apply this style:

```
<div class="card card-inverse" style="background:#000;">
  <div class="card-block">
    <h4 class="card-title">Card title</h4>
    <p class="card-text">Some basic description text for your card should
appear in this section.</p>
    <a href="#" class="btn btn-primary">Button</a>
  </div>
</div>
```

Again, this variation is pretty easy to apply with a couple of small changes:

- On the `<div>` with the `.card` class, add a second class named `.card-inverse`.
- This will only inverse the text in the card. You need to set the `background color` yourself. For speed, I just did an inline CSS style in the demo code. I'd recommend actually creating a CSS class in your stylesheet for your own project, which is a nicer way to do things.

That's all you need to do. Once you're done, your card should look like this:

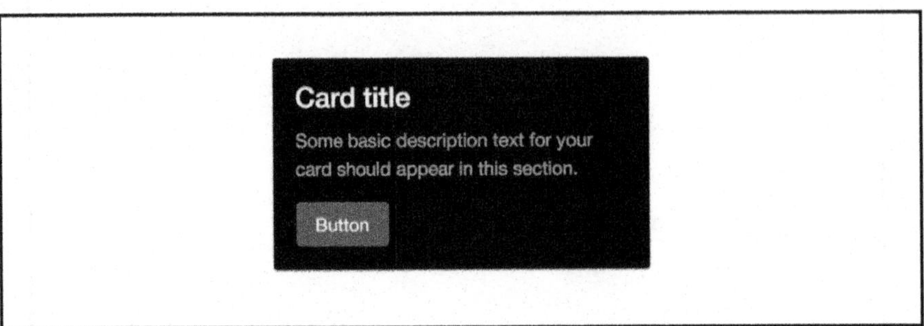

In this case, you do need to specify the custom background color. However, Bootstrap does have some background color variations that you can use if you want to add an additional CSS class. The naming convention for these options is just like buttons and labels. Let's take a look at what the code will look like:

```
<div class="card card-inverse card-primary">
  <div class="card-block">
    <h4 class="card-title">Card title</h4>
    <p class="card-text">Some basic description text for your card should
appear in this section.</p>
  </div>
</div>
<div class="card card-inverse card-success">
  <div class="card-block">
    <h4 class="card-title">Card title</h4>
    <p class="card-text">Some basic description text for your card should
appear in this section.</p>
  </div>
</div>
<div class="card card-inverse card-info">
  <div class="card-block">
    <h4 class="card-title">Card title</h4>
    <p class="card-text">Some basic description text for your card should
appear in this section.</p>
```

```
    </div>
  </div>
  <div class="card card-inverse card-warning">
    <div class="card-block">
      <h4 class="card-title">Card title</h4>
      <p class="card-text">Some basic description text for your card should
  appear in this section.</p>
    </div>
  </div>
  <div class="card card-inverse card-danger">
    <div class="card-block">
      <h4 class="card-title">Card title</h4>
      <p class="card-text">Some basic description text for your card should
  appear in this section.</p>
    </div>
  </div>
```

This is a bunch of code, but there are only a couple of things that change from our previous card example:

- All I've done is add an additional CSS class to the `<div>` with our base `.card` class on it. Let's review each one in the following points.
- The **Primary** card uses the `.card-primary` class and is blue.
- The **Success** card uses the `.card-success` class and is green.
- The **Info** card uses the `.card-info` class and is light blue.
- The **Warning** card uses the `.card-warning` class and is yellow.
- The **Danger** card uses the `.card-danger` class and is red.

Once you've set up the above code, your cards should look like this in the browser:

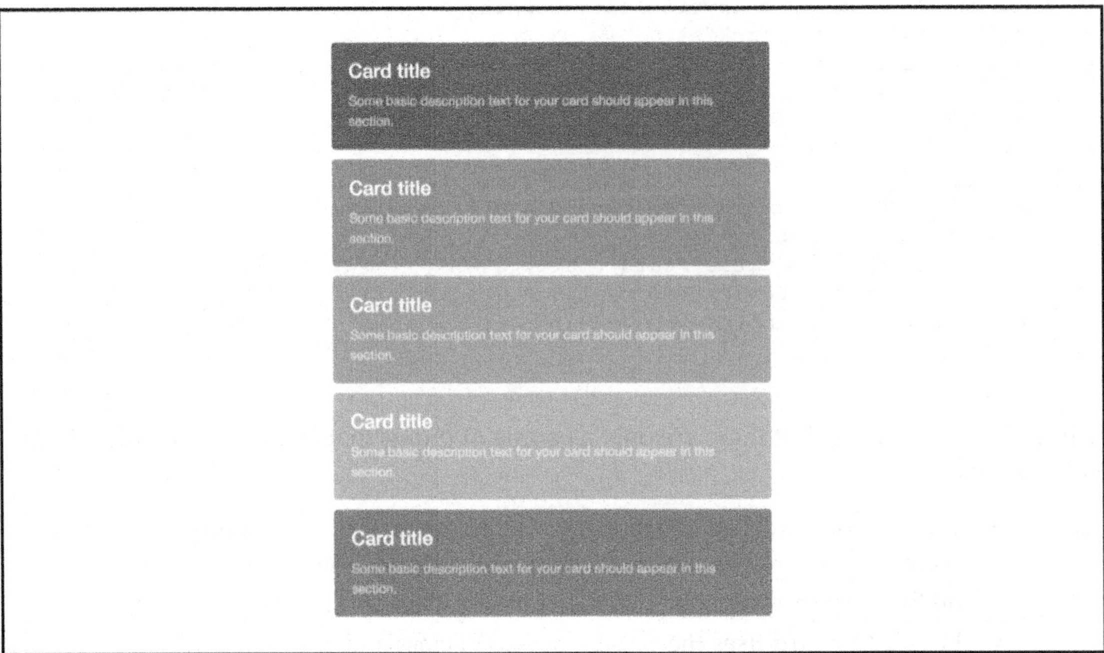

That concludes the basic and advanced styling you can do with the Card component. Why don't we take a break from learning for a bit and actually build some Cards in our blog project.

Adding a location card to the Contact page

Let's jump back into our project by adding a simple Card component to the **Contact** page. Reopen `contact.ejs` in your text editor and head down to the main body that we recently updated with a contact form. Find the following column code for that section:

```
<div class="col-md-12">
```

We're going to split this full width column into two separate columns. Change the class on the previous snippet of code to `.col-md-8` and add a new `<div>` with a class of `.col-md-4` on it. When you're done, the body of the page code should now look like this:

```
<div class="col-md-8">
      <form>
        <fieldset class="form-group">
```

```
          <label>Email</label>
          <input type="email" class="form-control" placeholder="Enter
email">
          <small class="text-muted">We'll never share your email with
anyone else.</small>
        </fieldset>
        <fieldset class="form-group">
          <label>Name</label>
          <input type="text" class="form-control" placeholder="Name">
        </fieldset>
        <fieldset class="form-group">
          <label>Message</label>
          <textarea class="form-control" rows="3"></textarea>
        </fieldset>
        <button type="submit" class="btn btn-primary">Submit</button>
      </form>
    </div>
    <div class="col-md-4">
    </div>
```

Now that the column is set up, let's insert a Card component into our new column. Enter the following code into the second column in the layout:

```
<div class="card">
  <div class="card-header">
    Address &amp; Phone
  </div>
  <div class="card-block">
    <ul class="list-unstyled">
      <li>Mike Smith</li>
      <li>1234 Street Name</li>
      <li>Vancouver, BC</li>
      <li>Canada V7V 1V1</li>
      <li>604.123.1234</li>
    </ul>
  </div>
</div>
```

Once you've inserted the Card component code, save your file and check it out in a browser. It should look like this:

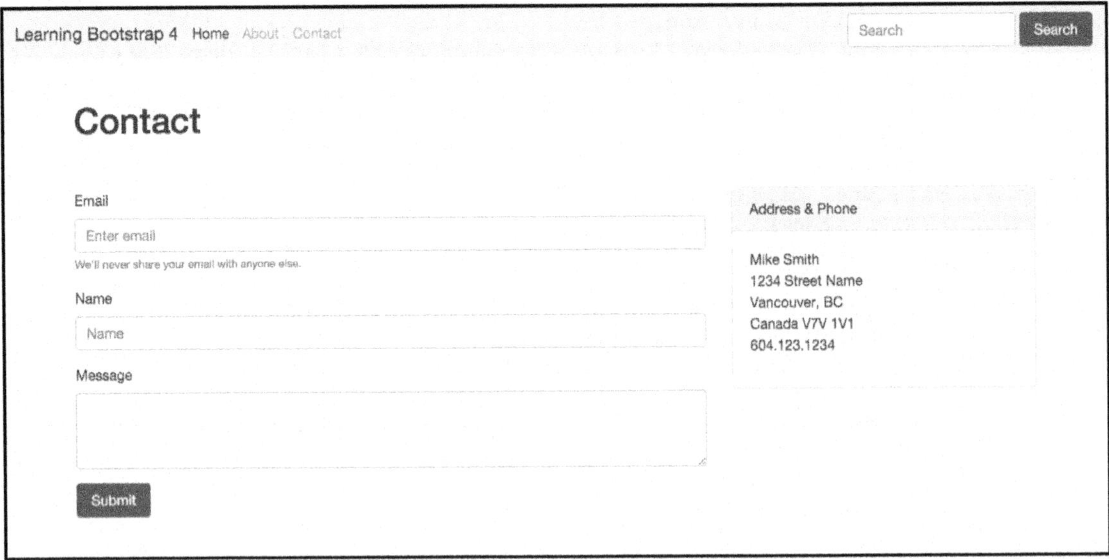

Now the **Contact** page is starting to take more shape. Let's add the Card component to a few other pages before we move on to our next Content component.

Updating the Blog index page

Now that we've covered the card component, it's time to set up the main layout for our Blog index page. The design is going to rely heavily on the Card component, so let's get to it. First of all, open up `index.ejs` in your text editor and find the body of the page section. The left column will look like this:

```
<div class="col-md-8">
```

Within this `<div>` currently is some filler text. Delete the filler text and insert the following Card component, which will be our first Blog post:

```
<div class="card">
  <img class="card-img-top img-fluid" src="img/image.jpg" alt="Card image
cap">
  <div class="card-block">
    <h4 class="card-title">Post title</h4>
    <p><small>Posted by <a href="#">Admin</a> on January 1, 2016 in <a
href="#">Category</a></small></p>
    <p class="card-text">Some quick example text to build on the card title
and make up the bulk of the card's content.</p>
    <a href="#" class="btn btn-primary">Read More</a>
```

```
  </div>
</div>
```

Now that we've added our first card to the Blog roll, let's break down what's happening:

- I've started by including a photo I took in Nova Scotia a few summers ago. I've given it a class of `.img-fluid` so it stretches the width of the card.
- From there, I've set up my card exactly like I taught you previously, but in this case, I've added some real content for a blog.

Let's go ahead and add the rest of the Card component code for the blog roll. Insert the following code after the first Card in the left column:

```
<div class="card">
  <div class="card-block">
    <h4 class="card-title">Post title</h4>
    <p><small>Posted by <a href="#">Admin</a> on January 1, 2016 in <a
href="#">Category</a></small></p>
    <p>Pellentesque habitant morbi tristique...</p>
    <a href="#" class="btn btn-primary">Read More</a>
  </div>
</div>
<div class="card">
  <img class="card-img-top img-fluid" src="img/image.jpg" alt="Card image
cap">
  <div class="card-block">
    <h4 class="card-title">Post title <span class="label label-
success">Updated</span></h4>
    <p><small>Posted by <a href="#">Admin</a> on January 1, 2016 in <a
href="#">Category</a></small></p>
    <p class="card-text">Some quick example text to build on the card title
and make up the bulk of the card's content.</p>
    <a href="#" class="btn btn-primary">Read More</a>
  </div>
</div>
<div class="card">
  <div class="card-block">
    <h4 class="card-title">Post title</h4>
    <p><small>Posted by <a href="#">Admin</a> on January 1, 2016 in <a
href="#">Category</a></small></p>
    <p>Pellentesque habitant morbi tristique senectus...</p>
    <a href="#" class="btn btn-primary">Read More</a>
  </div>
</div>
```

That's a long chunk of code. The filler text is just in there to give you an idea. Feel free to remove that or replace it with actual text. Now that we've filled out the left column with a good amount of content, your page should look like this:

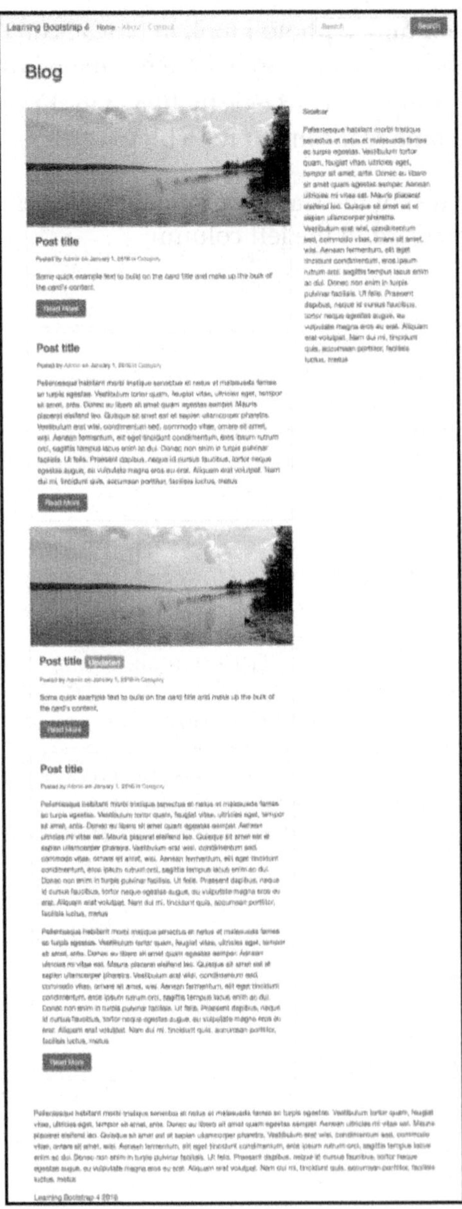

Now that the main blog roll content is complete, let's also add the right column content.

Adding the sidebar

Let's add some more content to the index page by adding the sidebar. We'll also use the Card component here, but in this case, some different variations of it. Go back to `index.ejs` and remove the filler text from the second column. Instead, insert the following Card code:

```
<div class="card card-block">
  <h5 class="card-title">Recent Posts</h5>
  <div class="list-group">
    <button type="button" class="list-group-item">Cras justo odio</button>
    <button type="button" class="list-group-item">Dapibus ac facilisis
in</button>
    <button type="button" class="list-group-item">Morbi leo risus</button>
    <button type="button" class="list-group-item">Porta ac consectetur
ac</button>
    <button type="button" class="list-group-item">Vestibulum at
eros</button>
  </div>
  <div class="m-t-1"><a href="#">View More</a></div>
</div>
```

You'll notice in this Card I'm using a different variation, which is the List Group option. To do this, follow these steps:

- Create a new `<div>` with a class of `.list-group` inside your card.
- Inside, insert a `<button>` with a class of `.list-group-item` on it for every item of your list. I've added five different options.

Once you're done, save your file and it should look like this in the browser:

As you can see, that will draw a nice-looking sidebar list component. Let's fill out the rest of the sidebar by inserting the following code after the first Card component:

```
<div class="card card-block">
  <h5 class="card-title">Archives</h5>
  <div class="list-group">
    <button type="button" class="list-group-item">Cras justo odio</button>
    <button type="button" class="list-group-item">Dapibus ac facilisis
in</button>
    <button type="button" class="list-group-item">Morbi leo risus</button>
    <button type="button" class="list-group-item">Porta ac consectetur
ac</button>
    <button type="button" class="list-group-item">Vestibulum at
eros</button>
  </div>
  <div class="m-t-1"><a href="#">View More</a></div>
</div>
<div class="card card-block">
  <h5 class="card-title">Categories</h5>
  <div class="list-group">
    <button type="button" class="list-group-item">Cras justo odio</button>
    <button type="button" class="list-group-item">Dapibus ac facilisis
in</button>
    <button type="button" class="list-group-item">Morbi leo risus</button>
    <button type="button" class="list-group-item">Porta ac consectetur
ac</button>
    <button type="button" class="list-group-item">Vestibulum at
eros</button>
  </div>
  <div class="m-t-1"><a href="#">View More</a></div>
</div>
```

This will produce two more List Group Card components for the sidebar of your blog project. Once it's all done, the entire page should now look like this:

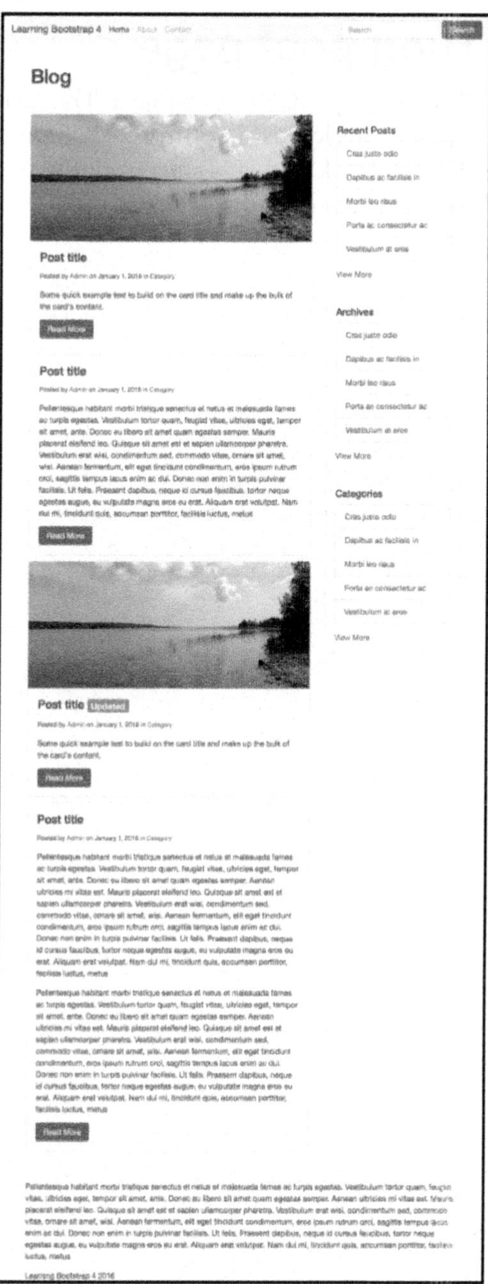

That concludes the user of the Card component on the index page. The last page we need to set up with the Card component is our Blog post page.

Setting up the Blog post page

The index page is a list of all the Blog posts in our project. The last page we need to setup is the Blog post page, which is just a single post in our project. Open up the `blog-post.ejs` template you created earlier in the book and let's start updating some code. Head down to the page body section and find this line of code:

```
<div class="col-md-8">
```

Currently, you'll see some filler text in that `<div>`; let's replace it with the following code:

```
<div class="card">
  <div class="card-block">
    <p><small>Posted by <a href="#">Admin</a> on January 1, 2016 in <a
href="#">Category</a></small></p>
    <p>Pellentesque habitant morbi tristique senectus et...</p>
    <p><code>&lt;p&gt;this is what a code sample looks
like&lt;/p&gt;</code></p>
    <p>Pellentesque habitant morbi tristique senectus et netus...</p>
    <!-- pre sample start //-->
    <h4>pre sample code</h4>
    <pre>This is what code will look like</pre>
    <!-- pre sample end //-->
    <!-- image //-->
    <h4>responive image</h4>
    <p><img src="img/image.jpg" class="img-fluid" alt="Responsive
image"></p>
    <!-- table //-->
    <h4>table</h4>
    <table class="table">
      <thead>
        <tr>
          <th>#</th>
          <th>First Name</th>
          <th>Last Name</th>
          <th>Username</th>
        </tr>
      </thead>
      <tbody>
        <tr>
          <th scope="row">1</th>
          <td>john</td>
          <td>smith</td>
          <td>@jsmith</td>
        </tr>
        <tr>
          <th scope="row">2</th>
```

```
              <td>steve</td>
              <td>stevens</td>
              <td>@steve</td>
            </tr>
            <tr>
              <th scope="row">3</th>
              <td>mike</td>
              <td>michaels</td>
              <td>@mike</td>
            </tr>
          </tbody>
        </table>
      </div>
    </div>
```

There's a good chunk of things going on in this code. I've thrown in a few other components we've already learned about so you can see them in action. The Card component has the following things included inside it:

- Text, `<code>` and `<pre>` tags
- Tables
- Images

Let's also update this template to use the same sidebar code as the index page. Copy the right column code from the index template and paste it into the same location in the blog post template.

When you are done, the page should now look like this:

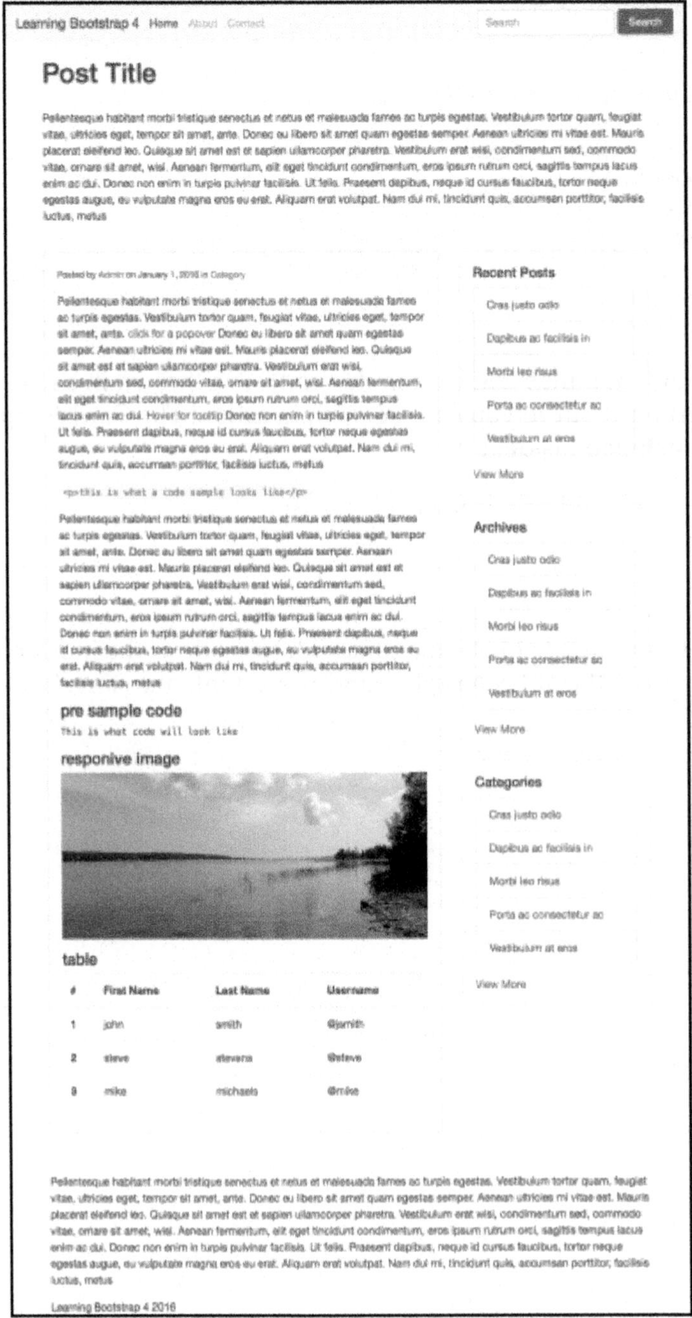

As you can see, we're using a single Card component to hold all of the content for the body of the page. We're also using the same Card components for the sidebar that we copied over from the index page. Now that we've added the Cards to all of our page templates, let's get back to learning about some other Content components in Bootstrap 4.

How to use the Navs component

The Navs component in Bootstrap can be displayed in a couple of different ways. The default view for the component is just a simple unstyled list of links. This list can also be transformed into tabs or pills for ways of organizing your content and navigation. Let's start by learning how to create a default Nav component:

```
<ul class="nav">
  <li class="nav-item">
    <a class="nav-link" href="#">Link 1</a>
  </li>
  <li class="nav-item">
    <a class="nav-link" href="#">Link 2</a>
  </li>
  <li class="nav-item">
    <a class="nav-link" href="#">Link 3</a>
  </li>
</ul>
```

The most basic version of the Nav component is built using the preceding code:

- The component is based on an unordered list with a class of `.nav`
- Each `<li>` tag in the list requires a class of `.nav-item`
- Nested inside the `<li>` tag must be an `<a>` tag with a class of `.nav-link`

Once you've completed adding that code it should look like this in the browser:

Link 1
Link 2
Link 3

As I mentioned, this is just a basic unstyled list of links. One easy change you can make is to display the list of links inline horizontally. To achieve this, you just need to add a class named `.nav-inline` to the `<ul>` tag, like this:

```
<ul class="nav nav-inline">
```

This will display all the links in a horizontal line. Why don't we move on to something a little more exciting, such as converting this list into tabs.

Creating tabs with the Nav component

Converting the basic list to tabs is easy to do by adding a couple of things to our code. Take a look at this sample:

```
<ul class="nav nav-tabs">
  <li class="nav-item">
    <a class="nav-link active" href="#">Link 1</a>
  </li>
  <li class="nav-item">
    <a class="nav-link" href="#">Link 2</a>
  </li>
  <li class="nav-item">
    <a class="nav-link" href="#">Link 3</a>
  </li>
</ul>
```

I've made two changes to the code, let's review them now:

- On the `<ul>` tag, I removed the `.nav-inline` class and added `.nav-tabs`. This will render the list as tabs.
- I then added a class of `.active` to the first link so that it is the selected tab when the page loads.

After you've coded that up, it should look like this in the browser:

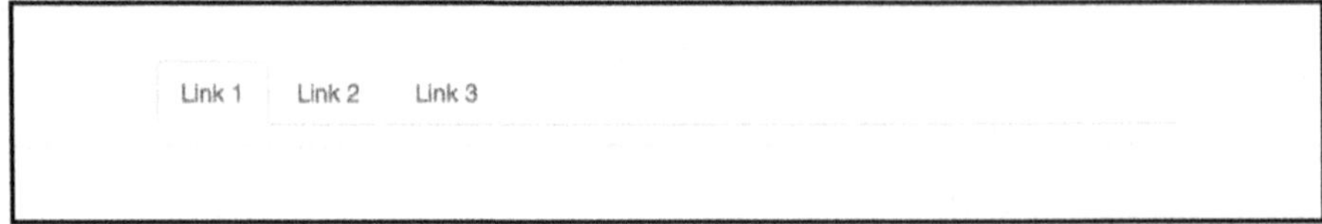

Just like that you can render the list as a set of tabs. The next variations you'll want to try are pills.

Creating a pill navigation

Changing the style of the Nav component to Pills is actually really easy. Take a look at the following sample code:

```
<ul class="nav nav-pills">
  <li class="nav-item">
    <a class="nav-link active" href="#">Link 1</a>
  </li>
  <li class="nav-item">
    <a class="nav-link" href="#">Link 2</a>
  </li>
  <li class="nav-item">
    <a class="nav-link" href="#">Link 3</a>
  </li>
</ul>
```

Let's breakdown what is new here. I've only made one change to the code. I've removed the `.nav-tabs` class from the `<ul>` tag and replaced it with a `.nav-pills` class. This is the only change you need to make.

Save your file with the changes and it should look like this in the browser:

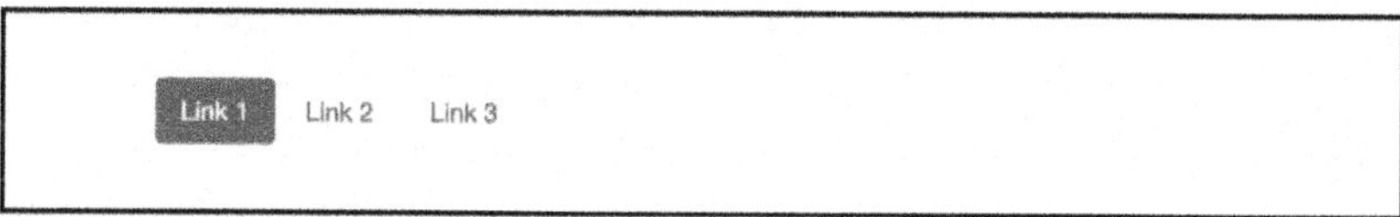

The preceding example is the default display for Nav pills. There is another variation you can try though, which are stacked pills. This pattern is commonly used in sidebar navigations. To create this version, update the following line of code:

```
<ul class="nav nav-pills nav-stacked">
```

Here I've simply added a class of `.nav-stacked` to the `<ul>` tag to stack the pills. Here's how it will look in the browser:

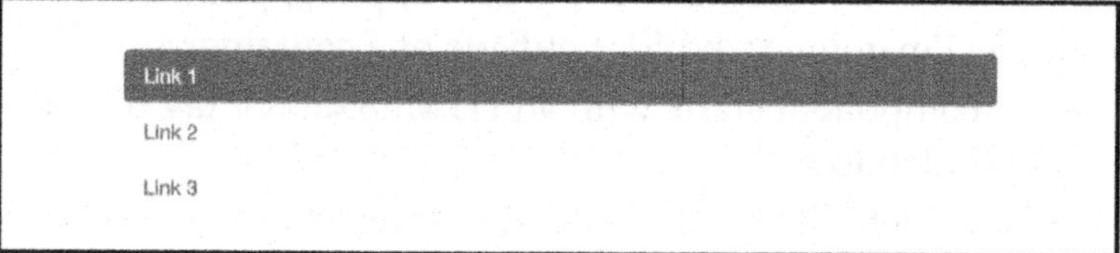

That concludes the Nav component in Bootstrap 4. As you learned, it's pretty easy to create a few different styles of navigation with a simple list of unordered links. In the next section, we'll review the more complicated navigation component, which is the Navbar.

Using the Bootstrap Navbar component

The Navbar component is a staple of Bootstrap that gets used all the time. In the past, this component has required a decent amount of markup to get it working. I'm glad to report that in Bootstrap 4 they have simplified this component and made it easier to use. Let's start by going over a basic example of the Navbar:

```
<nav class="navbar navbar-light bg-faded">
  <a class="navbar-brand" href="#">Navbar</a>
  <ul class="nav navbar-nav">
    <li class="nav-item active">
      <a class="nav-link" href="#">Home</a>
    </li>
    <li class="nav-item">
      <a class="nav-link" href="#">Page 1</a>
    </li>
    <li class="nav-item">
      <a class="nav-link" href="#">Page 2</a>
    </li>
    <li class="nav-item">
      <a class="nav-link" href="#">Page 3</a>
    </li>
  </ul>
</nav>
```

You may notice some similarities here with the Nav component. The Navbar uses some of the same code, but you can extend it further and combine additional components into it. Let's start by breaking down this basic example:

- A Navbar component can be used outside or inside of a `<div>` with a `.container` class on it. If you want the Navbar to be flush with the edges of the browser, you should not include it inside a `.container` `<div>`. However, if you do want the default padding and margins applied, put it inside the `<div>`. For this example, I'm going to build it outside of a container.
- The Navbar component starts with an HTML5 `<nav>` tag that has the following CSS classes added to it.
- `.navbar` is the default class that always needs to appear on the component.
- `.navbar-light` is the color of component you want to use. There are some other variations you can pick from.

- `.bg-faded` is a utility class that you can use to make the background lighter. This is an optional class.
- The first element inside of a Navbar is the Brand. The Brand should be the title for your project. To render the element, create an `<a>` tag and give it a class of `.navbar-brand`. The anchor text for this link should be the name of your project or website. Keep in mind, using the Brand is optional.
- The core part of the Navbar is the list of navigation links. This is created with an unordered list, similar to the Nav component. In this case, your `<ul>` tag should have classes of `.nav` and `.navbar-nav` included.
- The nested `<li>` and `<a>` tags should use the same `.nav-item` and `.nav-link` classes from the Nav component.

This will create a basic Navbar component for you. This is how it should look in the browser:

Navbar Home Page 1 Page 2 Page 3

Now that you've learned how to build a basic Navbar, let's learn how to extend the component further.

Changing the color of the Navbar

In Bootstrap 3, you could invert the color scheme of the Navbar. However, in Bootstrap 4 you have multiple options for coloring the Navbar component. All that is needed to edit is some of the classes on the `<nav>` tag that wrap the component. Let's take a look at the code for some of the different color options:

```
<nav class="navbar navbar-inverse">
  ...
</nav>
<nav class="navbar navbar-primary">
  ...
</nav>
<nav class="navbar navbar-success">
  ...
</nav>
<nav class="navbar navbar-warning">
  ...
```

```
</nav>
<nav class="navbar navbar-info">
  ...
</nav>
<nav class="navbar navbar-danger">
  ...
</nav>
```

As you can see, we're reusing the keywords for color variations that we've used in other components. Let's break down each variation of the Navbar component:

- `.navbar-inverse` will color the component black and grey
- `.navbar-primary` will color the component blue
- `.navbar-success` will color the component green
- `.navbar-warning` will color the component yellow
- `.navbar-info` will color the component light blue
- `.navbar-danger` will color the component red

Once you're done coding that up, the navbars should look like this in the browser:

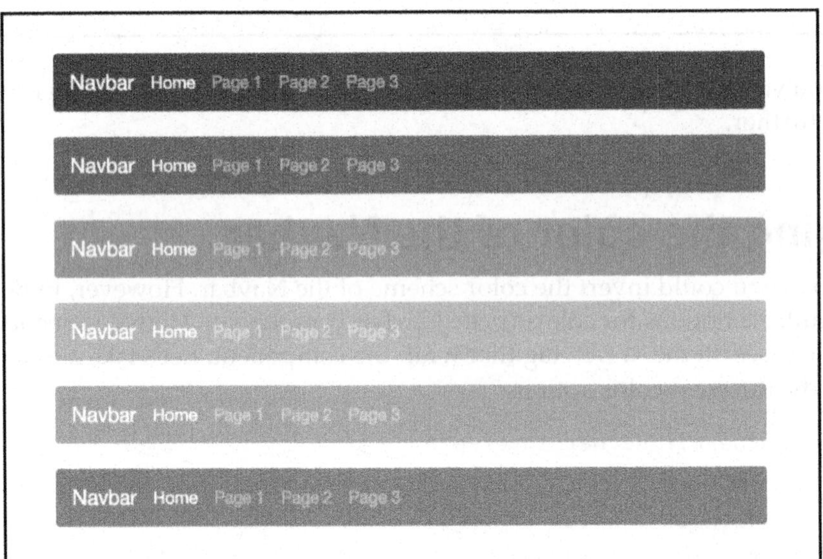

As you can see, we now have the Navbar in a whole range of colors you can choose from. Let's learn what else we can add to this component.

Making the Navbar responsive

Being that Bootstrap is a mobile-first framework, it would only make sense that you need the ability to make the Navbar component responsive. Let's check out the basic code for this:

```
<nav class="navbar navbar-light bg-faded">
    <button class="navbar-toggler hidden-sm-up" type="button" data-
toggle="collapse" data-target="#responsive-nav">
      ≡
   </button>
   <div class="collapse navbar-toggleable-xs" id="responsive-nav">
      <a class="navbar-brand" href="#">Navbar</a>
      <ul class="nav navbar-nav">
        <li class="nav-item active">
          <a class="nav-link" href="#">Home</a>
        </li>
        <li class="nav-item">
          <a class="nav-link" href="#">Page 1</a>
        </li>
        <li class="nav-item">
          <a class="nav-link" href="#">Page 2</a>
        </li>
        <li class="nav-item">
          <a class="nav-link" href="#">Page 3</a>
        </li>
      </ul>
    </div>
</nav>
```

There's a few different things in the code here that you need to be aware of:

- After the opening `<nav>` class, you need to insert a `<button>` with the CSS classes `.navbar-toggle` and `.hidden-sm-up`. The first class says this button will toggle the navigation. The second class says only show the responsive navigation for sizes above small. You also need to include the data attribute `data-toggle="collapse"` to all the Nav to collapse. Finally, you need to add a data-target, which will point to the area you want to be collapsible. I've given that an ID of `#responsive-nav`.
- Next, head down to your list of links and wrap a `<div>` around them. This section needs CSS classes named `.collapse` and `.navbar-toggleable-xs`. You also need to give it an ID of `responsive-nav` to tie it to the button from the previous step.

That's it; once you code this up shrink your browser window to a small size and your bar should switch to look like this. Oh, and don't forget that the code ≡ in the button will render a hamburger menu icon in the responsive Navbar:

That concludes the Navbar component in Bootstrap 4. I know this has been a long chapter, but we only have a few more components to go over.

Adding Breadcrumbs to a page

The Breadcrumbs component is a pretty easy one to use in Bootstrap. Let's check out the code for how to render one:

```
<ol class="breadcrumb">
  <li><a href="#">Home</a></li>
  <li><a href="#">Page 1</a></li>
  <li class="active">Page 2</li>
</ol>
```

As you can see, the code for this component is pretty basic, let's review it:

- The Breadcrumb component uses an ordered list or `<ol>` tag as its base.
- Within the ordered list, you simply just need to create a list of links. The last item in the list should have a class of `.active` on it.

Adding Breadcrumbs to the Blog post page

For this example, let's actually add some Breadcrumbs to our Blog post page template. Open up `blog-post.ejs` and add the following code after the container `<div>` at the top:

```
<div class="row m-t-1">
    <ol class="breadcrumb">
      <li><a href="#">Home</a></li>
      <li><a href="#">Blog</a></li>
      <li class="active">Post Title</li>
    </ol>
  </div>
```

This code should come before the page title and once you make the update, your page should now look like this at the top:

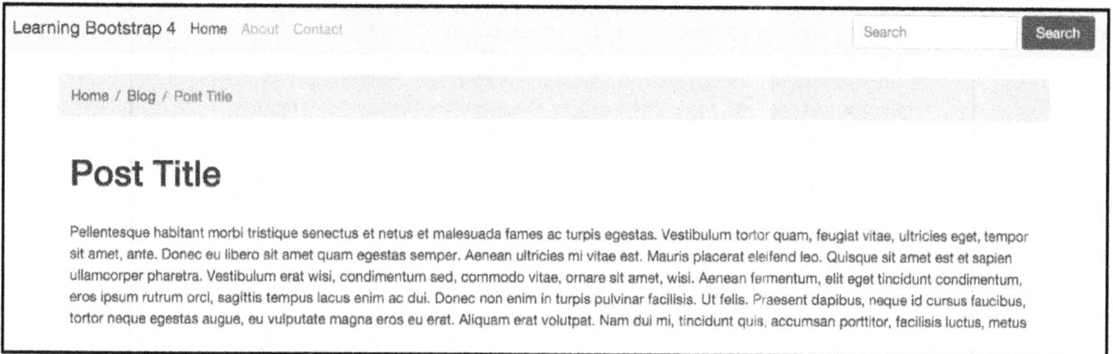

There, now we've added a nice Breadcrumb to our blog post template. Let's move on to adding Pagination to our page templates.

Using the Pagination component

Let's continue adding some more components to our templates by learning how to use the Pagination component. For our blog project, we want to use the Pager version of the component. Open up `index.ejs` and insert the following code after the last Card component in our blog feed:

```
<nav>
  <ul class="pager m-t-3">
    <li class="pager-prev"><a href="#">Older Posts</a></li>
    <li class="pager-next disabled"><a href="#">Newer Posts</a></li>
  </ul>
</nav>
```

The Pager is wrapped in an HTML5 `<nav>` tag and uses an unordered list as its base:

- The `<ul>` tag should have a class of `.pager` added to it.
- The first list item in the group should have a class of `.pager-prev` on it.
- The second list item should have a class of `.pager-next` on it. In this case, I've also added the class `.disabled` which means there are no more posts to go to.

After you've added this code to your index template, it should look like this in the browser:

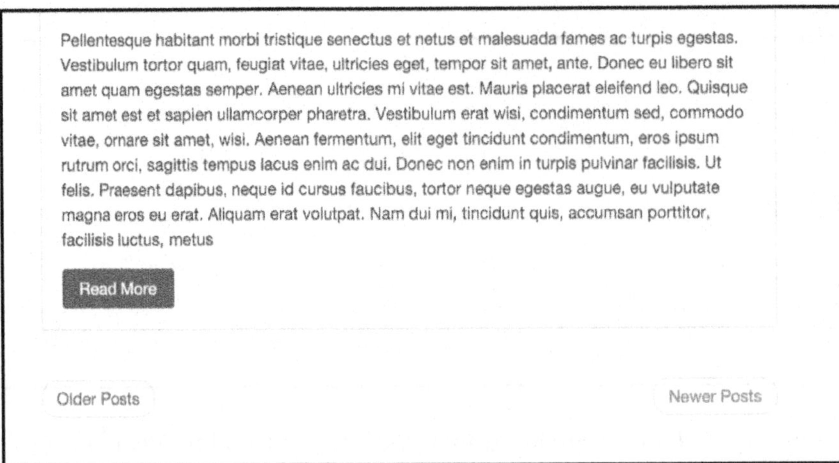

Let's also add this component to the Blog post page template.

Adding the Pager to the Blog post template

Open up `blog-post.ejs` and paste the same snippet of code from previously at the bottom of the left column, right after the end of the Card component. I won't bother posting another screenshot, as it should look the same as the previous example. Let's continue by learning how to use another component.

How to use the List Group component

This is the last main content component we need to go over for this chapter. Let's get right into it by reviewing the code needed to render a List Group:

```
<ul class="list-group">
  <li class="list-group-item">Item 1</li>
  <li class="list-group-item">Item 2</li>
  <li class="list-group-item">Item 3</li>
  <li class="list-group-item">Item 4</li>
</ul>
```

Like the components before it, this one is based off of an unordered list:

- The `<ul>` tag needs a class of `.list-group` on it to start
- Each `<li>` needs a class of `.list-group-item` on it

Once you're done, your List Group should look like this in the browser:

As you can see, with some minimal coding you can render a decent looking component. You may have missed it, but we actually already used this component when we were building our sidebar on the index and blog post page templates. Open up one of them in a text editor and you'll see the following code, which is a List Group:

```
<div class="card card-block">
  <h5 class="card-title">Recent Posts</h5>
  <div class="list-group">
    <button type="button" class="list-group-item">Cras justo odio</button>
    <button type="button" class="list-group-item">Dapibus ac facilisis
in</button>
    <button type="button" class="list-group-item">Morbi leo risus</button>
    <button type="button" class="list-group-item">Porta ac consectetur
ac</button>
    <button type="button" class="list-group-item">Vestibulum at
eros</button>
  </div>
  <div class="m-t-1"><a href="#">View More</a></div>
</div>
```

That concludes the use of the List Group component. That also concludes the Content components chapter.

Summary

This has been a really long chapter but I hope you have learned a lot. We have covered Bootstrap components including buttons, button groups, button dropdown, forms, input groups, dropdowns, Jumbotron, Label, Alerts, Cards, Navs, Navbar, Breadcrumb, Pagination, and List Group. Our blog project is really starting to take shape now, too. In the next chapter, we'll dive into some JavaScript components in Bootstrap 4 that will include Modal, Tooltips, Popovers, Collapse, and Carousel.

7
Extending Bootstrap with JavaScript Plugins

In this chapter, we're going to dive deeper into Bootstrap components by learning how to extend the framework using JavaScript plugins. You may remember that back in the first chapter we included `bootstrap.min.js` in our template. This file contains a number of JavaScript components that come with Bootstrap. In this chapter, we'll go over how to use some of these components, including: Modals, Tooltips, Popovers, Collapse, and Carousel. Let's get right to it by learning how to create a Modal in Bootstrap 4.

Coding a Modal dialog

Modals go by a number of different names; you may also know them as dialogs, popups, overlays, or alerts. In the case of Bootstrap, this component is referred to as a Modal and that is how I'll be referring to it throughout the book. A Modal is made up of two required pieces of code. The first is a button, and here's the basic code required to render it:

```
<button type="button" class="btn btn-primary" data-toggle="modal" data-
target="#firstModal">
  Open Modal
</button>
```

As you can see, this is a basic Button component with a few attributes added to it:

- The first is the `data-toggle` data attribute, which needs to be set to `modal`. This tells the browser that this `<button>` is attached to a Modal component.
- The second is the `data-target` attribute, which should be an ID. It doesn't really matter what you name this, I've called it `#firstModal`. It's important to note this ID name as it will be tied in later. Also make sure that the ID name is unique.

Once you've coded this up, it should look like a regular button in the browser:

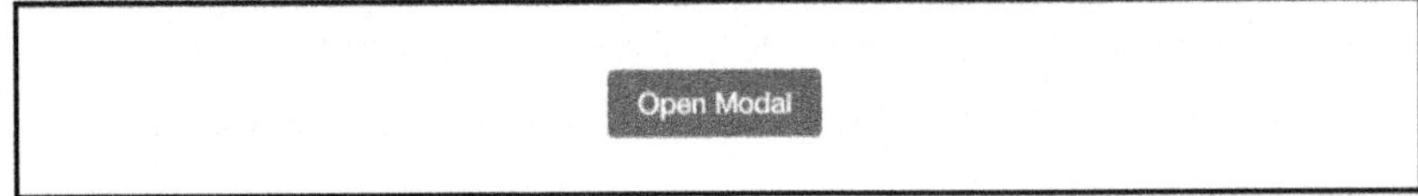

Coding the Modal dialog

The second part of the Modal component is the dialog. This is the part that will pop up in the browser once you click the button. Let's take a look at some basic code for creating the dialog:

```
<div class="modal fade" id="firstModal" tabindex="-1" role="dialog" aria-
hidden="true">
  <div class="modal-dialog" role="document">
    <div class="modal-content">
      <div class="modal-header">
        <button type="button" class="close" data-dismiss="modal" aria-
label="Close">
          <span aria-hidden="true">&times;</span>
        </button>
        <h4 class="modal-title">Dialog Title</h4>
      </div>
      <div class="modal-body">
        Some copy for your modal.
      </div>
      <div class="modal-footer">
        <button type="button" class="btn btn-secondary" data-
dismiss="modal">Close</button>
        <button type="button" class="btn btn-primary">Save</button>
      </div>
    </div>
  </div>
</div>
```

This is a bigger piece of code and there are a few things going on here that I need to explain to you:

- The entire dialog is wrapped in a `<div>` with a required class of `.modal`. There's also an optional `.fade` class there, which will fade the dialog in. Note the ID on this `<div>` because it's important. The ID value needs to match the `data-target` attribute you set on the button. This is how we tell the browser to link that button with this dialog. Finally, there are a couple of other attributes that are required by

Bootstrap including `tabindex`, `role`, and `aria-hidden`. Make sure you include those with their corresponding values.

- Inside the first `<div>` we have a second one with a class of `.modal-dialog` on it; make sure you include that.
- Next, the interior of the Modal is split into three parts: header, body, and footer.
- Inside our `.modal-dialog`, add another `<div>` with a class of `.modal-header` on it. Within this section you'll notice another button. This button is the **Close** or **X** icon for the Modal; although not required, it's a good idea to include this.
- After the button you need to include a header tag, in this case a `<h4>`, with a CSS class of `.modal-title` on it. Here you should enter the title for your Modal.
- The next section is another `<div>` for our body and it has a class of `.modal-body` on it. Within this section you should enter the body copy for your Modal.
- Finally, we have the footer section, which is another `<div>` with a class of `.modal-footer` on it. Inside this section you'll find two buttons that you need to include. The first is the white button labeled **Close** which when clicked will close the Modal. Note that the `<button>` tag has a data attribute called `data-dismiss` on it and its value is `modal`. This will close the Modal. The second button is a primary button that would be used as a Save button if you were hooking in the actual functionality.

After coding all that up, go to the browser and click on your button. You should then see a Modal that looks like this:

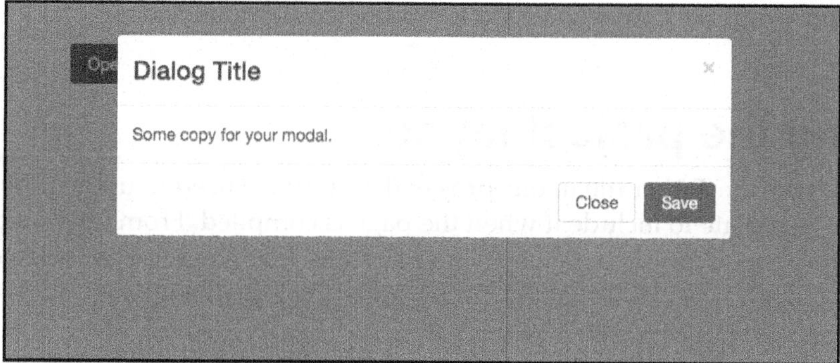

As you can see, our Modal has popped up over the button. You can read the Modal title and body and see the footer buttons as well as the **Close** or **X** button in the top-right corner. You may have noticed that you didn't actually have to write any JavaScript to make this Modal work. That is the power of the Bootstrap framework; all of the JavaScript is already written for you and you can simply call the Modal functionality by using the HTML data attributes, which makes things much easier. That concludes the lesson on Modals; next let's move on to learning how to use Tooltips.

Coding Tooltips

A Tooltip is a marker that will appear over a link when you hover over it in the browser. They are pretty easy to add with data attributes in Bootstrap, but we do need to make some updates to get them working. In Bootstrap 4 they have started using a third-party JavaScript library for Tooltips called Tether. Before we go any further, head over to the Tether website below and download the library:

`http://github.hubspot.com/tether/`

Once you've downloaded the library, unzip it and open the main directory where you'll see a number of files. Navigate to the `/dist/js` directory and find the file named `tether.min.js`:

Now copy `tether.min.js` into the `/js` directory of our blog project. This is the only file you need from Tether's directory, so you can keep the rest of the files or delete them. Once the file is in our project directory we need to update our template.

Updating the project layout

Now that we have the Tether file in our project directory we need to update our `_layout.ejs` template to include it when the page is compiled. From the root of our project directory, open up `_layout.ejs` and insert the following line of code near the bottom after jQuery. It's critical that the Tether file is loaded after jQuery, but before `bootstrap.min.js`:

```
<script src="js/tether.min.js"></script>
```

Save the file and make sure you recompile your project so that this is imported into all of your HTML files. Once that's done, you will now be able to use Tooltips on any page that is included in our project.

How to use Tooltips

Now that we've included the Tether library, we can learn how to actually use Tooltips in Bootstrap. Let's try them out on one of our project files. Open up `index.ejs` in your text editor and find a section of code that is just text, like this:

```
<p>Pellentesque habitant morbi tristique senectus et netus et malesuada
fames ac turpis egestas...</p>
```

Once you've found that section of code, let's wrap an `<a>` tag around the first three words with the following attributes on it:

```
<p><a href="#" data-toggle="tooltip" >Pellentesque habitant morbi</a>
tristique senectus et netus et malesuada fames ac turpis egestas.</p>
```

This is the basic markup needed to render a Tooltip. Let's breakdown what is happening here:

- The `data-toggle` attribute is required to tell the browser that this is a Tooltip. The value should be set to `tooltip`.
- The `title` attribute is also required and the value will be the text that appears in your Tooltip. In this case, I have set it to `This is a tooltip!`.

Before we can test this out in the browser, we need to add something else to our `_layout.ejs` template. Open that file in your text editor and insert the following code after the Tether library:

```
<script src="js/bootstrap.min.js"></script>
<script>
  $("a").tooltip();
</script>
```

In Bootstrap 4, Tooltips need to be initialized before you can use them. Therefore, I'm using a little jQuery here to say that all `a` tags should be initialized to use the Tooltip method, which will activate all link tags for use with a Tooltip. This is a little trick you can use so you don't have to use an ID to indicate every Tooltip you want to initialize. Once you've completed this step, save all your files, recompile them, and then view your project in the browser; it should look like this when you rollover the link anchor text:

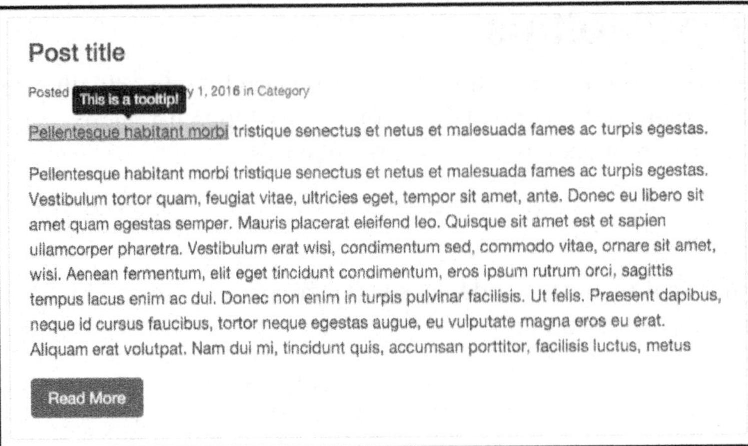

How to position Tooltips

By default, in Bootstrap the position for Tooltips is above the anchor text. However, using the `data-placement` attribute will allow you to place the tip above, below, left, or right of the anchor text. Let's take a look at the code required to render the different versions:

```
<p><a href="#" data-toggle="tooltip"  data-placement="top">Pellentesque
habitant morbi</a> tristique senectus et netus et malesuada fames ac turpis
egestas.</p>
<p><a href="#" data-toggle="tooltip"  data-placement="bottom">Pellentesque
habitant morbi</a> tristique senectus et netus et malesuada fames ac turpis
egestas.</p>
<p><a href="#" data-toggle="tooltip"  data-placement="right">Pellentesque
habitant morbi</a> tristique senectus et netus et malesuada fames ac turpis
egestas.</p>
<p><a href="#" data-toggle="tooltip"  data-placement="left">Pellentesque
habitant morbi</a> tristique senectus et netus et malesuada fames ac turpis
egestas.</p>
```

As you can see, I've added the `data-placement` attribute to each link tag. The following values will control the position of the Tooltip when you hover over it:

- Top: `data-placement="top"`
- Bottom: `data-placement="bottom"`
- Right: `data-placement="right"`
- Left: `data-placement="left"`

Adding Tooltips to buttons

It's also quite easy to add a Tooltip to a button by using the same data attributes as links. Let's take a look at how to code a simple button with a Tooltip above it:

```
<button type="button" class="btn btn-primary" data-toggle="tooltip" data-
placement="top" data-original->This is a button tooltip!</button>
```

Here you'll see a basic button component, but with the Tooltip data attributes:

- I've added the `data-toggle` attribute with a value of `tooltip`
- You can optionally include the `data-placement` attribute; if you leave it out it will default to top
- You need to include the `data-original-title` attribute and the value will be the Tooltip message

Updating the layout for buttons

To get Tooltips on buttons working, you need to initialize them the same way you did the links in the previous section. Open up `_layout.ejs` again in your text editor and include the following line of code. The entire section of JavaScript should now look like this:

```
<script>
  $("a").tooltip();
  $("button").tooltip();
</script>
```

Like we did with the link tags, we'll initialize all button tags to use the Tooltip component if called in the HTML template. Let's take a look at how our Tooltip on a button should look in the browser when it's done correctly:

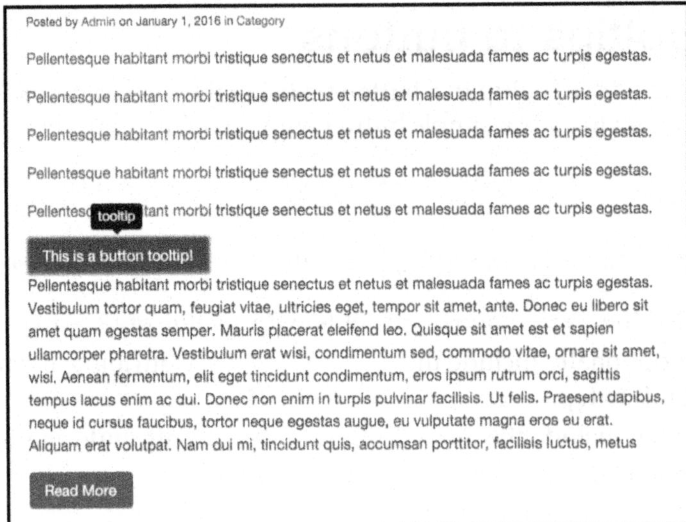

Avoiding collisions with our components

Until now we've only used the Tooltip JavaScript component so our code is solid. However, in the next section, we will introduce a different component called Popovers. We need to do some clean up of our JavaScript code so that the two don't collide with each other and give us unwanted results.

Since this is the case, we should go back to `_layout.ejs` and edit the code by providing a specific ID for each Tooltip that you want to use in your project. Our script should now look like this:

```
<script>
  $("#tooltip-link").tooltip();
  $("#tooltip-button").tooltip();
</script>
```

Note that I removed the `a` and `button` selectors and replaced them with IDs named `#tooltip-link` and `#tooltip-button`. Now we also need to update our link and button code on the index template to include these IDs.

```
<p><a id="tooltip-link" data-toggle="tooltip" >Pellentesque habitant
morbi</a> tristique senectus et netus et malesuada fames ac turpis
egestas.</p>
```

```
<button type="button" id="tooltip-button" class="btn btn-primary" data-
toggle="tooltip" data-placement="top" data-original->This is a button
tooltip!</button>
```

As you can see, I've included the ID for each element in the preceding code. Now we are safe to start introducing new components without any worry of collisions occurring in the JavaScript. Let's move on to the component in question; Popovers.

Using Popover components

Popover components are similar to Tooltips but allow for more content to be included. Popovers are also revealed on a click action, not a hover action like Tooltips. Let's take a look at the basic code to render a Popover. First, let's make sure we add this Popover to our project, so open up `index.ejs` again and find another filler line of code to add this new component. When you do, enter the following code into the template:

```
<p><a id="popover-link" data-toggle="popover"  data-content="This is the
content of my popover which can be longer than a tooltip">This is a
popover</a>. Pellentesque habitant morbi tristique senectus et netus et
malesuada fames ac turpis egestas. Vestibulum tortor quam, feugiat vitae,
ultricies eget, tempor sit amet, ante.</p>
```

As you can see, there are a few new things we need to go over here:

- First of all, you'll notice I've given the link tag this ID; `popover-link`.
- In this case, `data-toggle` is set to `popover`.
- The `title` attribute is required and will be the title for your Popover.
- Finally, we have a new attribute named `data-content`. The value for this should be the copy you want to appear on the Popover.

Updating the JavaScript

Like we did with Tooltips, we also need to update the JavaScript for this new component. Open up `_layout.ejs` again and insert the following line of code after the Tooltip JavaScript:

```
$("#popover-link").popover();
```

This code will initialize a Popover component on the element with the `#popover-link` ID on it. Once you've completed that, save both files and go to your browser. Find the link you created for the Popover and click it. This is what you should see in the browser:

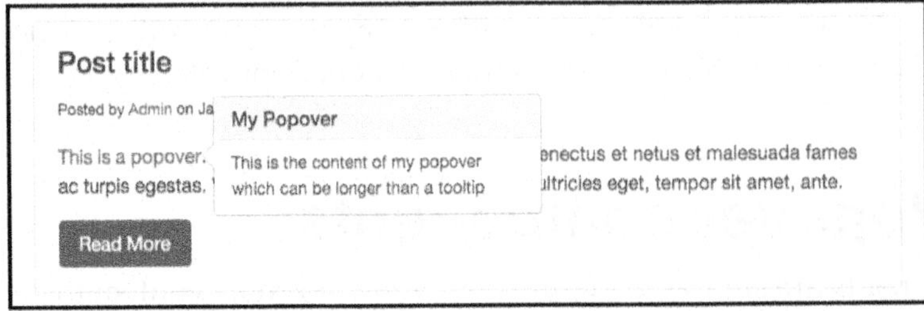

As you can see, the Popover component has more to it than the Tooltip. It includes a title and content. You should use this component if you need to give more context than can be achieved through the use of a regular Tooltip.

Positioning Popover components

Again, like Tooltips, it is possible to control the position of a Popover component. This is done in the same way by using the `data-placement` attribute on the link tag. Here's the code for each variation:

```
<p><a id="popover-link" data-placement="top" data-toggle="popover"  data-
content="This is the content of my popover which can be longer than a
tooltip">This is a popover</a>. Pellentesque habitant morbi...</p>

<p><a id="popover-link" data-placement="bottom" data-toggle="popover"
data-content="This is the content of my popover which can be longer than a
tooltip">This is a popover</a>. Pellentesque habitant morbi...</p>

<p><a id="popover-link" data-placement="right" data-toggle="popover"  data-
content="This is the content of my popover which can be longer than a
tooltip">This is a popover</a>. Pellentesque habitant morbi...</p>

<p><a id="popover-link" data-placement="left" data-toggle="popover"  data-
content="This is the content of my popover which can be longer than a
tooltip">This is a popover</a>. Pellentesque habitant morbi...</p>
```

Since this works in exactly the same way as for Tooltips, I won't bother breaking it down any further. Simply include the `data-placement` attribute and give it one of the four positioning values to control where the Popover appears when clicked.

Adding a Popover to a button

A Popover component can also be easily added to a button. Open up the index template again and insert the following button code:

```
<p><button type="button" id="popover-button" class="btn btn-primary" data-
toggle="popover"  data-content="This is a button popover example">Popover
Button</button></p>
```

As you can see, this markup is very similar to the Tooltip button. Let's break it down again:

- The button tag needs an ID of `popover-button` to be added
- As with the link, set the `data-toggle` attribute to `popover`
- Include a value for `title` and the `data-content` attribute

As with the previous examples, don't forget to update the JavaScript!

Adding our Popover button in JavaScript

The last thing we need to do is update the JavaScript to initialize our new Popover button. Open up `_layout.ejs` and insert the following line of code after the Popover link JavaScript:

```
$("#popover-button").popover();
```

Once that is complete, save both files and open up the index page in your browser. Locate the button you inserted and click it. Your Popover should look like this:

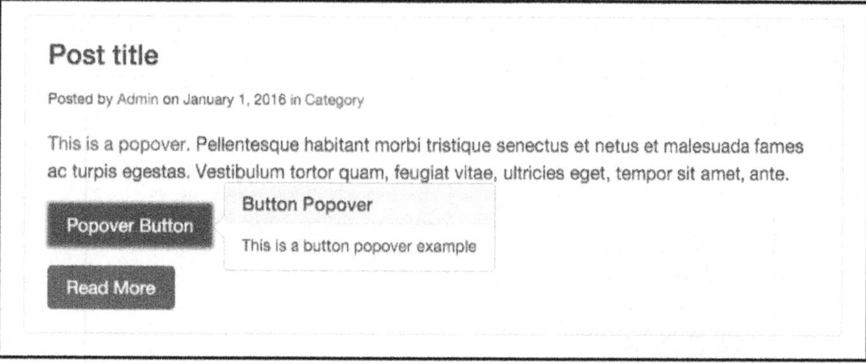

As you can see, you now have a button with a Popover component attached to it. This can be useful for calling out something important with a button, and then once it has been clicked it reveals a message to your users. I have a couple more JavaScript components I would like to review with you; the next one is the Collapse component.

Using the Collapse component

I find that the Collapse component's name is a bit confusing. What it really means is a collapsable section that can be shown or hidden on a click action. Let's start by creating a simple collapsable section of text on the `index.ejs` template. Open that template and insert the following code wherever you like:

```
<p><a class="btn btn-primary" data-toggle="collapse" href="#collapse-link"
aria-expanded="false">Collapse Link Trigger</a></p>
```

The Collapse component is broken into two parts. The first is the trigger to show or hide the collapsable content. The second is the actual content you want to show or hide. Let's review it in more detail to show how to code this up:

- The first part is the trigger for the collapsable content, and I have chosen to use a link that has some button classes on it
- The link requires the `data-toggle` attribute with a value of `collapse` on it
- The `href` for the link needs to be a unique ID name, in this case, `#collapse-link`
- Finally, we set the `aria-expanded` value to `false` because we want the collapsable content to be hidden on page load

On page load, your new component should just appear like a regular button:

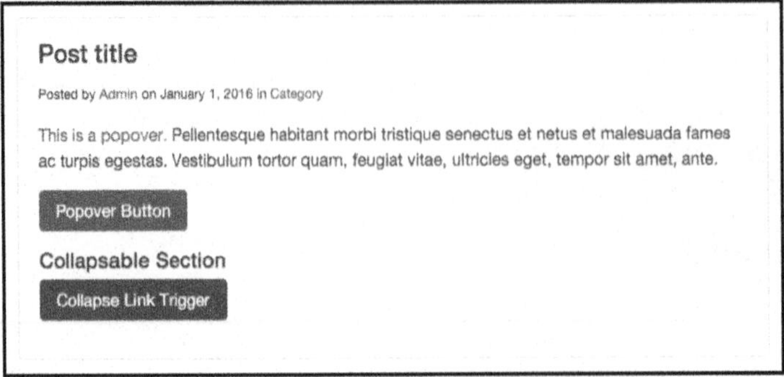

Coding the collapsable content container

Now that the trigger for the Collapse is set up, we need to code the content container. After the link tag, insert the following code:

```
<div class="collapse" id="collapse-link">
  <p class="alert alert-warning">This is some collapsable text.</p>
</div>
```

Here's how to assemble this section of code:

- We start with a `<div>` that needs to have a CSS class of `collapse` on it. You also need to include an ID here. This should match the ID you set as the `href` in the trigger link; in this case, `#collapse-link`.
- Within the `<div>` you can include any content you want. This content will be the hidden, collapsable content that you will show or hide when the trigger is clicked. To make the example really obvious, I've wrapped a warning Alert around some text to make it stand out.

After you've coded this up and saved your file, head to the browser, find the button, and click it. You should see the following in your window once you click the trigger link:

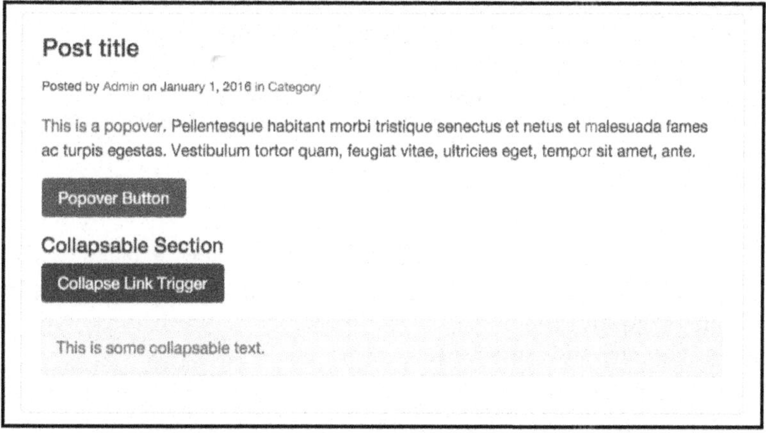

This is only a simple example of how you can code up the Collapse component. Using additional code and setup, you can use this component to create an Accordion.

Coding an Accordion with the Collapse component

In the previous section, I taught you a pretty simple way to use the Collapse component. The same component can be used to create a more complex version, which is the Accordion. Let's take a look at the basic code to create an Accordion:

```
<div id="accordion">
  <div class="panel panel-default">
    <div class="panel-heading" role="tab" id="headerOne">
      <h4 class="panel-title">
        <a data-toggle="collapse" data-parent="#accordion"
href="#sectionOne" aria-expanded="true" aria-controls="sectionOne">
          Section #1
        </a>
      </h4>
    </div>
    <div id="sectionOne" class="panel-collapse collapse in" role="tabpanel"
aria-labelledby="headerOne">
      This is the first section.
    </div>
  </div>
  <div class="panel panel-default">
    <div class="panel-heading" role="tab" id="headerTwo">
      <h4 class="panel-title">
        <a class="collapsed" data-toggle="collapse" data-
parent="#accordion" href="#sectionTwo" aria-expanded="false" aria-
controls="sectionTwo">
          Section #2
        </a>
      </h4>
    </div>
    <div id="sectionTwo" class="panel-collapse collapse" role="tabpanel"
aria-labelledby="headerTwo">
      This is the second section.
    </div>
  </div>
  <div class="panel panel-default">
    <div class="panel-heading" role="tab" id="headerThree">
      <h4 class="panel-title">
        <a class="collapsed" data-toggle="collapse" data-
parent="#accordion" href="#sectionThree" aria-expanded="false" aria-
controls="sectionThree">
          Section #3
        </a>
      </h4>
```

```
    </div>
    <div id="sectionThree" class="panel-collapse collapse" role="tabpanel"
aria-labelledby="sectionThree">
      This is the third section.
    </div>
  </div>
</div>
```

Now that might look like a ton of code, but it's actually a repeating pattern that is pretty easy to put together once you understand it. Let me breakdown everything that is happening here:

- The entire component is wrapped in a `<div>` with an ID on it. In this case, I'm using `#accordion`.
- Each section of the Accordion is a `<div>` with a class of `.panel` on it. I've also included the `.panel-default` class to just do the most basic styling.
- Each panel is made up of a heading and a body or section. Let's cover the header first. Create another `<div>` with a class of `.panel-heading` on it. Also include the `role` attribute with a value of `tab` and you need to give your header a unique ID, in this case, `#headerOne`.
- Inside the header include a header tag, in this case, a `<h4>`, with a class of `.panel-title`.
- Finally, nested inside the header tag, code a link that has a few attributes that you need to include:
    - `.collapsed` is required for the Accordion component.
    - `data-toggle` is also required.
    - `data-parent` should be the same ID that you set on the first `<div>` for the accordion.
    - `href` will be a link to the body of the section that will be collapsable. In this case, it is called `sectionOne`.
    - `aria-expanded` should be set to `true` because we want this section to be open on page load. The other links should be set to `false`, unless you want them to be open on page load.
    - `aria-controls` should also match the ID name of the corresponding section.
    - Now that the header has been broken down, let's cover the body of the panel.

- After the header, insert another <div> with an ID of #sectionOne on it. It should also have a class of .panel-collapse and .collapse on it. Include the attribute role with a value of tabpanel on it. Finally, include aria-labelled by attribute with the value of sectionOne.
- Inside this <div> include the content of the section that you want to display.

For the next sections, you need to repeat what you did for the first panel. Simply copy and paste and then you need to change a few things:

- Change headerOne to headerTwo
- Change sectionOne to sectionTwo
- Change up the header title and content of the body for the second section

Do the same for the third section, and then the Accordion component is done. Once you're done, this is what it should look like in the browser:

Section #1
This is the first section.
Section #2
Section #3

That completes the Collapse and Accordion components. We have one more to go, which is the Carousel component.

Coding a Bootstrap Carousel

Carousel is a popular component used on many different types of websites. We're going to build a Carousel in the Blog Post template of our project. Let's start by opening up blog-post.ejs from the project directory in your text editor. After the page title block of code, insert the following markup:

```
<div id="carousel-example-generic" class="carousel slide" data-
ride="carousel">
  <ol class="carousel-indicators">
    <li data-target="#carousel-example-generic" data-slide-to="0"
class="active"></li>
    <li data-target="#carousel-example-generic" data-slide-to="1"></li>
    <li data-target="#carousel-example-generic" data-slide-to="2"></li>
  </ol>
```

```
  <div class="carousel-inner" role="listbox">
    <div class="carousel-item active">
      <img src="..." alt="First slide">
    </div>
    <div class="carousel-item">
      <img src="..." alt="Second slide">
    </div>
    <div class="carousel-item">
      <img src="..." alt="Third slide">
    </div>
  </div>
  <a class="left carousel-control" href="#carousel-example-generic"
role="button" data-slide="prev">
    <span class="icon-prev" aria-hidden="true"></span>
    <span class="sr-only">Previous</span>
  </a>
  <a class="right carousel-control" href="#carousel-example-generic"
role="button" data-slide="next">
    <span class="icon-next" aria-hidden="true"></span>
    <span class="sr-only">Next</span>
  </a>
</div>
```

This is a larger component like the Accordion so let's go through it section by section:

The Carousel component starts with a `<div>` and it needs a unique ID. In this case, `#carouselOne`. Also include the following classes: `.carousel` and `.slide`. Finally, you need to add the attribute `data-ride` with a value of `carousel`.

Adding the Carousel bullet navigation

The first thing we need to add to the Carousel is the bullet or indicator navigation. It's made up of an ordered list. Here's the code, then we'll break it down:

```
<ol class="carousel-indicators">
  <li data-target="#carouselOne" data-slide-to="0" class="active"></li>
  <li data-target="#carouselOne" data-slide-to="1"></li>
  <li data-target="#carouselOne" data-slide-to="2"></li>
</ol>
```

Here's how the Carousel navigation works:

- On the `<ol>` tag allocate a class of `.carousel-indicators`.
- Each `<li>` in the list needs to have a few things:
    - The `data-target` needs to be the same ID that you gave to your

root Carousel `<div>`, in this case, `#carouselOne`.

- Include the `data-slide-to` attribute and the first value should be 0. Increase it by one for each list item after the first.

Including Carousel slides

The next step is to include the actual Carousel slides. I'm not going to include images in the code, that will be up to you to insert, but don't worry, I'll show you where to put them. Here's the code for the section that wraps the slides:

```
<div class="carousel-inner" role="listbox">
  ..
</div>
```

Give that `<div>` a class of `.carousel-inner` and add the `role` attribute with a value of `listbox`. Inside this `<div>` you're going to add another section for each image slide in the Carousel. Here's the code for one slide in the Carousel:

```
<div class="carousel-item active">
  <img src="..." alt="First slide">
</div>
```

Let's breakdown what's happening here in the code:

- In this case, insert a `<div>` tag with the classes `.carousel-item` and `.active`

Note you should only include the `.active` class on the first slide. This is where the Carousel will start on page load.

- Inside the `<div>`, insert an `img` tag with the following attributes:
  - Insert the `src` attribute and the value should be the path to the image file for the slide
  - Optionally, include an `alt` attribute with a value for the image

Adding Carousel arrow navigation

The last thing we need to add to the Carousel is the arrow navigation. Here's the code for rendering the arrows:

```
<a class="left carousel-control" href="#carouselOne" role="button" data-
slide="prev">
  <span class="icon-prev" aria-hidden="true"></span>
  <span class="sr-only">Previous</span>
</a>
<a class="right carousel-control" href="#carouselOne" role="button" data-
slide="next">
  <span class="icon-next" aria-hidden="true"></span>
  <span class="sr-only">Next</span>
</a>
```

Let me explain how the arrow navigation works:

- The left and right arrow navigation is based on `href` tags.
- The first will be the left arrow; code a link with the following classes on it: `.left` and `.carousel-control`.
- The `href` for the link should be set to the main ID for the Carousel, in this case, `#carouselOne`.
- Set the `role` attribute to `button`.
- Finally, set the `data-slide` attribute to `prev`.
- Within the link, add a `<span>` with a class of `.icon-prev` on it. This will render the arrow icon. Include the `aria-hidden` attribute and set it to `true`.
- Lastly, you can include another optional `<span>` for accessibility reasons. If you want to include it, give it a class of `.sr-only`. Within the `<span>` include the text `Previous`.
- Now let's go over the differences for the right arrow:
    - Code another link tag and switch the `.left` class to `.right`.
    - Change the `data-slide` attribute value to `next`.
    - In the first `<span>` tag change the class value to `.icon-next`.
    - If you included the accessibility `<span>` tag change the text to `Next`.

That completes the setup of the Carousel component. Fire up the project server and view the Blog Post page in the browser, and it should look like this:

That concludes the chapter on JavaScript components in Bootstrap. In this chapter, I taught you how to code up the following components: Modals, Tooltips, Popovers, Collapse, Accordion, and the Carousel. In the next chapter, I'll teach you how to use **Sass** in Bootstrap.

Summary

In this chapter, we have covered all components in Bootstrap that rely on JavaScript. This included: Modals, Tooltips, Popovers, Collapse, and Carousel.

In the next chapter, we will see how in Bootstrap 4 the framework has moved from Less to Sass as its CSS preprocessor. We will cover the basics of using Sass in a Bootstrap theme. I'll also explain how you can customize or use existing variables, or write your own.

8

Throwing in Some Sass

Up until now we've covered a bunch of different Bootstrap components and how to use them. In this chapter, we're going to change gears and learn about Sass, which will allow you to customize the look and feel of your components. I'll start by introducing some Sass basics that you need to know, move on to writing some basic code, and then show you the power of using variables in your components to save yourself valuable time when creating your web app or project.

Learning the basics of Sass

Sass stands for **Syntactically Awesome Style Sheets**. If you've never used or heard of Sass before, it's a CSS preprocessor. A preprocessor extends regular CSS by allowing the use of things such as variables, operators, and mixins in CSS. Sass is written during the development stage of your project and it needs to be compiled into regular CSS before you deploy your project into production. I'll cover that in more detail in the next section but don't worry because Harp.js makes this really easy to do.

Up until version 4 of Bootstrap, the CSS preprocessor used was actually Less. For a good while both Sass and Less were popular in frontend design circles. However, over the last few years, while Sass has emerged as the best choice for developers, the Bootstrap team decided to make the change in version 4. If you are familiar with Less but have never used Sass, don't worry as they are pretty similar to use so it won't take much to get you up-to-speed.

Using Sass in the blog project

As I mentioned in the previous section, Sass is part of the development process and the browser cannot read it in its native format. Before you can deploy the project, you need to convert or compile the Sass files into regular CSS files. Normally this would require you to install a Ruby gem and you would have to manually compile your code before you can test it. Luckily for us, Harp.js actually has an Sass compiler built into it. So when you run the `harp compile` command to build your templates, it will also build your Sass files into regular CSS. I bet you're starting to like Harp even more after learning that.

Updating the blog project

Before we go any further, we need to make a few updates to our blog project to set it up for Sass. Head to your project directory and navigate to the CSS directory. In this directory, create a new file called `custom.scss`.

The file extension used for Sass files is `.scss`.

What we're doing here is creating a custom style sheet that we are going to use to overwrite some of the default Bootstrap look-and-feel CSS. To do this, we need to load this custom file after the Bootstrap framework CSS file in our layout file. Open up `_layout.ejs` in the root of the project directory and insert the following line of code after `bootstrap.min.css`. Both lines together should look like this:

```
<link rel="stylesheet" href="css/bootstrap.min.css">
<link rel="stylesheet" type="text/css" href="css/custom.css">
```

Note here that I'm using the `.css` file extension for `custom.css`. This is because, after the files are compiled, the template will be looking for the actual CSS file, not the Sass file. The critical part is just that the actual filenames match and that you use `.css` in the layout file. Before we go any further, let's test out our Sass file to make sure it is set up properly. Open up `custom.scss` in your text editor and add the following code:

```
body {
   background: red;
}
```

This is just a simple way to make sure that Sass is compiling to CSS and is being inserted into our layout. Compile your project and launch the server. If you've done everything correctly the background for your homepage should be red and look like this:

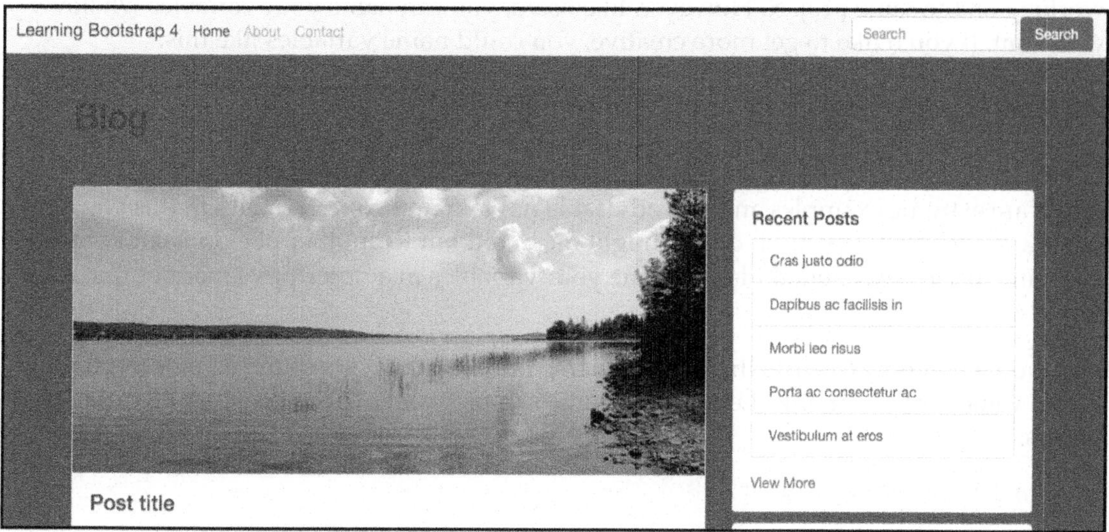

Hopefully this is what you're seeing and you can confirm you've set up your file correctly. Once you've successfully done this, delete the CSS we entered in the Sass file.

It's perfectly acceptable to write regular CSS in Sass files. Ideally, you want to combine regular CSS code with Sass syntax to take full advantage of the preprocessor.

Now that you've finished setting up your files, let's start to learn a little bit more about using Sass in your project.

Using variables

In Sass, variables are called by using the `$` sign character. If you're familiar with Less, the `@` symbol is used for variables. So in that case, all you would need to do is use `$` instead of `@`. To write a variable, start with the `$` sign and then insert a descriptive keyword that can be anything you like. Here are a few examples of generic variable names:

```
$background-color
$text-size
$font-face
```

```
$margin
```

I've named these pretty generically and they actually match some CSS property names. This is a good idea and they are easy to reuse and make sense of if multiple developers are working on the same project. However, like I said, you can name your variables whatever you want. If you'd like to get more creative, you could name variables like this:

```
$matts-best-color
$awesome-background-color
$fantastic-font-face
```

These are extreme examples and it is advisable not to name your variables in this way. To you `$awesome-background-color` might mean red but to another person it could mean anything. It's always a good idea to name your variables in a descriptive manner that makes sense.

I've shown you how to write the variable name but the other side of the equation is the actual value for the variable. Let's add in some sample values for our first set of variable names:

```
$background-color: #fff;
$text-size: 16px;
$font-face: helvetica, sans-serif;
$margin: 1em;
```

You write Sass variables the same way that you would write CSS properties. It's also worth noting that you should enter your variables at the very top of your style sheet so that they can be used in all of the CSS you write after them.

Using the variables in CSS

Now that we've written some variables, let's actually insert them into some CSS. After the variables in `custom.scss`, enter the following code:

```
body {
   background: $background-color;
   font-size: $text-size;
   font-family: $font-face;
   margin: $margin;
}
```

So instead of using actual values for our CSS properties, we're using the variable names that we set up. This starts to get more powerful as we add more CSS. Let's reuse some of these variables:

```
body {
   background: $background-color;
   font-size: $text-size;
   font-family: $font-face;
   margin: $margin;
}

h1 {
   font-size: 36px;
   font-family: georgia, serif;
}

h2 {
   font-size: $text-size;
   font-family: $font-face;
}
```

In this example, you can see a few things going on that I should explain:

- For the `<h1>` tag, I'm not using any variables. I'm using regular CSS property values.
- For the `<h2>` tag, I'm reusing the same variables to insert the `font-size` and `font-family` values.

As your style sheet grows longer, I'm sure you'll see the value in this strategy. For example, if I decide I want to change my `font-size` to `24px`, all I need to do is change the value for the `$text-size` variable to `24px`. I don't have to go through my entire style sheet and change all the values individually. These are just the basics of what you can do with variables. Let's look at a more advanced use case.

Using other variables as variable values

That might sound like a bit of a mouthful, but you can actually use a variable as the default value for another variable. A good example of where you might want to do this is when you are defining a color palette. You can switch the hex values to readable names and then use them for your other variables. This is much easier to scan and understand when you are debugging your code. Here's an example of what I mean:

```
$black: #000;
$white: #fff;
$red: #c00;

$background-color: $white;
$text-color: $black;
```

```
$link-color: $red;
```

Let me break down what is happening here for you:

- First I've created three color variables for `black`, `white`, and `red`
- Next I've created three CSS property variables for `background-color`, `text-color`, and `link-color`; the values for these CSS property variables are the color variables

Instead of using hex number values for the CSS property variables, I used a color keyword variable which is much easier to read and understand. That concludes the introduction to variables in Sass. Next we'll learn about importing different files into `custom.css` and using partials.

Importing partials in Sass

Just as you can do in `Harp.js`, you can use partials in Sass. If you've forgotten what a partial is, it's a little snippet of code that is saved into a different file and then imported into the main CSS theme or layout, in the case of Harp. This can be handy for making your CSS modular and easier to manage. For example, it would make a ton of sense to break every Bootstrap component into its own CSS file and then use the `@import` directive to bring them all into a single master theme, which is then included in your project. Let's go over an example of how you could do this for a single component. In your project, go to the `/css` directory and create a new sub-folder called `/components`. The the full path should be:

```
/css/components
```

In the `/components` directory, create a new Sass file and name it `_buttons.scss`. Make sure you always insert an underscore at the start of the filename of a partial. The compiler will then ignore these files as the underscore means it is being inserted into another file. Enter the following at the top of the file as a marker:

```
/* buttons */
```

Save the buttons file and then open up `custom.scss` and add the following line of code to the file:

```
@import "components/_buttons.scss";
```

That line of code uses the `@import` rule, which will allow us to import the `_buttons.scss` file into our main theme file that we are calling `custom.scss`. As I've mentioned, the reason you need to do this is for maintainability. This makes the code much easier to read and to add/remove components, which is just another way of saying it makes it more modular.

Before we can test this out to make sure it works, we need to add some code to our `_buttons.scss` file. Let's add some simple CSS to change the primary button as an example:

```
.btn-primary {
  background-color: green;
}
```

After adding this code, save the file and do a `harp compile`. Then launch the server and check out the home page; the buttons will be green like this:

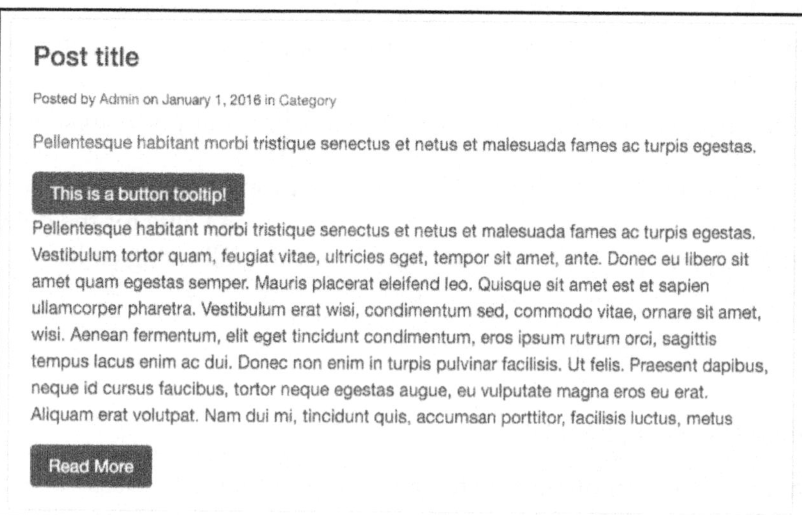

After testing that out, you may want to take that custom code out unless you want the buttons to remain green. That's just a simple example of how you can use partials to make your Bootstrap components more modular. I'll get into that topic in greater depth in a future chapter but for now we are going to focus on using Sass mixins.

Using mixins

Writing something in CSS, such as, for example, browser vendor prefixes, can be really tedious. Mixins allow you to group CSS declarations together so that you can reuse them through your project. This is a great because you can include the code for, say, a border-radius, using one line of code instead of multiple lines for each browser. To start, open up custom.scss and insert the following code at the top of the file:

```
@mixin border-radius($radius) {
  -webkit-border-radius: $radius;
     -moz-border-radius: $radius;
      -ms-border-radius: $radius;
          border-radius: $radius;
}
```

Let's go over a few things that are happening here:

- A mixin is always started in Sass with the @mixin keyword
- Following that, you want to include the property name to target as well as set a variable, in this case $radius
- We then apply the $radius variable to each browser prefix instance

We've set up the mixin to handle the border-radius property but we still need to add the corner value to an element. Let's change the border-radius value for the default Bootstrap button. Open up _buttons.scss and insert the following code:

```
.btn {
  @include border-radius(20px);
 }
```

Let me explain what is happening here:

- I'm targeting all Bootstrap buttons by inserting the .btn class
- Inserting the @include keyword will grab the border-radius mixin
- Lastly, I've provided a value of 20px, which will make our buttons look really rounded on each end

Save your file, run the harp compile command, and then, when you view the project in the browser, it should look like this:

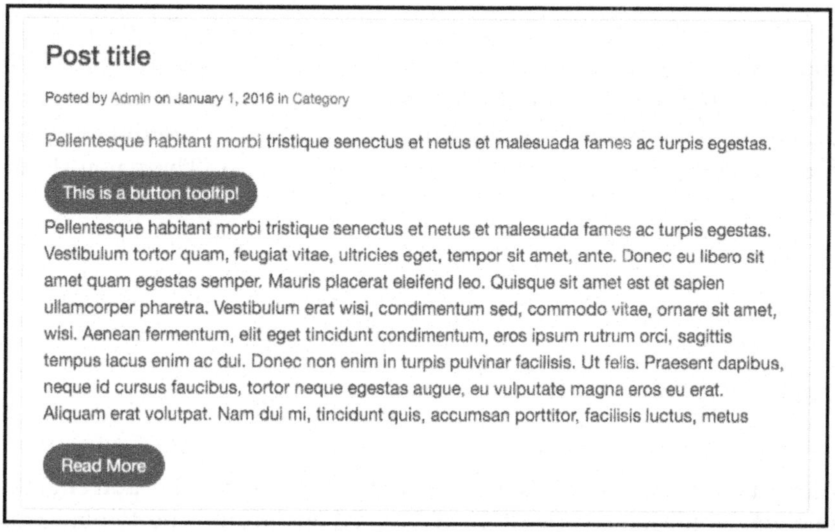

Post title

Posted by Admin on January 1, 2016 in Category

Pellentesque habitant morbi tristique senectus et netus et malesuada fames ac turpis egestas.

This is a button tooltip!

Pellentesque habitant morbi tristique senectus et netus et malesuada fames ac turpis egestas. Vestibulum tortor quam, feugiat vitae, ultricies eget, tempor sit amet, ante. Donec eu libero sit amet quam egestas semper. Mauris placerat eleifend leo. Quisque sit amet est et sapien ullamcorper pharetra. Vestibulum erat wisi, condimentum sed, commodo vitae, ornare sit amet, wisi. Aenean fermentum, elit eget tincidunt condimentum, eros ipsum rutrum orci, sagittis tempus lacus enim ac dui. Donec non enim in turpis pulvinar facilisis. Ut felis. Praesent dapibus, neque id cursus faucibus, tortor neque egestas augue, eu vulputate magna eros eu erat. Aliquam erat volutpat. Nam dui mi, tincidunt quis, accumsan porttitor, facilisis luctus, metus

Read More

That concludes a fairly simple example of how to use mixins in Bootstrap 4. You can use them for many other reasons but replacing CSS3 vendor prefixes is one of the most common and useful. Next we'll cover a slightly more complicated topic in Sass, which is the use of operators.

How to use operators

Sass allows you to perform basic math operations in CSS, which is useful for a number of reasons. First of all, you can use the following operators `+`, `-`, `*`, `/`, and `%`. To give you an understanding of how you can use operators in CSS, let's learn how to convert a pixel-based grid into percentages. We'll create two columns in pixels and then use some Sass to convert them to percentages. Open up `custom.scss` and insert the following code:

```
.left-column {
  width: 700px / 1000px * 100%;
}

.right-column {
  width: 300px / 1000px * 100%;
}
```

Now, I've created two columns here. The `.left-column` class will have a width of 70% after we compile this Sass operator. The `.right-column` class will have a width of 30%. So if we add those together we'll get roughly a three-quarter layout with a larger column on the left and a smaller column on the right. Run a `harp compile` command to build this code and then open up `custom.css` in the `/www/css folder`. There you should find the following code:

```
.left-column {
  width:70%;
}

.right-column {
  width:30%;
}
```

As you can see, our Sass operators have been converted into regular percentage values. That's just one way you can use operators in Sass; I'd encourage you to play around more with them. Next we're going to learn how to set up a library of Sass variables that you can use to create a Bootstrap theme.

Creating a collection of variables

One of the main things you'll want to do when using Sass in Bootstrap is to create a library of global variables that can be used throughout your theme. Think of things such as colors, backgrounds, typography, links, borders, margins, and padding. It's best to only define these common properties once and then you can reuse them through different components. Before we go too far, we need to create a new `.scss` file. Open up your text editor, create a new file, and call it `_variables.scss`. Save that file to the `/css/components` directory. For now, you can just leave it blank.

Importing the variables to your custom style sheet

Now that we've created the variables Sass file, we need to import it into our custom style sheet. Open up `custom.css` in your text editor and paste the following line of code at the top of the file:

```
@import "components/_variables.scss";
```

It's important to note that this file must be at the top of your custom style sheet file. The variables will cascade through all the code that follows them so they must load first. Let's start filling out our variables file with a color palette.

Adding a color palette

Save the custom style sheet and then go back to the variables file. Let's start by inserting a color palette into the variables file like this:

```
$red: #e74c3c;
$red2: #c0392b;
$blue: #3498db;
$blue2: #2980b9;
$green: #2ecc71;
$green2: #27ae60;
$yellow: #f1c40f;
$yellow2: #f39c12;
$purple: #9b59b6;
$purple2: #8e44ad;
$white: #fff;
$off-white: #f5f5f5;
$grey: #ccc;
$dark-grey: #333;
$black: #000;
```

As you can see, I've set up a palette of several colors that I'll use through my components and later my theme. Here are a few key points to keep in mind:

- It's good to have two variations for your key colors. This comes in handy for a component such as a button where `$red` would be the static color and `$red2` would be the hover or active color for the button.
- I'm guessing you can already see how using variable names such as `$purple` is much more readable than hex values in a long style sheet.

Adding some background colors

The next thing you should add to your collection of variables is background colors. As we move through this variables file, we're going to create a variable for all properties that get used over and over again in our style sheet.

Add the following background color variables to the file:

```
$primary-background: $white;
$secondary-background: $off-white;
$inverse-background: $black;
```

Let me explain, as best practice, how I have set this up:

- First of all, I'm using the color variables we just set up as the values for our new background color variables. This keeps things simple and it also allows you to change the color and have it cascade through all your other variables. This is a great time-saving tip.
- At the very least, it's a good idea to define a `primary`, `secondary`, and `inverse` background color variable. Note how I'm reusing the same language here that Bootstrap uses. This is a good practice to follow. Feel free to define additional background colors if you think you'll need them in your project.

Setting up the background color variables is pretty simple. Next let's set up our base typography variables.

Setting up variables for typography

The next section of variables we are going to set up is for the base typography styles. Insert the following code after the background colors:

```
$body-copy: helvetica, arial, verdana, sans-serif;
$heading-copy: helvetica, arial, verdana, sans-serif;
$base-font-size: 16px;
$font-size: 1em;
$base-line-height: 1.75;
```

Let me explain why I'm setting the following variables for the typography:

- For consistency, it's good to have a body and heading typeface. In this case, I'm using the same font stack for both but you could easily change the heading variable to something else. As you are coding your CSS, it's really easy to think of the `font-family` in either the body or heading version, compared with trying to remember the entire font stack for each, which also involves much more typing.
- For the `$base-font-size` variable, we are going to use a pixel value. This is one of the only places you'll see pixels and it's set to the base em size that everything else will work off. Remember that ems are a relative sizing unit, so if you ever want to make all your components a little bigger or smaller, you can just tweak this one pixel value.

- We also need a `$font-size` variable, which will be set to `1em`. This is a base unit and it can easily be changed in other selectors by using Sass operators. The reason we set it to `1em` is because it simply makes the math easy to do.
- Finally, I set the `$base-line-height` to `1.75` because I like a little extra line spacing in my copy. You could choose to leave this out if you are fine with the Bootstrap default, which is closer to `1.5`.

Now that we've set up our typographyvariables, let's move on to coding our text colors.

Coding the text color variables

As with the background colors, we need to set up some common color styles for text, as well as defining some colors for base HTML tags such as `<pre>` and `<code>`. Insert the following markup after the typography variables in the file:

```
$primary-text: $black;
$light-text: $grey;
$loud-text: $black;
$inverse-text: $white;
$code-text: $red;
$pre-text: $blue;
```

Let me break down how each variable is set up:

- As in the background color variables, we are using a variable name for the value of our text color variables. I've included a variable called `$primary-text` and set it to black, following the same naming convention that was previously established.
- I've added `$light-text` and `$loud-text` variables so we can easily apply lighter or darker text throughout our components.
- I've also included an `$inverse-text` variable to be used with the corresponding background color.
- Finally, I've set up default colors for the `<pre>` and `<code>` tags, which we will use to overwrite the default colors so they match our theme and color palette.

That finishes off the color variables that I recommend setting up. Feel free to add more if you have other uses you want to cover. Next we'll continue with some text colors by adding links.

Coding variables for links

An extension of basic text colors will be colors for links in our project. Go ahead and add the following code after the text colors in the file:

```
$primary-link-color: $purple;
$primary-link-color-hover: $purple2;
$primary-link-color-active: $purple2;
```

In this case, I've decided to only define a primary link color to keep things simple. In your own projects, you will likely want to come up with a couple more variations.

- For the static link color, I'm using the `$purple` color variable.
- For the hover and active states of the primary link, I'm using `$purple2`. As I previously mentioned, this is an example of why it's a good idea to have two variations of each color in your palette.

Like I said, I've kept the link variables simple. It's nice to try and keep your set of variables as compact as possible. If you have too many then it starts to defeat the purpose of using them as it will be harder to remember them in your code. Next let's cover the variables we should set up for borders.

Setting up border variables

Another CSS property that gets used often is borders. That makes it a great candidate for Sass variables. Insert the following code after the link colors in the file:

```
$border-color: $grey;
$border-size: 1px;
$border-type: solid;
$border-focus: $purple;
```

Let me explain why I've set up the border variables in this manner:

- When you are deciding on a value for `$border-color`, you should pick a color that you think will get used the most often in your components. Something like `$grey` is always a safe bet in most designs.
- As with the color value, you should set the `$border-size` to the most common border size you anticipate using. It's also a good idea to set this to `1px` because you can easily do the math to apply a Sass operator if you want a thinner or thicker border.

- Again for the `$border-type`, set it to the value you will use the most, which is probably going to be solid.
- Finally, set up a common `$border-focus` color. This is primarily used in form inputs once they are active. It's a good idea to pick a contrasting color for this variable so it really stands out when the input is in focus.

That concludes all the border variables I would recommend including. Next let's include some basic layout variables.

Adding variables for margin and padding

For consistent spacing throughout your designs, it's a good idea to use variables for `margin` and `padding` so that you can standardize on size. These properties are also used often so it's smart to make them variables that can be reused. Add the following code after the border markup:

```
$margin: 1em;
$padding: 1em;
```

All I'm doing here is setting a base size (for both `padding` and `margin`) `1em`. Again, it's a good idea to set both of these to `1em` because it is easy to do the math if you want to use Sass operators to increase or decrease the values of specific components. Those are the last variables that I would recommend adding to your variables file. However, we should add at least one mixin to the file before we are finished.

Adding mixins to the variables file

Since mixins will also be used through a number of your components, you should define them in this variables file. Then they will be available to all the CSS code that follows them in the custom theme file. At the very least, I would recommend setting up a mixin for `border-radius`, which I will show you how to do next. You may also want to include additional mixins for other CSS3 features.

Coding a border-radius mixin

We talked a little bit about mixins earlier but let's review them again now that we are actually applying them to our project. Insert the following code after the layout variables in your file:

```
@mixin border-radius($radius) {
  -webkit-border-radius: $radius;
     -moz-border-radius: $radius;
      -ms-border-radius: $radius;
          border-radius: $radius;
}
```

In Less, it is possible to set a global value for all your `border-radius` in a mixin. However, with Sass you have to set up the above formula but then on the actual selectors that follow you have to set the actual `border-radius` value. An example of that would look like this:

```
.my-component {
  @include border-radius(5px);
 }
```

In this example, I've added the `border-radius` mixin to a CSS class called `.my-component`. The component will have a `border-radius` of `5px` applied to it. You will need to repeat this step on any CSS class or component where you want to apply the `border-radius` mixin. That concludes our variables Sass file. We went over a bunch of code there, so let's see what it all looks like together. I've also included some CSS comments in the following code to help remind you what each section does:

```
/* variables */

/* color palette */
$red: #e74c3c;
$red2: #c0392b;
$blue: #3498db;
$blue2: #2980b9;
$green: #2ecc71;
$green2: #27ae60;
$yellow: #f1c40f;
$yellow2: #f39c12;
$purple: #9b59b6;
$purple2: #8e44ad;
$white: #fff;
$off-white: #f5f5f5;
$grey: #ccc;
$dark-grey: #333;
$black: #000;
```

```
/* background colors */
$primary-background: $white;
$secondary-background: $off-white;
$inverse-background: $black;

/* typography */
$body-copy: helvetica, arial, verdana, sans-serif;
$heading-copy: helvetica, arial, verdana, sans-serif;
$base-font-size: 16px;
$font-size: 1em;
$base-line-height: 1.75;

/* text colors */
$primary-text: $black;
$light-text: $grey;
$loud-text: $black;
$inverse-text: $white;
$code-text: $red;
$pre-text: $blue;

/* links */
$primary-link-color: $purple;
$primary-link-color-hover: $purple2;
$primary-link-color-active: $purple2;

/* border */
$border-color: $grey;
$border-size: 1px;
$border-type: solid;
$border-focus: $purple;

/* layout */
$margin: 1em;
$padding: 1em;

/* border-radius mixin */
@mixin border-radius($radius) {
  -webkit-border-radius: $radius;
     -moz-border-radius: $radius;
      -ms-border-radius: $radius;
          border-radius: $radius;
}
```

Now that we have all our variables and mixins set up, let's go ahead and start to learn how to apply them. We'll continue to build on the button example we started earlier by extending it into a custom look and feel.

Customizing components

Let's first start by customizing a single component; later on I'll talk about creating a theme where you customize all the components in Bootstrap. To get started, we'll build on the button component we started to work on earlier. In this next step we are going to expand on the CSS we have added to fully customize the component. What you want to do is overwrite all the CSS classes and properties that you want to change. In some cases, this might only be a few things but in other scenarios you may want to change quite a bit.

Customizing the button component

To start, open up `_buttons.scss` located in `/css/components` in our project directory. The first thing we need to customize is the base `.btn` CSS class. Once we have applied some changes there, we'll add more CSS to control the look and feel of the different button variations. Insert the following CSS at the top of the file for the base button class:

```
.btn {
  background-color: $grey;
  border-color: $grey;

  @include border-radius(20px);
}
```

To keep things simple, I'm only going to overwrite a few properties. You're totally free to get more creative and change additional properties to make your buttons look different from the Bootstrap default link. Let's break down what I've done:

- First I've set the `background-color` and `border-color` to use the `$grey` from our color palette. This is a good time to point out that if you want to do a full theme you need to overwrite all the Bootstrap default colors on all components to match your color palette.
- Next I've inserted the `border-radius` mixin and given it a value of `20px`. This will make the buttons really rounded. I'm going for this look so you can clearly see that the button has been customized.

Once you have saved these changes, go to the terminal and run the `harp compile` command from the root of the project directory. Then fire up the server and open the home page of the project that has a bunch of buttons on it. Your buttons should now look like this:

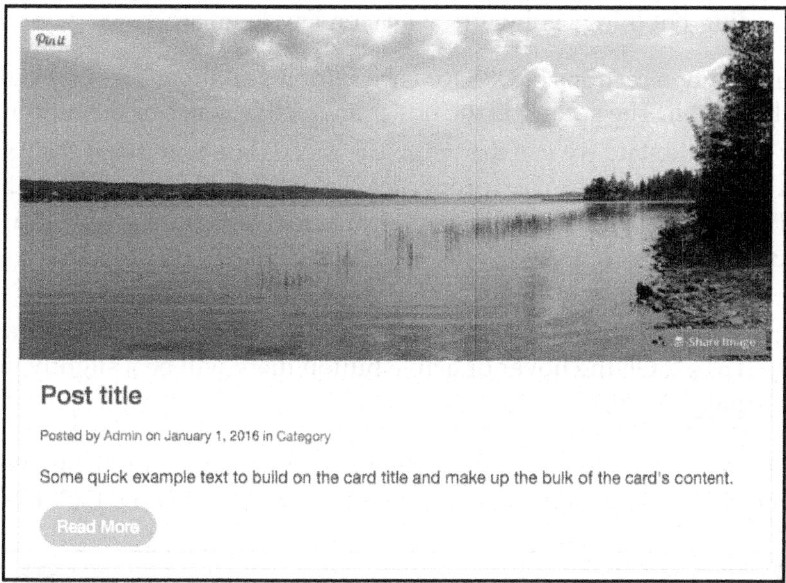

Now that might not look too useful, but it's important that we customize the base `.btn` class first; now we'll continue building the component out by applying our color palette to all of the different button variations.

Extending the button component to use our color palette

In this next section, we will extend the button component further by applying our color palette to all the different Bootstrap button variations. Before we get to all the different button types, let's start by customizing the `.btn-primary` variation. Enter the following code in the `_buttons.scss` file after the base `.btn` styles:

```
.btn-primary {
   background-color: $purple;
   border-color: $purple;
}

.btn-primary:hover,
.btn-primary:active {
   background-color: $purple2;
   border-color: $purple2;
}
```

There are a few different things going on so let's review them all:

- There are two sections of CSS for each button variation. The first is the static state of the button. The second is the hover and active states of the button.
- For the static state we use the `.btn-primary` class and insert the `background-color` and `border-color` properties. I want to make my primary button purple so I've inserted the `$purple` Sass variable to overwrite the Bootstrap default color.
- For the other states, we have `.btn-primary:hover` and `.btn-primary:active`. In this case, I'm using the second purple color variable which is `$purple2`. On the hover or active button there will be a slightly darker shade of purple.

Save the file, run a `harp compile` in the terminal, and then open up the home page in your browser. If everything was coded correctly, your buttons should now look like this:

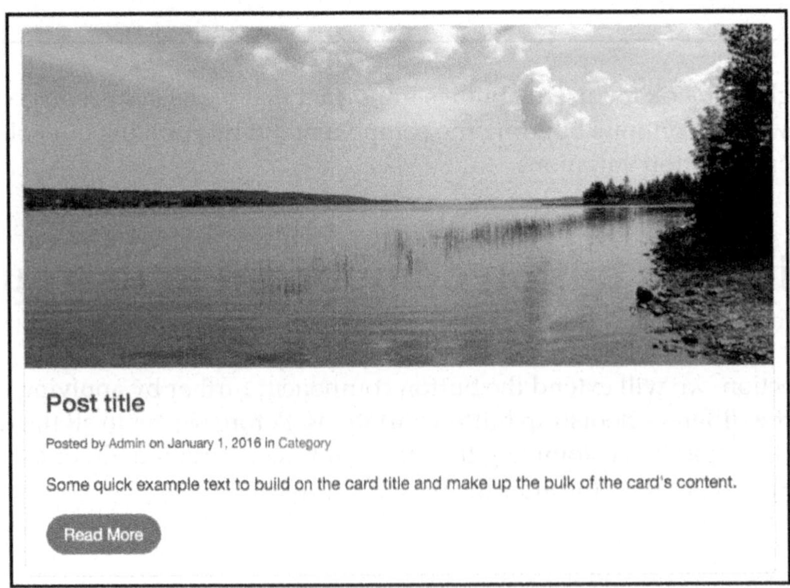

As you can see, the primary button is now purple! It's as simple as that; you can start to apply a custom look and feel to the button component. Let's build out the rest of the button color variations by entering the following code into the `_buttons.scss` file:

```
.btn-secondary {
  background-color: $off-white;
  border-color: $off-white;
```

```
}

.btn-secondary:hover,
.btn-secondary:active {
   background-color: $grey;
   border-color: $grey;
}

.btn-success {
   background-color: $green;
   border-color: $green;
}

.btn-success:hover,
.btn-success:active {
   background-color: $green2;
   border-color: $green2;
}

.btn-info {
   background-color: $blue;
   border-color: $blue;
}

.btn-info:hover,
.btn-info:active {
   background-color: $blue2;
   border-color: $blue2;
}

.btn-warning {
   background-color: $yellow;
   border-color: $yellow;
}

.btn-warning:hover,
.btn-warning:active {
   background-color: $yellow2;
   border-color: $yellow2;
}

.btn-danger {
   background-color: $red;
   border-color: $red;
}

.btn-danger:hover,
.btn-danger:active {
```

```
        background-color: $red2;
        border-color: $red2;
    }
```

That's a bunch of code but it should be fairly easy to understand. I've simply followed the same steps I completed for the primary button for every other button variation. Along the way, I've replaced the default Bootstrap color values with our custom color palette. Once you're done, all of your buttons should now look like this:

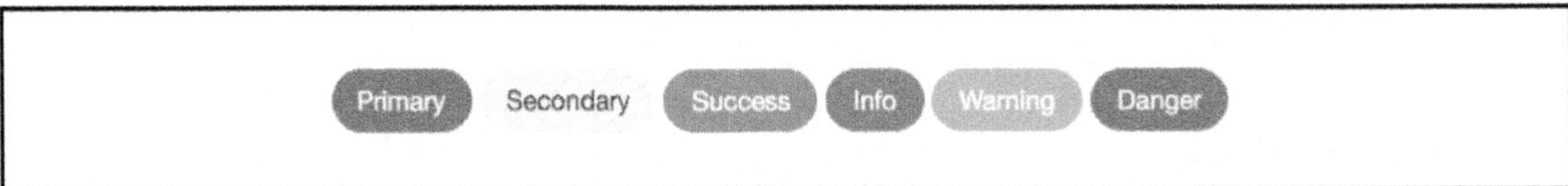

We've now successfully customized the entire button component. As I mentioned earlier, there may be additional things you might want to do to the buttons. However, at the very least, we've done enough to show how you can make the component your own. The next step in this process is to go through every Bootstrap component one by one and apply the same customization process. We call this writing your own Bootstrap theme.

Writing a theme

Creating your own Bootstrap theme is a bit of an undertaking. The good news is that once you've done it you can reuse a ton of the code for future themes. That's where the real power in making your code modular comes into play. Instead of starting over from scratch each time, you can reuse old code and just extend it. In the last section, we learned how to customize the button component that was the start of our own theme. Let's first start by looking at some common Bootstrap components that you'll want to customize for your own themes.

Common components that need to be customized

There are many ways that you can theme Bootstrap. In some cases, you may only need to customize a few components to get a unique look and feel going. However, you may want to do a more thorough theming process so that your theme doesn't resemble the default Bootstrap look at all. In this section, let's start by listing some of the common components you will most likely want to customize.

Next we'll go through the process of writing the code to customize a few so you get an idea as to how it works. Here's a list of components that I would recommend customizing:

- Buttons
- Drop-downs
- Alerts
- Navbar
- Typography
- Tables

This list is just a starting place. If you want to create a unique theme, you should really try to customize all Bootstrap components. At the very least, you should change them to use your custom color palette, typography, and layout styles. We've already covered buttons so let's jump into customizing the drop-down component, which is an extension of the button.

Theming the drop-down component

The drop-down component requires a medium-sized amount of customization so it's a good starting place to get an idea of what is involved in this process. It also builds on the code we wrote for the button so it's a natural second step. It's important to note that some components will require a good amount of CSS to customize them, while others will only need a little bit. Let's start by creating a new Sass file for drop-downs. From your project folder, create a new file called `_dropdown.scss` in the `css/components` directory. You can leave the file blank for now, just save it.

Once you've created the new Sass file for the drop-down component, we need to import it into our main theme is called `custom.scss`. Open up the custom style sheet in your text editor and insert the following line of code after the `@import` for the button component:

```
@import "components/_dropdown.scss";
```

Now we are ready to start coding our custom drop-down styles. Open up `_dropdown.scss` in your text editor and let's insert this first section of CSS:

```
.dropdown-menu {
   color: $primary-text;
}
```

As with the buttons in the previous section, I'm only going to change the most basic properties to demonstrate how you can customize the component. Feel free to customize additional properties to get a more unique look and feel.

Let's break down what is happening here. The drop-down component is made up of the base `.dropdown-menu` CSS class. This controls how the menu will look. Here I've simply changed the text color to use for the `$primary-text` variable.

We also need to do some work on the list of links that appear in our drop-down menu. Insert the following CSS after the first section you just entered:

```
.dropdown-item:focus,
.dropdown-item:hover {
   color: $primary-text;
   background-color: $secondary-background;
}
```

Let me break down what is happening here:

- These CSS classes control the hover and focus states for each list item in our drop-down menu. Again, I've set it to use our `$primary-text` font color.
- When you hover on a list item, the background color changes. I've changed that background color to use our `$secondary-background` color variable. In this case you should use the background color variable, not a customized color variable. The reason for this is it's easier to keep track of what background colors you are using as you progress through the writing of your code.

The last thing we need to do is update the actual drop-down button trigger with some additional code. Enter the last part of CSS into the file:

```
.open > .btn-primary.dropdown-toggle:focus {
   background-color: $purple2;
   border-color: $purple2;
}
```

When the drop-down button trigger is clicked the `.open` CSS class will dynamically be inserted into the HTML code. This initiates a unique variation on the button class, a drop-down toggle focus. That may sound complicated but what you need to know is that you need to set this selector to our `$purple2` color so it matches the rest of the button.

I've overwritten the `background-color` and `border-color` properties to use `$purple2` from our color palette.

That's it, the drop-down component has now been themed to match our look and feel. If you preview it in the browser it should look like this when the menu is open:

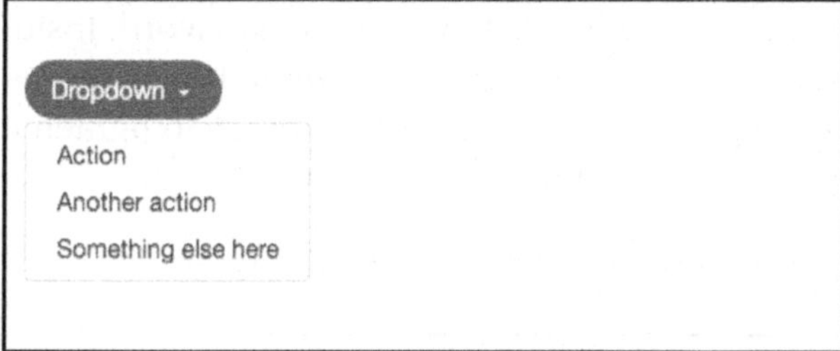

Now that we've finished with the drop-down component let's move on to learning how to theme the alerts component.

Customizing the alerts component

The alerts component in Bootstrap is fairly easy to theme. As with the button component, it comes in a few variations. Let's start by coding up the CSS for the default color method. Create a new file called `_alerts.scss` and save it to the `css/components` directory. Don't forget to import it into `custom.scss` with the following line of code:

```
@import "components/_alerts.scss";
```

Once you've set up the file, let's get started with the code for the success alert component:

```
.alert-success {
   color: $green;
   background-color: lighten( $green, 30% );
   border-color: lighten( $green, 30% );
}
```

What you're now seeing should start to look familiar. However, I have introduced something new that I need to explain:

- This is the success alert so it should be green in color. The first thing I've done is change the text color to use the green from our palette with the `$green` variable.
- For the `background-color` and `border-color` properties, I'm using something new, a Sass function. In this case, I want a green color that is slightly lighter than my text. Instead of introducing another green color variable, I can use a Sass function to lighten the base `$green` variable color.

- To create the function, you use the `lighten` keyword. Inside the brackets you need to include the variable name you want to target, in this case `$green`, and finally include a percentage value for how much to lighten it by. This is a nice little trick to save you having to create more variables.

Once you code this up it should look like this in the browser:

This is a success alert message

As you can see, we are using the green color values from our color palette. Let's continue and customize the colors for the rest of the alert bar variations. Enter the following code into the `_alerts.scss` file:

```
.alert-info {
   color: $blue;
   background-color: lighten( $blue, 30% );
   border-color: lighten( $blue, 30% );
}

.alert-warning {
   color: $yellow;
   background-color: lighten( $yellow, 30% );
   border-color: lighten( $yellow, 30% );
}

.alert-danger {
   color: $red;
   background-color: lighten( $red, 30% );
   border-color: lighten( $red, 30% );
}
```

The other alerts follow the same pattern as the success version. They should look like this in the browser when you are done:

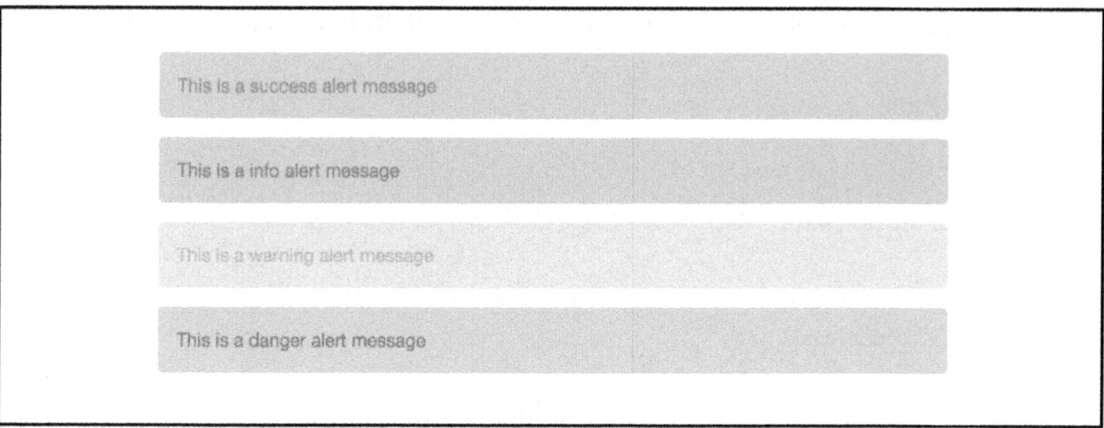

As you can see, the alerts are now using our color palette. Let's move on to the last component that I will show you how to customize, which is typography.

Customizing the typography component

The typography component isn't difficult to customize. We'll build off the base variables we set up to apply them to the appropriate HTML tags. As we did with our other components, start with creating a new file called `_typography.scss` and save it to the `css/components` directory. Once you do this, import the file into `custom.scss` with the following line of code:

```
@import "components/_typography.scss";
```

Let's start customizing the type by applying some styles to the base header tags:

```
h1, h2, h3, h4, h5, h6 {
   font-family: $heading-copy;
   color: $primary-text;
}
```

Here I've simply used the `$heading-copy` variable and applied it to all the HTML heading tags. This will allow our custom heading typeface to be used for all headers. I've also added the `$primary-text` variable so that our headers are using the correct text color. Next let's take a look at a few miscellaneous text styles that you will likely want to overwrite:

```
small {
   color: $light-text;
}

pre {
   color: $pre-text;
}

code {
   color: $code-text;
}
```

As we did with our base variables, I'm now applying some of them on actual selectors. Let's break it down:

- For the `<small>` HTML tag, I want it to look more subtle so I've set the text color to use the `$light-text` variable.
- I purposely set up color text variables for the HTML `<pre>` and `<code>` tags. I've now applied the `$pre-text` and `$code-text` variables to these tags.

That covers some of the basic typography styles you're going to want to customize. There are more you could add but I will let you explore these on your own. That also goes for all the Bootstrap components. We have only scratched the surface of the level of customizing you can do for your Bootstrap theme. However, I think I've given you a good introduction to what you need to do for coding your own Bootstrap themes.

Summary

That brings this chapter to a close. We've covered a ton of new content in this chapter including: the basics of Sass, how to use Sass in Bootstrap, how to create a library of Sass variables, how to apply those variables to customize Bootstrap components, and, finally, how to start writing your own Bootstrap theme. In the final chapter, I'll provide some advice on moving from Bootstrap version 3 to 4.

9
Migrating from Version 3

Version 4 of Bootstrap is a major update. Almost the entire framework has been rewritten to improve code quality, add new components, simplify complex components, and make the tool easier to use overall. We've seen the introduction of new components such as Cards and the removal of a number of basic components that weren't heavily used. In some cases, Cards present a better way of assembling a layout than a number of the removed components. Let's jump into this chapter by showing some specific class and behavioral changes to Bootstrap in version 4.

Browser support

Before we jump into the component details, let's review the new browser support. If you are currently running on version 3 and support some older browsers, you may need to adjust your support level when migrating to Bootstrap 4. For desktop browsers, Internet Explorer version 8 support has been dropped. The new minimum Internet Explorer version that is supported is version 9.

In terms of mobiles, iOS version 6 support has been dropped. The minimum iOS supported is now version 7. The Bootstrap team has also added support for Android v5.0 Lollipop's browser and **WebView**. Earlier versions of the Android Browser and WebView are not officially supported by Bootstrap.

Big changes in version 4

Let's continue by going over the biggest changes to the Bootstrap framework in version 4.

Switching to Sass

Perhaps the biggest change in Bootstrap 4 is the switch from Less to Sass. This will also likely be the biggest migration job you will need to take care of. The good news is you can use the sample code we've created in the book as a starting place. Luckily, the syntax for the two CSS pre-processors is not that different. If you haven't used Sass before, there isn't a huge learning curve that you need to worry about. Let's cover some of the key things you'll need to know when updating your stylesheets for Sass.

Updating your variables

The main difference in variables is the symbol used to denote one. In Less we use an `@` symbol for our variables, while in Sass you use the `$` symbol. Here are a couple of examples for you:

```
/* LESS */

@red: #c00;
@black: #000;
@white: #fff;

/* SASS */

$red: #c00;
$black: #000;
$white: #fff;
```

As you can see, that is pretty easy to do. A simple find and replace should do most of the work for you. However, if you are using `@import` in your stylesheets, make sure this retains an `@` symbol.

Updating @import statements

Another small change in Sass is how you import different stylesheets using the `@import` keyword. First, let's take a look at how you do this in Less:

```
@import "components/_buttons.less";
```

Now let's compare how we do this using Sass:

```
@import "components/_buttons.scss";
```

As you can see, it's almost identical. You just need to make sure you name all your files with the `.scss` extension. Then update your file names in the `@import` to use `.scss` and not `.less`.

Updating mixins

One of the biggest differences between Less and Sass is mixins. Here we'll need to do a little more heavy lifting when we update the code to work for Sass. First, let's take a look at how we would create a border-radius, or round corner, mixin in Less:

```
.border-radius (@radius: 2px) {
  -moz-border-radius: @radius;
  -ms-border-radius: @radius;
  border-radius: @radius;
}
```

In Less, all elements that use the `border-radius` mixin will have a border radius of 2px. That is added to a component, like this:

```
button {
.border-radius
}
```

Now let's compare how you would do the same thing using Sass. Check out the mixin code:

```
@mixin border-radius($radius) {
  -webkit-border-radius: $radius;
  -moz-border-radius: $radius;
  -ms-border-radius: $radius;
  border-radius: $radius;
}
```

There are a few differences here that you need to note:

- You need to use the `@mixin` keyword to initialize any mixin
- We don't actually define a global value to use with the mixin

To use the mixin with a component, you would code it like this:

```
button {
@include border-radius(2px);
}
```

This is also different from Less in a few ways:

- First, you need to insert the `@include` keyword to call the mixin
- Next, you use the mixin name you defined earlier, in this case, `border-radius`
- Finally, you need to set the value for the `border-radius` for each element, in this case, `2px`

Personally, I prefer the Less method as you can set the value once and then forget about it. However, since Bootstrap has moved to Sass, we have to learn and use the new syntax. That concludes the main differences that you will likely encounter. There are other differences and if you would like to research them more, I would check out this page:

`http://sass-lang.com/guide.`

Additional global changes

The change to Sass is one of the bigger global differences in version 4 of Bootstrap. Let's take a look at a few others you should be aware of.

Using REM units

In Bootstrap 4, px has been replaced with rem for the primary unit of measure. If you are unfamiliar with rem it stands for **root em**. Rem is a relative unit of measure where pixels are fixed. Rem looks at the value for font-size on the root element in your stylesheet. It then uses your value declaration, in rems, to determine the computer pixel value. Let's use an example to make this easier to understand:

```
html {
font-size: 24px;
}

p {
font-size: 2rem;
}
```

In this case, the computed font-size for the `<p>` tag would be **48px**. This is different from the **em** unit because **ems** will be affected by wrapping elements that may have a different size. However, **rem** takes a simpler approach and just calculates everything from the root HTML element. It removes the size cascading that can occur when using **ems** and nested, complicated elements. This may sound confusing, but it is actually easier to use em units. Just remember your root font-size and use that when figuring out your rem values.

What this means for migration is that you will need to go through your stylesheet and change any px or em values to use ems. You'll need to recalculate everything to make sure it fits the new format if you want to maintain the same look and feel for your project.

Other font updates

The trend for a long while has been to make text on a screen larger and easier to read for all users. In the past, we used tons of small typefaces that might have looked cool but were hard to read for anyone visually challenged. To that end, the base font-size for Bootstrap has been changed from **14px** to **16px**. This is also the standard size for most browsers and makes the readability of text better. Again, from a migration standpoint, you'll need to review your components to ensure they still look correct with the increased font size. You may need to make some changes if you have components that were based on the **14px** default font-size in Bootstrap 3.

New grid size

With the increased use of mobile devices, Bootstrap 4 includes a new smaller grid tier for small screen devices. The new grid tier is called extra small and is configured for devices under **480px** in width. For the migration story this shouldn't have a big effect. What it does do is allow you a new breakpoint if you want to further optimize your project for smaller screens.

That concludes the main global changes to Bootstrap that you should be aware of when migrating your projects. Next, let's take a look at components.

Migrating components

With the release of Bootstrap 4, a few components have been dropped and a couple of new ones have been added. The most significant change is the new Cards component. Let's start by breaking down this new option.

Migrating to the Cards component

With the release of the Cards component, the Panels, Thumbnails, and Wells components have been removed from Bootstrap 4. Cards combines the best of these elements into one and even adds some new functionality that is really useful. If you are migrating from a Bootstrap 3 project, you'll need to update any Panels, Thumbnails, or Wells to use the Cards component instead. Since the markup is a bit different, I would recommend just removing the old components altogether, and then recoding them using the same content as Cards.

Using icon fonts

The GLYPHICONS icon font has been removed from Bootstrap 4. I'm guessing this is due to licensing reasons as the library was not fully open source. If you don't want to update your icon code, simply download the library from the GLYPHICONS website at:

`http://glyphicons.com/`

The other option would be to change the icon library to a different one such as Font Awesome. If you go down this route, you'll need to update all of your `<i>` tags to use the proper CSS class to render the icons. There is a quick reference tool that will allow you to do this called **GlyphSearch**. This tool supports a number of icon libraries and I use it all the time. Check it out at: `http://glyphsearch.com/`.

Those are the key components you need to be aware of. Next let's go over what's different in JavaScript.

Migrating JavaScript

The JavaScript components have been totally rewritten in Bootstrap 4. Everything is now coded in ES6 and compiled with Babel, which makes it easier and faster to use. On the component side, the biggest difference is the Tooltips component. The Tooltip is now dependant on an external library called **Tether**, which you can download from:

`http://github.hubspot.com/tether/.`

If you are using Tooltips, make sure you include this library in your template. The actual markup looks to be the same for calling a Tooltip but you must include the new library when migrating from version 3 to 4.

Miscellaneous migration changes

Aside from what I've gone over already, there are a number of other changes you need to be aware of when migrating to Bootstrap 4. Let's go through them all below.

Migrating typography

The `.page-header` class has been dropped from version 4. Instead, you should look at using the new display CSS classes on your headers if you want to give them a heading look and feel.

Migrating images

If you've ever used responsive images in the past, the class name has changed. Previously, the class name was `.image-responsive` but it is now named `.image-fluid`. You'll need to update that class anywhere it is used.

Migrating tables

For the table component, a few class names have changed and there are some new classes you can use.

If you would like to create a responsive table, you can now simply add the class `.table-responsive` to the `<table>` tag. Previously, you had to wrap the class around the `<table>` tag. If migrating, you'll need to update your HTML markup to the new format.

The `.table-condensed` class has been renamed to `.table-sm`. You'll need to update that class anywhere it is used.

There are a couple of new table styles you can add called `.table-inverse` or `.table-reflow`.

Migrating forms

Forms are always a complicated component to code. In Bootstrap 4, some of the class names have changed to be more consistent. Here's a list of the differences you need to know about:

- `control-label` is now `.form-control-label`
- `input-lg` and `.input-sm` are now `.form-control-lg` and `.form-control-sm`
- The `.form-group` class has been dropped and you should instead use `.form-control`

You likely have these classes throughout most of your forms. You'll need to update them anywhere they are used.

Migrating buttons

There are some minor CSS class name changes that you need to be aware of:

- `btn-default` is now `.btn-secondary`
- The `.btn-xs` class has been dropped from Bootstrap 4

Again, you'll need to update these classes when migrating to the new version of Bootstrap. There are some other minor changes when migrating on components that aren't as commonly used. I'm confident my explanation will cover the majority of use cases when using Bootstrap 4. However, if you would like to see the full list of changes, please visit:

`http://v4-alpha.getbootstrap.com/migration/.`

Summary

That brings the final chapter of the book to a close! Thank you for taking the time to read it and I hope I've successfully brought you up-to-speed on how to use Bootstrap 4.

Index

A

Accordion
  coding, with Collapse component 182
advantages, Bootstrap 4
  card component 8
  Flexbox 8
  improved grid system 8
  Internet Explorer 8 support dropped 9
  normalize.css, rebooting 9
  other updates 9
Alerts button
  dismiss button, adding 136
alerts component
  customizing 213, 214
Alerts component
  using 135, 136

B

background colors
  adding, to collection of variables 199, 200
base template
  converting, to generator 13
basic table
  setting up 101
blog contact page
  form, adding to 124
blog home page
  coding 72
  content, adding 75, 77
  index.ejs template, writing 72
  layout, on mobile devices 78
  layout, testing 75
  spacing CSS classes, using 73
Blog index page
  sidebar, adding 151, 152
  updating 148
Blog post page
  Breadcrumbs component, adding to 164
  Pagination component, adding to 166
  setting up 154
blog post template
  blog post body, adding 85
  blog post feature, adding 85
  coding 84
blog project page grids
  _data.json, updating 79
  coding 79
  new page templates, creating 80
blog project
  compiling 35
  css directory, creating 28
  data JSON file, creating 30
  EJS files 29
  fonts directory, creating 28
  footer, setting up 34
  header, setting up 32, 33
  img directory, creating 29
  js directory, creating 29
  layout, setting up 31
  partial directory, creating 29
  running 36
  Sass, using in 190
  setting up 28
  updating 124, 190, 191
  viewing 36
Bootstrap 7, 8
Bootstrap 4
  advantages 8
  forms, coding 118
Bootstrap documentation
  reference 24
Bootstrap Flexbox layout grid
  Sass variable, updating 52, 53

setting up 52
Bootstrap JavaScript 10
Bootstrap source files
downloading 23
reference 23
border variables
setting up 202
border-radius mixin
coding 204
borders
adding, to table 104, 105
Breadcrumbs component
adding 164
adding, to Blog post page 164
Bundler
about 25
reference 25
button component
using 109
button component
customizing 206
extending, to use color palette 207
button dropdown
coding 115, 116
button groups
using 114
buttons
examples 109
layout, updating for 175
Popover component, adding to 179
Tooltip, adding to 175

C

card component 8
Card component
Card title, moving 139
color scheme, inverting of 143, 144
header, adding to 141, 142
location, adding to Contact page 146, 147
text alignment, modifying 140, 141
using, for layout 137, 138
Carousel arrow navigation
adding 187
Carousel bullet navigation
adding 185
Carousel component
coding 184
Carousel slides
including 186
changes to Bootstrap, in version 4
@import statements, updating 218
browser support 217
buttons, migrating 224
components 221
font updates 221
forms, migrating 224
global changes 220
icon fonts, using 222
images, migrating 223
JavaScript, migrating 222
migration, to Cards component 222
mixins, updating 219
new grid size 221
REM units, using 220
switching to Sass 218
tables, migrating 223
typography, migrating 223
variables, updating 218
checkboxes 111
adding, to inline form 127, 128
inserting, into form 122
collapsable content container
coding 181
Collapse component
Accordion, coding with 182
using 180
collection of variables
creating 198
collisions
avoiding, with components 176
color palette
inserting, into variables file 199
color scheme
inverting, of Card component 143, 144
color
changing, of Navbar component 161
column classes
mixing, for different devices 70, 71
selecting 68
columns

adding, to layout 67
extra large columns 68
extra small column 67
large column 68
medium column 67
offsetting 71
small column 67
components
collisions, avoiding with 176
customizing 206
contact page template
coding 80
contact page body, adding 81, 82
containers
working with 63, 64, 65
Content Delivery Network (CDN) 9
CSS framework 7
CSS
images, aligning with 100
variables, using in 192
custom style sheet
variables, importing to 198

D

description list
using 97, 98
devices
column classes, mixing for 70, 71
different sized drop-down buttons
creating 117
display headings
using 93, 94
documentation
running 26
drop-down component
theming 211, 212

E

Embeddable JavaScript (EJS) 15, 29
extra large column 68
extra small column 67

F

Flexbox project
basic three-column grid, creating 55
custom theme, adding 54
full-width layouts, creating 57, 58
setting up 53, 54
Flexbox
about 8, 40
basics 39, 40
child sections, stretching to fit parent container 42
direction, modifying 42, 43, 44
equal-height columns, creating 46, 48, 49, 51, 52
ordering 40, 41
wrapping 45
form component 92, 93
form fields
width, controlling of 129, 130
forms
adding, to blog contact page 124
checkboxes, inserting to 122
coding 118
file input form field, adding 121
radio buttons, inserting to 122
select dropdown, adding 120
setting up 118
textarea, inserting into 121
framework files
implementing 9, 10

G

generator
base template, converting to 13
Glyph-icons
reference 222
Glyphicons icon set 15
GlyphSearch
reference 222
Grunt
about 22
installing 22

H

Harp project
compiling 16
CSS, inserting 14
deploying 16

deploying, Surge used 17
JavaScript, inserting 14
layout, setting up 15
previewing 16
setting up 14
Harp.js
installing 13, 27
need for 27
Harp
about 13
reference 13
Sass, adding in 14
header
adding, to Card component 141, 142
headings
about 92
customizing 94
hover state
adding, to rows 105
HTML framework 7
HTML5 Doctype 11

I

image shapes
using 99
images
aligning, with CSS 100
making responsive 98, 99
styling 98
inline form
checkboxes, adding to 127, 128
creating 126
labels, hiding in 127
radio buttons, adding to 127, 128
size, modifying of input 128
inline lists
creating 97
inputs
validation, adding to 130, 131

J

JavaScript files
used, for implementing framework 10
JavaScript framework 7
JavaScript
Popover button, adding in 179
Jekyll
about 25
reference 25
jQuery
about 10
reference 10
JSON files
setting up 29
Jumbotron component
using 132

L

Label component
adding 134, 135
labels
hiding, in inline form 127
large column 68
layout
Card component, using for 137, 138
columns, adding to 67
creating, without container 65
rows, inserting into 66
updating, for buttons 175
lead class
using 95
Less 8
links
variables, coding for 202
list component 92
List Group component
using 166, 167
lists
description list 97, 98
inline lists, creating 97
unstyled list, coding 95, 96
working with 95

M

mailing list section
converting, to partial 86
margin
variables, adding for 203
Material Design 8
medium column 67

mixins
adding, to variables file 203
using 196
Modal dialog
coding 169, 170
multiple containers
using, on single page 65

N

Navbar component
color, changing of 161
making responsive 163, 164
using 160
Navs component
pill navigation, creating 159
tabs, creating with 158
using 157, 158
Node 20
Node.js
download link 13
installing 20
reference 20
normalizing 12
npm
about 20
updating 21, 22

O

operators
using 197, 198
outlined buttons
creating 111

P

padding
variables, adding for 203
page template
creating 35
Pagination component
adding, to Blog post page 166
using 165
paragraphs 92
partials
importing, in Sass 194
pop-up menu
creating 116
Popover button
adding, in JavaScript 179
Popover component
JavaScript, updating 178
Popover component
about 176
adding, to button 179
positioning 178
using 177
preformatted text 92

R

radio button group
creating 112
radio buttons 111
adding, to inline form 127, 128
inserting, into forms 122
Reboot
about 9
basics 91
rebooting 12
responsive meta tag
structuring 12
responsive utility classes
using 79
responsive web design
reference 12
root em 91, 220
rows
hover state, adding to 105
inserting, into layout 66
Ruby
about 23
installing 23

S

Sass
about 8, 38
adding, in Harp 14
basics 189
partials, importing in 194
using, in blog project 190
screen reader only 127
select dropdown

adding, to forms 120
simple three-column layout
creating 68
single blog post
designing 58, 59
single page
multiple containers, using on 65
small column 67
spacer classes
creating 74
spacing classes 73
starter template
about 11
HTML5 Doctype 11
responsive meta tag, structuring 12
static site generator
Harp.js 27
setting up 26
using 12
static websites
issues 12
Surge
about 16
installing 17
reference 16
used, for deploying Harp project 17

T

table component 92
table header
inversing 103
table rows
color-coating 106
tables
borders, adding to 104, 105
coding 101
inversing 102, 103
making responsive 107
striped rows, adding 104
tabs
creating, with Nav component 158
Tether
about 222
reference 222
text color variables
coding 201
textarea
inserting, into form 121
theme
writing 210
tools
about 19
Bundler gem 25
Grunt 22
Node.js 20
Ruby 23
Tooltip 222
adding, to buttons 175
coding 172
positioning 174
using 173
typography component
customizing 215
typography
using 93
variables, setting up for 200, 201

U

unstyled list
coding 95, 96

V

validation
adding, to inputs 130, 131
variables file
color palette, inserting into 199
mixins, adding to 203
variables
adding, for margin 203
adding, for padding 203
coding, for links 202
importing, to custom style sheet 198
setting up, for typography 200, 201
using 191
using, in CSS 192
using, in variable values 193
vertical button group
creating 114

W

WebView 217
width

  controlling, of form fields 129, 130

X

XHTML 11

Lightning Source UK Ltd.
Milton Keynes UK
UKOW05f1908200318
319760UK00004BA/246/P

9 781785 881008